P

An Assessment of the

RIVATIZATION

of Child Welfare Services

Challenges and Successes

MADELYN FREUNDLICH ■ SARAH GERSTENZANG

Washington, D.C. CWLA Press

CWLA Press is an imprint of the Child Welfare League of America. The Child Welfare League of America is the nation's oldest and largest membership-based child welfare organization. We are committed to engaging people everywhere in promoting the well-being of children, youth, and their families, and protecting every child from harm.

CHILD WELFARE LEAGUE OF AMERICA, INC.
HEADQUARTERS
440 First Street NW, Third Floor
Washington, DC 20001-2085
E-mail: books@cwla.org

CURRENT PRINTING (last digit)
10 9 8 7 6 5 4 3 2 1
Printed in the United States of America
Cover and text design by James D. Melvin
Edited by Julie Gwin
ISBN # 0-87868-876-5

CONTENTS

TABLES

Acknowledgments

The authors gratefully acknowledge the Annie E. Casey Foundation, without whose support this study would not have been possible. The Annie E. Casey Foundation's grant to Children's Rights provided the critical resources needed to undertake this in-depth study. We also acknowledge the invaluable assistance provided by the consultants who advised us on various aspects of the project: Charlotte McCullough, MEd; Sara Rosenbaum, JD; and Alexandra Bowie, JD.

Particular appreciation is extended to members of the study's Advisory Board, who provided ongoing consultation and critical feedback on the case studies. In addition to Ms. McCullough, these advisors were James Beougher, Director, Child and Family Administration, Michigan Family Independence Agency, Lansing, MI; Fred Chaffee, Chief Executive Officer, Arizona's Children Association, Tuscon, AZ; Phil Coltoff, Executive Director and Chief Executive Officer, Children's Aid Society, New York, NY; and Jan McCarthy, Director of Child Welfare Policy, Georgetown University Child Development Center, Washington, DC.

We also thank Jennine Meyer, Policy Associate, Children's Rights, for her tireless proofreading of this manuscript. Last but not least, our deepest appreciation goes to Carmen Hernandez, Policy Assistant, Children's Rights, whose administrative support has been unflagging. Without her expertise, this document could not have been produced.

Introduction

Public child welfare agencies increasingly are contracting with the private sector to provide services and benefits to children that public agencies provided previously. Based on the assumption that market competition produces greater efficiency and economy, agencies are embracing privatization as a strategy for providing higher quality child welfare services at a lower cost. Although the history of privatization is more extensive in the areas of child support enforcement and the administration of welfare benefits, the 1996 privatization of child welfare services in Kansas ushered in an era of heightened interest in privatizing family preservation, foster care, and adoption services. In the past, noncompetitive, quasi-grant arrangements typified the relationships between public and nonprofit agencies. Now, it is common to find that public child welfare functions are privatized through a variety of contractual arrangements that place full responsibility for previous public functions with private, nonprofit agencies. Practice, policy, and fiscal considerations have set the stage for the emergence of privatization as a trend in child welfare service delivery.

Despite the enthusiasm with which some quarters have embraced privatization, evaluation of privatization efforts generally has been limited to self-studies that lack the necessary objectivity for solid assessment. Importantly, there has been no cross-jurisdictional analysis of the types of privatization efforts (often combined with managed care features) being undertaken, the organizational and operational effects of the shift to the provision of services by the private sector, or the substantive outcomes achieved (or not achieved) for children and families with privatization of services. A limited understanding of the effect of privatization on the delivery of child welfare services and the outcomes and costs associated with those services exists.

At the same time, the growing interest in privatization of child welfare services has raised a number of questions, not the least of which is whether privatization is an appropriate approach to the delivery of these services. Some organizations, such as the National Association of Child Advocates (NACA) (2000), have expressed concerns that reliance on market competition in the context of privatizing human services is inappropriate given the nature of these services. Others argue that privatization benefits human services by bringing higher quality and greater efficiency to the service delivery process. They contend that the key issue is how (as opposed to whether) such an effort should be implemented. It is clear that very different perspectives exist on the privatization of child welfare services in Kansas, the site of the earliest and best-known effort. Although advocates point to good outcomes (such as the achievement of program outcomes at acceptable levels, generally positive client perceptions of new systems, and reduction in the number of full-time state employees in child welfare), others point to ongoing financial problems and indicators that suggest that success on a range of indicators has been elusive.

This book enhances understanding of efforts to privatize child welfare services, including the extent to which benefits are achieved through such approaches and the extent to which negative consequences exist for children and families and for the child welfare system itself. The book accomplishes this in three ways. First, in Part I, it examines the concept of privatization and explores exactly what is meant by the term and what, as a service delivery mechanism, privatization purports to do. Part I also examines the debate that has characterized considerations of privatization in general, in the context of social services overall, and in relation to child welfare services specifically. Finally, it considers some new aspects that have emerged to shape the nature of privatization in the child welfare arena.

Part II uses a case study approach to look closely at six different jurisdictions that have developed privatization initiatives. It examines two broad-based, statewide efforts—Kansas and Florida; two initiatives that were designed to meet the highly intensive needs of children and their families—Missouri and Hamilton County, Ohio; and a geographically targeted foster care initiative in Wayne County, Michigan. It also examines an effort in Maine to use privatization at the front end to serve families reported for abuse and neglect and for whom workers have assessed ongoing risk as low to moderate.

Part III synthesizes the lessons of the six case studies, offering 13 themes identified as common to many, if not all, of the initiatives studied. It offers specific recommendations that communities might consider if they choose to embark on a privatization effort. The book closes with a few observations on privatization in general and its effect in the child welfare arena.

Given the continuing interest in privatization, it is likely that many other jurisdictions will join the communities described here in designing and implementing their own efforts. It is hoped that documentation of the rich experiences of the communities that have implemented such efforts and learned what to do and what not to do can serve as a resource to inform future efforts.

PART I

What Is Privatization and What Does It Mean for Child Welfare?

Policymakers have increasingly used privatization at all levels of government as they have subscribed to the notion that market competition ensures a more efficient way to provide services (Cornell University Department of City & Regional Planning, 2000; Linowes, 1988). The theory is that innovation and cost reduction can be achieved only by reducing or eliminating government's "natural monopoly" in the provision of services (Morgan & England, 1988, p. 980). With that goal in mind, proponents of privatization place faith in the "magic of the marketplace" to solve the many problems besetting local and state governments (Morgan & England, 1988, p. 980). At the same time, advocacy for the shift from public to private provision of services is promoted on the purported strengths of the market: "efficiency, self-determination, consumer choice and cost effectiveness within an enterprise culture" (Samson, 1994, p. 81). Although the willingness to embrace privatization of government services may be attributable to a number of factors, one of the most powerful factors may be the "persistence of value-laden preferences for private solutions to public problems in the American context" (Rosenthal, 2000, p. 292).

This section examines the concept of privatization and the competing views regarding privatization in general and the privatization of social services more specifically. It then considers the many issues raised in connection with privatization of child welfare services. Finally, it examines certain aspects of child welfare privatization: performance-based contracting, integration of managed care principles into child welfare privatization initiatives, and the entry of for-profit groups into the arena of child welfare service provision.

What Is Privatization?

Although there is no single definition of *privatization*, the term generally has come to refer to a range of strategies that involve "the provision of publicly-funded services and activities by non-governmental entities" (Nightingale & Pindus, 1997, p. 1). Bailey (1987), for example, noted that, "although the concept is unclear, [*privatization*] might be tentatively defined as a general effort to relieve the disincentives toward efficiency in public organizations by subjecting them to the incentives of the private market" (p. 138). Accordingly, privatization generally refers to a broad range of activities designed to "shift into non-governmental hands some or all roles in producing a good or service that was once publicly produced or might be publicly produced" (Bendick, 1985, p. 103).

Bendick (1985) wrote that privatization may be conceptualized in one of two key ways. First, it may be viewed as a technique for "governmental load shedding," in which government divorces itself from both service delivery and financing (Bendick, 1985, p. 108). *Load shedding* (also known as *divestiture* or *denationalization)* involves the sale of at least 51% of a publicly owned enterprise to the private sector and is a far more common form of privatization in Western and Eastern Europe than in the United States (Atkan, 1995; Gormley, 1994-1995; Motenko, Allen, Angelos, & Block, 1995). Although some commentators maintain that load shedding is the only true form of privatization (see Samson, 1994), most view this approach as descriptive of privatization only in a very narrow sense (Atkan, 1995; Gormley, 1994-1995).

Alternatively, privatization may be viewed as a mechanism for changing the conduct of public business, so that government retains some level of funding responsibility but delegates provision of the service or production of the good (Bendick, 1985). When viewed as a mechanism for changing the conduct of public business (as opposed to the divorce of government from service delivery and financing), privatization may take a variety of forms:

> ■ **Contracting Out** (also called *outsourcing*). Contracting out is the most common form of privatization in the United States. It generally takes one of two forms: the transfer of management and operation of government services (such as refuse collection) to private entities, and the purchase of goods and services from the private sector (such as spare parts, lunches, transportation, and health and human services) (Atkan, 1995; Gormley, 1994-1995).

- **Franchising.** Franchising involves granting of monopoly privilege to a private entity to either produce a certain good or supply a specific service (such as mass transit) within a certain geographical area (Atkan, 1995).

- **Vouchers.** Vouchers provide consumers with direct access to certain goods and services that consumers wish to acquire, such as child care, housing, or health care. A government agency funds the service, but consumers receive certificates to "shop around" and buy the service from a private provider on the open market (Reason Public Policy Institute, 2000c).

A number of other activities also have been identified as falling within the scope of privatization, including:

- management contracts, under which a private entity operates a public facility;

- managed competition, in which public organizations and private entities participate in a bidding process that determines who will provide the service;

- volunteers, in which all or part of a government service is provided by nonpaid individuals;

- corporatization, in which the public entity is reorganized as a business that focuses on profit maximization and is freed from government procurement and management systems; and

- private infrastructure development and operation, in which a private entity builds, funds, and operates a public infrastructure, such as a road or airport, and charges usage fees (Reason Public Policy Institute, 2000c).

Depending on the forms they take, privatization initiatives will vary in the degree to which the public sector retains ownership, financial responsibility, and accountability (Starr, 1988). These forms fall along a spectrum from total privatization (as occurs with government load shedding or divestiture) to partial privatization (as is the case with vouchers or contracting out) (Starr, 1988). With the exception of divestiture, privatization is not self-implementing, and the government retains some administrative role, if not even greater administrative responsibility than it had in the past (Beecher, 1998). Specifically with regard to contracting out—the model most frequently used in the social services, in general, and in child welfare services in particular—government is likely to continue to finance services while private entities actually provide them.

The Privatization Debate

Workers and researchers can expect the enthusiasm for privatization as a mechanism for changing the essential structure government business to continue. As noted by the Cornell University Department of City & Regional Planning (2000), "Although empirical studies do not provide clear evidence on the costs and benefits of privatization, public perception and pressure for improved government efficiency will keep privatization on the government agenda" (p. 1). That said, people continue to debate the benefits of privatization in general, and the privatization of human services in particular. Likewise, they have not yet resolved the appropriateness of broader privatization of child welfare services.

Privatization in General

The concept of privatizing any type of government services has spawned considerable debate. Proponents view privatization as a key strategy for achieving the broader goal of decentralization of government functioning. They champion privatization on many grounds, but the most common are the greater efficiency of the private marketplace and the cost savings that can be realized when public services are privatized (Bennett, 1990; Kemp, 1991; Moore, A. T., 1997; Savas, 1982, 1987). Savas (1987, 1992), one of the most frequently cited advocates for U.S. privatization, for example, criticizes government service as unresponsive to individuals' needs (largely owing to its monopoly status) and argues that the private market is inherently more efficient because of economies of scale, higher productivity, and fewer legal restraints. Some attribute cost savings from privatization to a number of factors, including reduction in the size of government (Gormley, 1994-1995) and private providers' use of fewer staff and provision of less generous wage and benefit packages (Lopez-de-Silanes, Sheliefer, & Vishny, 1995; Savas, 1987; Stevens, 1984).

Proponents of privatization consistently characterize the private market as producing greater quality, offering increased consumer choice, and ensuring greater accountability (Bennett, 1990; Moore, A. T., 1997). Reed (1997), for example, argued that:

> the private sector exacts a toll from the inefficient for their
> poor performance, compels the service provider or asset
> owner to concern himself with the wishes of the customers,
> and spurs a dynamic, never-ending pursuit of excellence—all
> without the political baggage that haunts the public sector as
> elements of its very nature. (p. 2)

Proponents of privatization also emphasize the flexibility of the private sector, particularly its capacity to develop and eliminate services, its presumed ability to be more responsive to the needs of clients and communities, and the favorable reputation that the private sector enjoys, as opposed to the "stigma" of public agencies (Rosenthal, 2000). In a survey of Illinois county governments regarding factors that prompted their decision to privatize various government services, officials stated that they were most influenced by financial considerations and the quality of work, timeliness, and flexibility of the private sector (Reason Public Policy Institute, 1999).

Opponents of the privatization of government services, by contrast, contend that the very nature of public services make them inappropriate for privatization (Starr, 1988). They argue that in many cases, no meaningful opportunity exists to create the competition that lies at the heart of a privatized approach (Sclar, Schaeffer, & Brandwein, 1989; Starr, 1988). Opponents of privatization take issue with the presumed efficiency of private markets and contend that privatization is far less attractive economically than may be initially assumed. They point to hidden costs that result from limited information, the need to monitor the performance of private entities, and the possibility that private entities will bid low to secure initial contracts and raise prices later (Sclar et al., 1989; Starr, 1988). In addition, writers such as Savarese (1999) contend that efficiency comparisons are inevitably skewed because public services have been notoriously underfunded, and it is unlikely that private agencies would be any more effective if they were funded at the same level of resources that have flowed to the public sector. Other critics of privatization maintain that as inefficient as government services may appear to be, ample examples of waste and corruption exist in the private sector (Campbell, 2000; Hanrahan, 1983; Thayer, 1987). Gummer (1988), for example, argued that as opposed to the relative absence "of the most blatant forms of financial corruption" (pp. 107–108) at the federal government level, a much higher rate of corruption exists in contracts with private entities that provide public services.

Others argue that rather than taking a pro or con approach to the privatization of public services, the appropriateness of privatization should be examined based on certain government and private provider characteristics. Donahue (1989), for example, outlined three principles regarding the benefits of privatization, in general, and contracting out, in particular. His analysis suggests that privatization is likely to be more effective if tasks can be delineated, with specificity in advance and evaluation after the fact; if contractors can be relatively easily replaced when their performance is inadequate; and if the key governmental concern is the result, not procedures (Donahue, 1989). In addition, Donahue maintained that privatization is more promising if meaningful competition is present or can be developed, noting that "most of the kick in privatization comes in the greater scope for rivalry when functions are contracted out, not from private provision per se" (p. 220).

Kettl (1993) likewise viewed privatization as more appropriate under some circumstances than others, but he focused his analysis of contracting out on the strengths of government under certain circumstances. He contended that privatization is a more promising strategy when government knows what it is purchasing, who can provide what it wants to purchase, and how to evaluate what it wants to purchase (Kettl, 1993). Kettle doubted that competition, even when meaningful, would promote positive results if government does not have sufficient expertise to monitor and evaluate private contractors' performances. Finally, Gormley (1994–1995), echoing to some extent the principles articulated by Donahue, argued that privatization is most likely to yield positive results when private providers have considerable experience and enjoy high community regard; when government can easily intervene should private providers' performances "prove wanting"; and when private providers also offer "other useful public services" to the community (p. 222).

Privatization of Social Services

Just as people have embraced privatization in the broader environment of government services, a growing interest has existed in privatization of social services. The public debate about the quality of publicly provided social services and the pressures on public agencies to control budgets have heightened the interest in private market provision and management of social services that traditionally have been government provided (Blank, 2000). In its study of privatization of human services, the U.S. General Accounting Office (USGAO, 1997) found that privatization of social services generally has been "prompted by political leaders and top program managers,...responding to an increasing demand for public services and a belief that contractors can provide higher quality services more cost effectively than can public agencies" (p. 1). In its 1993 study of state social service agencies, the Council of State Governments found that almost 80% of state governments had expanded the service privatization in the preceding five years (Chi, 1994). Just as people debate the merits of privatization in general, however, decidedly different perspectives exist on the privatization of human services, including social services, and the extent to which a reliance on the market is appropriate in this area.

The Case For and Against Privatization of Social Services

Proponents of social service privatization contend that not only is it quite appropriate for the delivery of social services, it is extremely successful. Reed (2001), for example, wrote that "examples abound of the private sector doing a superior job in such areas as treating alcohol and drug abuse, training welfare recipients for jobs, providing adoption services, and managing public housing projects" (p. 1). Quoting from a study conducted by Stephen Moore of the Heritage Foundation, Reed (2001) noted:

> Through their small scale, non-bureaucratic nature, local knowledge and personal relationships, neighborhoods, families, churches, and voluntary associations can respond rapidly, accurately and in a more acceptable manner to local and individual needs in ways that large formal institutions such as government agencies cannot. (p. 1)

For neo-conservative proponents, expanding privatization and curtailing government-provided social services is the essence of equal opportunity and the open competition that promotes efficiency (Tuominen, 1991). For other proponents, the value of privatization rests in its capacity to strengthen communities (Starr, 1988). Berger and Neuhaus (1977), for example, viewed governments as "alienating megastructures" and argued that government's role should be to "empower" community organizations, churches, voluntary associations and other less formal institutions to "mediate" between government and individuals (p. 11). This emphasis downplays the rationales of efficiency and cost savings often advanced as the basis for privatization and highlights, instead, the value of local and smaller scale providers of social services (Berger & Neuhaus, 1977).

Critics of the privatization of social services argue that the competitive marketplaces that may exist in other service areas do not typically exist in the social services, and that as a result, privatization is an inappropriate strategy. NACA (2000), for example, takes issue with social service privatization on the following grounds:

- There tend to be only a few buyers and sellers, as opposed to the many buyers and sellers typically needed to support competition. The buyer in human services is a single government agency, and the few sellers of human services often hold a virtual monopoly.

- There tend to be significant market barriers to entry in human service provision, as opposed to the low entry barriers associated with competitive markets. Private entities attempting to enter the field must incur significant up-front costs to provide services that the public agency historically has provided.

Because the typical public public agency already has made the necessary initial investment and has an established capacity, it is often difficult for new providers to offer services in a more cost-effective manner than the public agency.

■ Insufficient information in human services often exists regarding the actual costs of services. When human services are privatized, lack of information may cause private providers either to overstate costs in an attempt to meet anticipated and unanticipated future cost increases or to underestimate costs and incur large overruns.

Similarly, a number of other commentators (see Bendick, 1989; Morgan & England, 1988) have argued that although the private market may work well for certain purposes, it does not work so well for other purposes. Bendick (1989), for example, distinguished the respective strengths of the public and private sectors and concluded that social services are more appropriately based in the public sector. In his view, private entities are likely to be strongest in providing specific services that do not require the exercise of professional judgment, such as garbage collection, the processing of payments, and computer systems design (Bendick, 1989). When services, however, move toward the "more complex, undefinable long-range and 'subjective' services [that are] characteristic of the social welfare field," private entities are hard pressed to successfully perform (Bendick, 1989, p. 105). He was particularly skeptical of the ability of the for-profit sector to handle the most difficult cases or manage systems involving complex objectives, because a key motivation for these entities is a fiscal return (Bendick, 1989). The high risks and high costs generally associated with complex cases, however, also may undermine the ability of nonprofit entities to perform at expected levels (Bendick, 1989). His analysis suggests that public agencies are best suited for the delivery of services to address complex client situations and service systems, a position that directly contradicts the rationale often advanced for privatization—that public agencies are too bureaucratic and unwieldy to deal effectively with complex problems.

Other critics of privatization focus on the difficulties that plague the development and maintenance of competitive markets that ensure that social service contractors have the capacity to respond to the diverse and challenging needs of social service clients. These critics point to the limited number of social service providers with trained staff to provide such services, the high cost of entering the human service field, and the demands in social services for ongoing continuity of care, such as long-term therapy or residential care (Nelson, 1992; O'Looney, 1993;

Smith & Lipsky, 1992). Some commentators, such as Milward (1994), argue that even when few barriers exist to entry, competition among nonprofits, nonetheless, tends to be limited because the incentives are insufficient to induce a large number of groups to enter or expand operations.

Critics are also skeptical about the actual degree of accountability that exists when social services are privatized. Milward (1994), for example, views the "short supply" (p. 78) of usable management information systems, auditing capability, and skilled contract managers as undermining meaningful accountability in efforts to privatize social services. The question becomes whether state and local governments have the capacity, in terms of both resources and expertise, to appropriately design, implement, and oversee privatization efforts (Beecher, 1998). Kramer and Grossman (1987), for example, argued that "government is seriously limited in its efforts to secure greater accountability and that service providers are generally able to maintain a relatively high degree of independence while serving as a vendor or public agent" (p. 42). Even when there are adequate systems to ensure accountability, the question often is "Accountability for what outcomes?" (Bardach & Lesser, 1996, p. 201). Although the expectation is that private contractors will be held accountable for results, Bardach and Lesser (1996) argued that, at most, accountability is "for a better quality of effort directed toward the results being measured" (p. 201) as opposed to higher quality outcomes.

Other critics of social service privatization focus less on issues related to ongoing accountability and more on the perceived effort of governments to foist their responsibilities onto the private sector. Smith and Lipsky (1992), for example, contended that the focus on accountability through government monitoring is misplaced, because the key issue is the failure of government to abide by its own obligations to pay in a timely way for the services that private agencies provide. This issue was dramatically illustrated in a February 2001 report that the New York City public child welfare agency owed private foster care contractors a total of $16 million, an amount outstanding since September of 2000, and that the public agency did not plan to pay the private contractors until the following month (Port, 2001).

Finally, some critics of social service privatization raise concerns about the blurring of the distinction between the public and private sectors and the effect on the rights and interests of the clients served (Morgan & England, 1988). First, concern exists regarding the commitment of private entities to serve clients who depend on their services in the face of diminished financial returns. Moe (1987), for example, questioned the legitimacy of delegating to private parties "activities of a purely public and governmental character" (p. 459) and specifically took issue with the right of private providers offering public services to seek bankruptcy, a right which public entities do not have (Moe, 1987). Second, the question exists of the extent to which private agencies have legal duties to the clients they serve. Sullivan (1987), for example, argued that privatization may undermine constitutional protections, because private entities, unlike public agencies, are not politically accountable nor are they bound by principles regarding the protection of citizens' rights. He concluded that "in the end, privatization and protection of civil liberties may prove to be mutually exclusive goals" (p. 466).

Issues of Quality, Efficiency and Cost Savings in Social Services

Principally, the arguments in favor of and against privatization have centered on the extent to which such efforts result in higher quality of services, greater efficiency, and budget reductions. Each of these issues warrants closer examination.

Quality. Both proponents and critics of social service privatization rely heavily on the issue of quality to make their respective cases. Proponents of privatization contend that quality services are more easily provided by the private sector because it has greater flexibility and does not have the bureaucratic complexity and constraints that characterize the public sector (Hatry & Durman, 1985; Nightingale & Pindus, 1997). Opponents of privatization contend that privatization leads to a lower quality of service as costs are forced down (Lowery, 1982; O'Looney, 1993). Scheslinger (1998), for example, argued that increased competition in the social service field tends to be price-focused, and with the emphasis on price that typically accompanies privatization, the quality of social services is likely to decline. Proponents of privatization, however, take issue with the presumed connection between pricing and quality. Blank (2000), for example, argued that "even when the private sector too strongly emphasizes price over quality" (p. 43), it is not necessarily true that the private sector will provide lower quality services and the government will provide higher quality services. Blank pointed out that public agencies have been known to provide services that both cost more than privately provided services and are of a lower quality.

Opponents of privatization express their greatest concerns about quality when for-profit entities provide social services. They argue that for-profit providers are likely to reduce services to enhance profits and "cream," that is, provide services to the easiest to serve and to those individuals most likely to benefit from their services (Nightingale & Pindus, 1997). These risks, it is contended, are greater when clients are highly vulnerable and their participation in services is involuntary (Hatry, 1983). These critics contend that assumptions that client satisfaction will be higher with privatized services (as an indicator of quality) are suspect because clients often have little information about service alternatives (Gilbert, 1984).

Efficiency. For proponents of the privatization of social services, one of the underlying assumptions is that privatization is inherently more efficient than government provision of services, and that with greater efficiency, higher quality will inevitably follow. Economists tend to take as givens that competition improves the market and that greater market competition reduces inefficiency (Blank, 2000). Opponents of privatization, however, point out that few data demonstrate that efficiency and greater competition actually improve social service delivery. Scheslinger (1998), in fact, argued that inefficiency may be an indicator of greater quality in social services. Blank (2000), similarly, argued that just as friendships and family relationships are often characterized as "highly inefficient transactions" (p. 39) because individuals simply spend time together, social service providers who take the time to talk with clients and learn more about them may provide better care. Blank pointed to the "efficiency/quality trade-off in the provision of social services" (p. 39) that must be taken into account when social services are privatized.

A study by Motenko and colleagues (1995) regarding the effects of privatization on nine social service agencies in Massachusetts suggests that direct services providers tend to view the drive toward greater efficiency as undermining the quality of their work. Social workers in the agencies that were studied, which included a range of public and private agencies serving the homeless, individuals with mental health and substance abuse problems, and the mentally retarded, described a deteriorating work environment as a result of a managed-care approach to privatization. They found that the increased demands for productivity reduced opportunities for staff collaboration on difficult cases, severely limited the ability of staff to provide mediation and advocacy services, and made it extremely difficult for staff to employ more generalist practice approaches in meeting clients' diverse needs. The researchers also found that although closer monitoring of professional staff existed, which might have translated into greater accountability, staff perceived this process to be primarily for the purpose of enhancing agencies' abilities to demonstrate cost-effectiveness and win new contracts, not to improve services.

Cost Savings. The arguments in favor of and against the privatization of social services also center on the capacity of privatization to reduce costs (Hatry & Durman, 1985; Nightingale & Pindus, 1997). The economic rationale is generally at the core of arguments made in behalf of privatization. It typically involves an intertwining of cost savings with maximization of efficiency (Morgan & England, 1988). Often, however, in the social services arena, proponents of privatization tend to present cost reduction as secondary to the ability of privatization to improve quality. Opinion varies as to whether, in reality, fiscal concerns or quality issues are the driving forces behind efforts to privatize (see Allen et al., 1989; USGAO, 1996a, 1996b).

Opponents of privatization typically do not argue that public agencies provide services in a more cost-effective manner. Instead, they contend that the private sector is not as economical as may be assumed. They point to the initial cost investments that private entities must make to offer services for which the public agency already has a developed capacity (NACA, 2000). They also argue that privatization itself generates new costs, particularly because privatization affects public sector employment, and resources must be mobilized as employees lose their jobs (Barr & McAllister, 1997).

A Middle Position: Not Whether But How to Privatize Social Services

Some commentators have argued that the key issue is not whether social services should be privatized but how (Hatry, 1983; Nightingale & Pindus, 1997). Nightingale and Pindus (1997), for example, wrote that "privatization is not inherently good or bad—the effectiveness of performance depends on implementation" (p. 1). They pointed to research that suggests that key factors associated with the success of privatization efforts are operational in nature: "clear accountability for results, clear criteria in contracts, and clear public objectives" (p. 2). Accordingly, they advised public agencies to simply "specify the roles of contractors, determine appropriate costs, and develop performance criteria that are tailored to the client population being addressed" (p. 13).

USGAO (1997), in its study of social service privatization, however, found that the very factors associated with successful implementation of privatization identified by writers such as Nightingale and Pindus posed "key challenges" (p. 1) to the privatization of these services. Specifically, USGAO (1997) found two key problems when public social service agencies privatize. First, these agencies frequently lacked experience in developing contracts "that specify program results in sufficient detail to effectively hold contractors responsible" (USGAO, 1997, p. 1–2). Specifically, USGAO found that unlike other service arenas, social services posed difficulties in terms of the complexity of tasks that make work requirements harder to clearly specify. Second, USGAO found that public social service agencies had problems monitoring contractors' performance in social service programs, particularly with regard to ensuring clients' access to service and the achievement of program goals without unintended negative consequences for clients. Specifically, USGAO (1997) found difficulties in measuring performance because "services cannot be judged on the basis of client outcomes; treatment approaches cannot be standardized, nor can the appropriateness of workers' decisions be effectively assessed" (p. 8). These findings suggest that the very dynamics that support successful privatization of social services may be the most difficult to achieve.

Privatization, Contracting Out, and Child Welfare

Despite the debate regarding the privatization of social services in general, the question as to whether child welfare services should be privatized has already been largely answered. As Rosenthal (2000) pointed out, state and local governments have paid private, voluntary agencies to provide child welfare services since the early 1800s. Historically, a reliance on nonprofits has existed in the child welfare arena (as well as certain other social services) in large part because of American "public's trust in the integrity, effectiveness, and selflessness of the non-profit sector" (Schuck, 1999, p. 4). Schuck (1999), however, contended that this trust has, at times, been misplaced, as some nonprofit providers operate no differently than for-profit entities. Nonetheless, "the settled acceptance of, and even preference for this alternative is a pivotal factor in many debates about the appropriate role of government" (Schuck, 1999, p. 4).

The Role of Privatization in Child Welfare

Given the historical, social, and cultural acceptance of the role of nonprofit organizations in the provision of child welfare services, it is not surprising that privatized service delivery has become the norm in this arena. A recent report by U.S. Department of Health and Human Services (USDHHS, 2001), which provided findings from a survey of local child welfare agencies, indicated that nationwide, child welfare agencies contract out 58% of all family preservation services, 42% of all residential treatment, and 52% of case management services for adoption. A brief review of historical developments illustrates the role that nonprofit agencies have come to play in child welfare services delivery.

The first significant growth in the number of public-private arrangements for the delivery of child welfare and other social services occurred between 1962 and 1974, as a result of amendments to the Social Security Act that allowed federal funding to be used to fund social services provided by private, nonprofit agencies. This development was a part of broad policy efforts to invest substantial levels of federal funds in mental health, health care, and social services as part of the War on Poverty (Rosenthal, 2000). By the mid-1970s, what is now known as privatization (in the sense of a purchase-of-service system involving individualized service agreements between public and private agencies) had become "an established fact" in the arena of child and family services (Rosenthal, 2000, p. 291). The enactment of the Adoption Assistance and Child Welfare Act of 1980 brought about a second significant increase in privately provided child welfare services as additional federal funds became available (Rosenthal, 2000). In Rosenthal's (2000) words, "an industry of services followed these events" (p. 292).

Beginning in the 1980s with the presidency of Ronald Reagan, a philosophical shift at the federal level moved away from the public commitment at the heart of the Great Society programs of the 1960s and 1970s and toward individual and private solutions to social problems (Kamerman & Kahn, 1989). This shift, embodied in federal and state budget cutbacks in social service programming and the involvement of managed care companies in the provision of Medicaid-funded health services (Motenko et al., 1995), set the stage for a third wave of growth in the privatization of child welfare services. Several studies documented the growth in privatized child welfare service delivery over this period of child welfare privatization. In 1993, for example, the Council of State Governments found that child care and the child welfare services of adoption, foster care, and independent living had been the highest growth areas for privatization over the preceeding five years (Chi, 1994). A federal study (USDHHS, 2001) found that family preservation and residential treatment services are increasingly being privatized through contracting out.

The new privatization of the 1990s took on a variety of forms and occurred in response to very different dynamics than those that characterized the public-private arrangements of the 1960s and 1970s. Whereas the earlier expansions of privatization were associated with the growth of the welfare state, contemporary privatization efforts largely have been the result of such forces as downsizing, government deregulation, and cost containment (Pierson, 1994; Rosenthal, 2000). Although these fiscal and regulatory issues have played primary roles in current privatization efforts, advocates of the new privatization, interestingly, tend to focus less on these factors and more on the purported capacity of the private sector to produce improved outcomes for children and families. Mountjoy (1999), for example, wrote that "[public] child welfare translates into an inefficient, costly, bureaucratic machine, with countless children lost in the cogs" (p. 1), as opposed to the efficiency and quality outcomes realized by private service providers. Snell (2000) similarly associated privatization with a range of positive outcomes, including "reducing the number of children and families involved with the state and ensuring permanency and safety for those children who really need to be protected" (p. 6). Snell argued that private agencies can "move children through the foster care system more quickly, ensure their safety, reduce the number of foster care placements, and reduce the caseload for social workers" (p. 6).

Child Welfare Privatization: Contracting Out

Contracting out, historically, has been the principal form of child welfare privatization. As the dynamics driving privatization have changed, however, contracting out has evolved. In the past, contracting out was largely noncompetitive, resembling quasi-grant arrangements more than contractual relationships (Hatry & Durman, 1985). As broader efforts toward privatization have been considered and implemented, contracting out has taken new forms. As this process has unfolded, contracting out has proven to be a highly diverse process, varying in nature and scope from one state to another as various privatization initiatives are designed and implemented. As the case studies in Part II illustrate, contracting out is not a single model of privatization but, instead, reflects multiple structural designs, none of which has emerged as a clearly preferable model (American Federation of State, County, and Municipal Employees, 2000; McCullough, 2001).

Given the long history of contracting out in the provision of child welfare services and its current status as the "premier privatization mechanism" (Morgan & England, 1988, p. 980), there has been and continues to be wide support for its increasing use. Some commentators, however, have raised questions regarding the advantages and disadvantages of this mechanism, particularly as newer forms of contracting out have emerged. These issues warrant consideration.

Proponents of contracting out have identified a range of benefits associated with this privatization approach (Ascher, 1987; DeHoog, 1984; Hartley, 1986; Moore, S., 1987; Savas, 1987). Specifically, they maintain that contracting out

- is efficient and effective because it promotes competition and, as a result of competitive bidding, drives down costs;

- results in better management, because decisionmaking is based on costs and benefits;

- reduces the number of government employees who are needed;

- reduces dependency on government, which, as a monopoly, is inherently inefficient and ineffective

- allows poor performance to be penalized; and

- fosters greater flexibility and responsiveness to consumers' needs because bureaucratic hierarchies are not involved.

Illinois, for example, recently expanded its contracting of child welfare services (Method, 2001). The reasons given were the greater flexibility and creativity in service provision that contracting out provides, including opportunities to experiment with new programs and approaches to improve outcomes for children and families; the latitude it gives states to discontinue contracts when performance is inadequate; and the opportunities that contracting out presents to use financial awards and penalties to promote goal achievement (Method, 2001).

There are, however, critics of contracting out, particularly as it has assumed a larger role in the delivery of child welfare services. Concerns are that contracting out presents the potential for corruption in awarding contracts; limits the ability of public agencies to respond in times of emergency when contractors default and seek bankruptcy protection; is not cost-free, because the public agency must monitor and enforce contracts with private agencies; creates an incentive for contractors to reduce costs through hiring poorly qualified staff; and can result in loss of jobs for public employees with costs to the public sector in the form of unemployment compensation (Atkan, 1995).

In her analysis of the effect of privatization on the employees of a number of New York City nonprofits that offered child and family services, mental health treatment, and services to the homeless and the elderly, Bernstein (1991) found that contracting out did not necessarily result in the benefits typically associated with the process (greater efficiency, better management, or greater flexibility). Among the problems that staff identified were lengthy waits for government reimbursement, the need to invest considerable energy and time in resolving billing problems rather than serving clients, frequent changes in government rules, multiple monitors, and the inability to use the required government reporting systems for internal management purposes with the result that contracting required "shadow" management information and accounting systems. Bernstein found that:

> repeatedly, managers describe situations in which aspects of
> the management of contracted services conflict with reality.
> In accepting these paradoxes, managers perceive their task as
> a game. This perception enables them to understand, get con-
> trol of, and keep in perspective contracted services. (p. 22)

Starr (1988) wrote that privatization through contracting out "diminishes the operational but not the fiscal or functional sphere of government action" (p. 12) and, as a result, raises as many questions as it answers. Governments may perceive benefits in their ability to shift complaints and claims to private entities, but clients may be placed at a disadvantage because private entities become "powerful claimants themselves" (Starr, 1988, p. 12). Starr questioned "whether this sort of partial privatization achieves any reduction in government spending or deficits" (p. 12).

Also at issue is whether contracting out child welfare services creates, to any meaningful extent, the competition that lies at the core of the presumed benefits of privatization. Many commentators believe that any such competition among child welfare agencies seeking a contract is extremely limited. Wulczyn and Orlebeke (1998), for example, wrote that:

> wherever child welfare services are provided by public agencies, competition plays little or no role in the evolution of the system. Even in areas of the country where child welfare services are more heavily privatized, the role of competition as a decisive influence has been somewhat muted, in part because public agencies have not yet managed contracts in ways that stimulate meaningful competition. For better or worse, the field has been "mission" dominated, rather than outcome dominated. (p. 14)

This issue raises questions not only about the nature of the competitive environment that can be created in relation to the provision of child welfare services but also about the extent to which outcomes can be used to create and support the desired level of competition.

New Aspects of Child Welfare Privatization

As contracting out has evolved, three new aspects of child welfare privatization have emerged: the use of performance-based incentives in contracts with private providers; implementation of managed care principles, including managed care-based financial methodologies; and extension of contracting out beyond the traditional nonprofit community to for-profit entities.

Contracting Out and Performance-Based Incentives

In contrast to earlier forms of contracting out, in which private agencies simply agreed to serve a certain number of children in return for payment based on a predetermined daily rate for each child's care, current models of contracting out often involve performance-based targets and incentives. With the advent of managed care in the health care arena and the extension of managed care principles to other human services, there has been increased focus on performance measurement or "performance targets." USGAO (1999) defined performance measurement as

> the ongoing monitoring and reporting of program accomplishments, particularly towards pre-established goals....Performance measures may address the type or level of program activities conducted (process), the direct products and services delivered by a program (outputs), and/or the results of those products and services (outcomes). (p. 6)

Typically, performance targets are stated as increases or decreases in a specified factor, such as, in the case of child welfare services, a reduction in the average length of time that children spend in foster care (Casey Outcomes and Decision-Making Project, 1998). Achievement of performance targets is determined through such methods as random sampling, "planned sampling," and consumer input (Office of Federal Procurement Policy, 1998).

Performance-based incentives connect payment to the achievement of pre-established goals, whether in the form of process indicators, outputs, or outcomes. Payment is tied to or contingent on the provider's ability to achieve goals that are defined at the time the contract is executed. Because payment is tied to predetermined outcomes, performance-based incentives highlight the need to define outcomes in a realistic and meaningful way. In the child welfare system, as in other service delivery systems, many agree that performance-based incentive strategies offer an opportunity to improve results for children and families (see LaFaive, 2000). The development and implementation of performance-based incentives, however, have presented a host of challenges as these processes have played out in one jurisdiction after another (discussed more specifically in Part II).

First, performance-based incentives require an understanding of which outcomes should be used. Specifically, this determination involves an assessment of which outcomes are realistic and whether adequate measures exist to assess the presence of the desired outcomes. As USDHHS (1999) noted, it is essential to determine whether existing outcome measures and data are "sufficiently strong to support performance-based financing" (p. 3). In that regard, the Alliance for Redesigning Government (1996) stressed that reaching agreement on outcomes for social services is difficult for several reasons:

- Determining which results are more important than others inevitably brings into play deeply held and often conflicting values.

- There has been a long history of developing new programs for new social problems, with the result that programs overlap and often have inconsistent objectives.

- Results related to well-being are, by their very nature, elusive.

- Public employees tend to view a focus on results as "shorthand for eliminating their jobs" (p. 7).

The literature suggests that there are strengths and weaknesses associated with the use of performance-based incentives. Mark Friedman (1996), for example, in a report from the Finance Project, urged caution in the use of performance-based incentives:

> Crafting money consequences to go with performance is tricky business. Pay for performance is an appealing concept, but hard to implement when the products are changes in human conditions; when performance is tied to the severity of client problems, not the quality of service delivery; and when there are often ready means to game the system. This means that we should not rush to implement pay for performance (or other rewards or penalty policies) before we know what good performance is. We need to build performance histories, and begin to measure and reward improvements on past performance. (p. 4)

Consistent with Friedman's (1996) observations, the National Research Council (Perrin & Koshel, 1997) emphasized the benefits of outcome measures in supporting a continuous improvement system and targeting technical assistance, as opposed to using such measures to determine how much, or even whether, a provider will be paid. In the report, Perrin and Koshel (1997) noted that

> if one measure or a combination of measures suggests that a given state is having unusual difficulty in making progress in meeting its...objectives, such information should trigger an alert that some additional resources or technical assistance is needed to overcome particular circumstances. (p. 4)

When the USDHHS Children's Bureau convened experts to consider the use of performance-based incentives in child welfare, the group identified a number of issues that were pertinent to state-level privatization efforts (USDHHS, 1999). Specifically, the participants focused on three areas in which questions remain to be resolved:

- The use of performance-based incentives in the context of providing a broad range of services to a population of children and families with widely varying needs. When designing a performance-based child welfare system, which services should be targeted? How can the design take into account the distortions that may occur inadvertently when one part of the system is emphasized at the expense of others?

- The potential effect of increased accountability on the children and families served through child welfare agencies. How can a performance-based incentive system be used to increase accountability and improve performance without punishing children and families when a contracting agency fails to perform well?

- The speed at which performance-based incentives should be put into place. The full effect of financing changes on the consumers of any human service, including child welfare, may not be apparent for some period of time. Can there be a "thoughtful, staged process for any new financing change" (USDHHS, 1999, p. 3) that permits an assessment of the effect on children, families, and service systems?

The issue of defining appropriate performance measures in child welfare, whether in the context of fiscal incentives or not, is a thorny one. Kansas Action for Children (1998) noted that "performance measurement has become a cottage industry in child welfare" (p. 9). For years, academic institutions, private foundations, and governments have struggled to define child welfare outcomes and develop strategies for effectively measuring them. Typically, certain child welfare domains have been highlighted: safety, permanency, child and family functioning, and client satisfaction (Wulczyn & Orlebeke, 1998). In a recent analysis of performance measurement in child welfare, Usher, Gibbs and Wildfire (1999) concluded that foundation-based efforts in this area have been "encouraging," in that they had shown that performance improvements were possible, however:

> They also suggest a need for caution in adopting a few simplistic performance indicators and ignoring changes in context that dictate adjustments in performance standards and expectations. The accomplishment of one set of goals (such as reduced admissions [into foster care]) can have repercussions for other performance indicators (such as length of stay). (pp. 13–14)

The process of refining performance indicators and measurement has continued, but it is not surprising that operational outputs, rather than service quality in the form of outcomes, are most often used as the performance indicators for privatized social services (Kansas Action for Children, 1999).

Second, implementation of performance-based incentives requires an understanding of the existing financial structure, the ways that incentives have been structured in the past, and the effects of past incentives (USDHHS, 1999). The relationship between fiscal structure and outcome may be quite complex and suggest a direct cause-effect relationship when, in fact, numerous variables are involved. It has been argued, for example, that contracts that provide per diem rates for children in foster care create incentives for private agencies to retain children in foster care as long as possible (Craig, Kulik, James, & Neilsen, 1998). From this perspective, changes in the payment structure, such as a set fee for the care of a child regardless of the length of the child's stay in foster care, should have the immediate effect of shortening children's foster care stays (see Craig et al., 1998). This premise, however, assumes that it is the financing structure that is determinative of the length of children's stay in foster care, when research suggests that a far more complicated set of factors relate to length of stay (see Barth, 1997; Testa, Shook, Cohen, & Woods, 1996).

Private providers of services, however, may find that performance-based contracting is far more beneficial than the use of financing mechanisms such as capitation, capped allocations, and case rates (discussed later). Under performance-based contracting, generally, less financial risk to providers exists even when the performance indicators may be questionable. On the other hand, performance-based contracting may penalize quality providers who work with more challenging clients and develop innovative approaches to services for clients with the most severe needs (Center for Assessment and Policy Development [CAPD], 1999). As noted earlier, commentators have pointed to the incentive for creaming that performance-based contracting may create (CAPD, 1999).

With that concern in mind, the argument is made that if performance-based incentives are used, service goals must be clearly defined and alternatives must be considered that can assist providers in achieving those goals without inadvertently creating a disincentive to serve (CAPD, 1999). As examples, performance-based contracts may be developed to encourage providers to put their "maximum efforts" into achieving certain outcomes, encourage providers to critically assess their current programmatic strategies in light of the desired outcomes for clients, or require providers to collect data on outcomes and use those data to refine their programs (CAPD, 1999, p. 1).

The Use of Managed Care Principles in Child Welfare Privatization

Kamerman and Kahn (1999) observed that given the growing concern with management problems and the importance of contract specifics and capacity to assess performance and outcome measures, it should not be surprising that a new approach to contracting via tighter management has caught the eye of public officials and child and family social service professionals. (p. 22)

The "new approach" that they mention involves a range of activities and practices that fall within "the managed care rubric" (Kamerman & Kahn, 1999, p. 22).

Drawing on the experiences of the health care arena (Jackson 1995), in the mid-1990s, child welfare agencies began to use managed care principles in the redesign of services for children and families in the child welfare system (USGAO, 1998a). Wulczyn and Orlebeke (1998) attributed the interest in managed care to mounting fiscal concerns in the wake of the devolution of responsibility for child welfare services to states and localities. In their study of four child welfare systems (Kansas; Hamilton County, Ohio; Tennessee; and District 13, Florida), the researchers found that the choice to use managed care approaches grew from frustrations regarding traditional payment systems, specifically with regard to programs that rewarded longer stays in foster care, the categorical nature of funding streams, and the inability to tie outcomes to fiscal rewards or penalties.

Feild (1996) similarly found that public child welfare agencies viewed managed care as a mechanism for aligning funding with program objectives, specifically with regard to reduction in children's length of stay in foster care and promotion of permanency for children. Interestingly, Feild also found that public child welfare agencies typically express relatively few concerns that under managed care arrangements, they will lose control with regard to service access and/or service quality—issues that have arisen in other service arenas that have moved to managed care approaches.

USGAO (1998a) found that 13 states had initiated child welfare managed care projects and that more than 20 other states had initiatives planned, although at the time, only about 4% of children in foster care were served under managed care arrangements. The Child Welfare League of America (CWLA, 1999) found in its survey of states conducted in late 1998 and early 1999 that 29 of the 49 states that responded (59%) had one or more child welfare initiatives under way or planned within the next year that could be considered managed care or privatization, although some respondents did not use those terms to describe their efforts.

The 2000–2001 survey conducted by CWLA (McCullough & Schmitt, 2002) found that 39 such initiatives were being implemented (33% were statewide, 38% were limited to one geographic area, and 28% were limited to a set number of children or specified agency contacts). CWLA (1999) estimated that the number of children served through such initiatives in 1999 was approximately 10% of the total child welfare population. In 2000, CWLA found that states were reporting projections of large numbers of children to be served through such initiatives in the following 12 months (125,000 children) and even larger numbers (210,000 children) when their initiatives were fully implemented

(McCullough & Schmitt, 2002). The CWLA 2000-2001 survey, however, also found that the target populations for these initiatives were broadening to include both children and families in the child welfare system and children referred by other systems (McCullough & Schmitt, 2002).

The Use of Managed Care Frameworks for Service Delivery. USGAO (1998a) found that public child welfare agencies were increasingly using managed care because of two of its features, both of which are consistent with privatization theory: the use of prepaid capitated payments to control costs and shift financial risk to providers, and the use of a single point of entry, such as a lead agency or managed care company, to enhance accountability for the delivery of quality service.

In its analysis of child welfare managed care arrangements, USGAO (1998a) found certain patterns in service organization and delivery:

- The majority of the arrangements expected private service providers to organize and coordinate a full array of services so that children and families had access to needed services.

- The public sector generally transferred case management responsibilities to private agencies.

- The public sector remained actively engaged at strategic points in the service delivery process.

- Public agencies used a variety of quality assurance activities to ensure that concerns about cost savings did not jeopardize the quality of or access to services.

- Despite the early interest in capitation (either for each referred client or for a defined population who resided in a geographical area), most public child welfare agencies limited the financial risk to which providers were exposed, either by capitating only part of the provider's payment and reimbursing other services on a fee-for-service basis or specifying in contracts a limit on the providers' financial risk.

USGAO (1998a) identified three major challenges in the implementation of managed care: (1) cash flow issues because states were making prospective payments but were receiving reimbursement under such funding sources as the federal Title IV-E program only after the services had been provided; (2) limited service and cost information, leading to difficulties in defining appropriate outcomes and setting adequate rates; and (3) dramatic shifts in the roles of public and private agency staff as the private sector assumed management and administrative functions.

In line with the USGAO findings, McCullough (1997, p. 15) wrote that few child welfare agencies that have implemented managed care approaches have had the information they needed regarding utilization, costs, or performance to make major systemic changes or to develop outcomes and protocols that reflect best practice. She observed that "without data on current utilization and outcomes linked to cost, it is very difficult to design and price a managed care or privatized reform initiative" (McCullough, 2001, p. 4). She noted that "most states simply do not have the capacity to track the services used, the outcomes, and the costs to serve an individual child and family over an episode of care," and many states cannot "even track and report accurate aggregate costs that are linked to utilization and outcomes" (McCullough, 2001, p. 4).

Consistent with these observations, Wulczyn and Orlebeke (1998) found in their study of four child welfare systems that had implemented prospective payment systems and other managed care strategies that "no site had completely adequate information to set baselines for payment and utilization levels" (p. 9). Although both public and private agencies have attempted to develop the information technology needed to successfully implement managed care initiatives, this area has continued to pose some of the most significant challenges to privatization (McCullough, 2001). These challenges arise both in relation to the data collection and management tasks of privatization and in terms of the relationship between such efforts and existing state information systems, such as SACWIS (McCullough, 2001).

On a note of greater optimism, however, McCullough (1997) observed that "as child welfare administrators become more familiar with the essential tools in the managed care toolbox" (p. 15), they can adopt and apply managed care principles to child welfare services and achieve both system reform and cost containment. McCullough recommended that certain steps be taken with regard to some of the key challenges in implementing managed care approaches:

- difficulties in defining outcomes: a greater focus on "symptom reduction" and "client satisfaction," as in the health care arena;

- problems with case management, utilization review, and "gate-keeping" as a result of the role of the courts in final decision-making regarding children and families: bringing the court system to "the table when managed care plans are being crafted";

- quality assurance: greater attention to accreditation and licensing; and,

- information systems: the development of timely, comprehensive data produced by a system that is "need-driven, flexible, user-friendly, and capable of generating useful reports for all users" (pp. 16–21).

Managed Care Financial Methodologies. A key aspect of managed care in child welfare is the use of distinctive financial methodologies (which often occur in conjunction with performance-based incentives). In contrast to the traditional noncompetitive, fee-for-service contracts that typified public/nonprofit agency arrangements in the past, child welfare systems increasingly are considering the use of capitated and other risk-shifting payment methods. Each of these methods involves prospective funding (unlike traditional fee-for-service arrangements, in which the provider is paid for services already provided). Wulczyn and Orlebeke (1998) pointed out that although financial models vary from state to state, several commonalities exist: a shift away from fee-for-service and per diem payments to prospective payment systems, mechanisms that shift financial risk from the public child welfare agency to private service providers, and greater flexibility so that providers have the latitude to spend dollars across service categories, regardless of funding source.

When applied to child welfare, these financial models are designed, in essence, to promote the provision of appropriate services for children and families and the discharge of children in a timely way from foster care. By the way of example, in the arena of foster care, the key goal typically is to shorten children's lengths of stay. To the extent that a provider is able to decrease a child's stay in foster care (based on defined length-of-stay standards), the provider may be able to use a larger portion of the payment received to develop new and creative services and programs, may receive a bonus or other fiscal incentive for achieving that goal, or in some cases, may simply be paid the agreed-on rate. To the extent that children's stays are longer, the provider may have little, if any, funding remaining for new service development or may be financially penalized. Key to such systems, however, is the level of funding. If adequately funded, incentives can work positively to support the development of creative service delivery models; if inadequately funded, incentives can result in children being "pushed through the system" in response to financial needs (Kansas Action for Children, 1998).

The major financial managed care–type methodologies that child welfare systems have used in privatization initiatives are capitation, capped allocations, and case rates. Under capitation, providers typically are required to deliver services for an annual fixed fee for each child in the defined service population. The rate is a per-child, per-month, population-based payment, and as a result, the rate remains fixed regardless of the number of children served. A new client does not generate new income. Under a pure capitated system, the mechanism provides for considerable flexibility in how the provider will allocate resources (Wulczyn & Sheu, 1998). On the other hand, the risk of financial loss is shifted entirely to the private provider (USGAO, 1998a; Wulczyn & Sheu, 1998). In child welfare, this prospect is particularly daunting because it is extremely difficult, if not impossible, to project the number of children and families within a given community who may enter the child welfare system or the level and duration of services that children and families will need (CWLA, 1999). These realities have made pure capitation systems unattractive to most child welfare systems and private providers.

As a consequence, some privatization efforts have modified the pure capitation approach and developed predictable, capitation-like financial methodologies. Capped allocations resemble capitation in that they are predetermined payments that cover all services to be provided (CWLA, 1999). They differ from capitation in that they are tied to the service needs of a targeted population as opposed to a general population of potential clients to be served.

As an alternative to capitation and capitation-like payment structures, a number of child welfare privatization initiatives have implemented a case rate approach. A case rate methodology pools funds and allocates money on a per-child basis, not as an annual payment, but as the rate for the total cost of care for each child (regardless of which services are provided) for the duration of the child's stay in the child welfare system (USGAO, 1998a). Unlike capitation, the case rate approach generates new income with each new client who is served. Although McCullough and Schmitt (2002) found that the case rate methodology is and continues to be the most common arrangement in child welfare privatization, the authors also found considerable variation in case rates among states for similar services to similar populations. Case rates in the 1998–1999 CWLA study, for example, were found to vary by more than $1,200 per child per month (CWLA, 1999).

Despite the differences among capitation, capped allocations, and case rates, each is viewed as creating financial incentives to move children out of the child welfare system as quickly as possible (Kansas Action for Children, 1998). Each, however, poses risks to service providers, and as a result, most child welfare privatization initiatives have developed risk-sharing processes in which both the private provider and the public funder bear some risk of financial loss. In its 1998–1999 survey of managed care and privatization initiatives, CWLA (1999) found that 74% percentage of these efforts included some risk-sharing arrangement; by the 2000–2001 survey, almost 95% of the reported initiatives used one or more types of risk-sharing arrangements (McCullough & Schmitt, 2002). USGAO (1998a) likewise, found that because of "the unknowns associated with the size of the population needing services and the scope and duration of those services" (p. 8), the large majority of public and private agencies that it surveyed had created mechanisms to limit the financial risk to any one party. Risk-limiting mechanisms included fixing payment for some services and reimbursing other services on a fee-for-service basis and, in the greater number of cases, limiting the level of financial risk that the service provider assumed through specific contract terms.

Wulczyn and Oberleke (1998) identified four risk-sharing arrangements that allocated certain kinds of risk to different parties:

- Arrangements in which public agencies continued to carry upside volume risk (the risk that admissions would exceed the level that had been anticipated and budgeted);

- Arrangements in which private providers assumed downside volume risk (that admissions would be lower than expected);

- Arrangements in which private agencies assumed unit cost risk (that changes in the cost of providing a unit of service would negatively affect the expenditure rate under a fixed-reimbursement contact); and

- Arrangements in which private agencies assumed at least some duration risk (that children would remain in foster care longer than expected, thus increasing expenditures beyond the budgeted level) and level-of-service expenditure risk (that clients would use higher levels of service, resulting in higher unit costs than expected). This risk-sharing arrangement was the common.

Risk limitations through contractual provisions are discussed more fully in the case studies in Part II. As an example, however, a contract with private providers may set a risk corridor, such as a percentage-shared risk factor of 10%. Under such a contract, a private provider would be responsible for all costs up to 110% above the case rate. Should costs reach or exceed 110% of the case rate, either the public agency would pay all excess costs or the public agency and the private provider would share equal responsibility for the excess. Likewise, if the provider's costs were 10% below the case rate, the provider would be allowed to retain the full savings. Should savings exceed 10% of the case rate, the provider either would be required to refund the excess savings to the public agency or the two agencies would share equally in the realized savings.

Typically, even when a capitated or case rate system is used, managed care and privatization initiatives included provisions for exempting some clients from the managed care arrangement, clients whose services are covered under fee-for-service payment arrangements. These approaches are discussed more fully in Part II.

For example, in Kansas, the financial methodology for serving children with high-end needs evolved over time. At the beginning of its privatization initiative, Kansas required foster care contracting agencies to make a special application for access to a catastrophic risk pool for a child with exceptional needs. In the second year of the foster care contract, Kansas changed the approach and set a $1,500 flat rate for each such child. Under the current system, each contractor is now allocated a fixed number of slots (ranging from 24 to 35) for which the contractor has 60 days from the date of referral to determine whether the child will be served outside the case rate on a fee-for-service basis (USGAO, 1998a).

It is important to note that as groups have developed models of child welfare privatization, no evidence has been found that any model (capitation, capped allocation, case rate, or risk sharing in its many forms) has resulted in cost savings (McCullough, 2001). In some cases, funds have been redirected and better results have been achieved, but these new systems consistently have been found to cost more than more traditional approaches to child welfare service delivery (McCullough, 2001).

For-Profit Entities' Provision of Traditional Public Services

A third trend seen in some privatization efforts is the emergence of for-profit entities as providers of child welfare services. Although relatively limited in child welfare today, for-profit entities have been far more active in adult and juvenile corrections and such social service fields as child support enforcement. The experiences of these systems in contracting with for-profits for service provision provides information that can be used to assess the potential strengths and weaknesses of for-profit privatization of child welfare services.

For-Profit Prisons and Correctional Facilities. The for-profit privatization of adult and juvenile correctional facilities has generated considerable debate. Questions about the appropriateness of for-profit management of prisons and other correctional facilities have persisted because the outcomes associated with prison privatization are not entirely clear. In one study of a privatized prison in which female inmates were housed, Logan (1991) found that conditions had generally improved. In another study, Hatry (1983) found somewhat higher quality in privately operated prisons than public ones, but found questionable results regarding lowered costs. Hart and colleagues (1997) found that the privatization of prisons led to lower costs but also found a higher level of violence in those facilities. USGAO (1996b), after reviewing studies and interviewing a number of key individuals, concluded that the results with regard to both quality and costs were mixed. USGAO (1996b) found that comparisons of operational costs indicated little difference between publicly and privately operated prisons or equivocal results that made a definitive conclusion impossible. With regard to quality comparisons, USGAO (1996b) found that too many questions existed about services in publicly and privately operated prisons to reach a conclusion regarding higher quality in either setting. Given these findings, USGAO (1996b) warned against generalizing the findings of any studies.

In the face of conflicting evidence, policymakers have disagreed about the ongoing privatization of prisons. Proponents of prison privatization most often cite the promise of substantial savings and assert that research demonstrates that privately operated prisons cost less (Bates, 2000a). One proponent (Moore, A. T., 1998), for example, argued that "the evidence is overwhelming that the private sector delivers quality correctional services at lower cost" (p. 2). On the other hand, Berger (1999), contended that privatized prisons have failed to create promised savings in the operations of prisons. He argued that private prisons have engaged in affirmative practices to heighten profit margins and diminish quality (such as skimping on food and reducing medical care). Other critics have pointed to staffing deficiencies in the form of high turnover (cited by some as three times the rate at public prisons), excessive overtime, and poor training (Greene, 2000). Bates (2000) concluded that "the real danger of privatization is not some innate inhumanity on the part of its practitioners but rather the added financial incentives that reward inhumanity" (p. 9).

The performance of one of the key entities in the field, Correctional Services Corporation (CSC, which became Prison Realty Corp. in January 1999 when it merged with another entity), has added to the concerns about prison privatization. A management company in the private corrections industry since 1989, CSC initially entered corrections by contracting for and operating adult prisons in Georgia and other states (*Atlanta Business Chronicle,* 1999). In 1996, it entered the youth service arena, assuming the operation of two youth training facilities in Florida (*Atlanta Business Chronicle*, 1999). In 1999, after a critical report by the U.S. Department of Justice, CSC agreed to pay $1.65 million to settle a lawsuit that alleged deficient management practice at a Ohio facility. That lawsuit claimed that CSC provided inadequate medical care for inmates, allowed guards to use excessive force, and classified inmates so improperly that violent offenders were easily able to attack other inmates (resulting in the murder of 2 prisoners and the stabbing of another 20 prisoners in the first year of the facility's operation) (*Atlanta Business Chronicle*, 1999; Greene, 2000). Such charges are not limited to CSC.

In 1999, the U.S. Department of Justice initiated a full-scale investigation of a juvenile correction facility in Jena, Louisiana, operated by Wackenhut Corrections Corporation (Greene, 2000). The department found a pattern of understaffing, physical abuse of youth, denial of access to telephones or recreation, and overuse of administrative segregation and isolation (Greene, 2000).

Child Support Enforcement Services by For-Profit Entities. Aside from adult and juvenile corrections, the relative effectiveness of the for-profit sector compared with the public or nonprofit sectors is also unclear. The principal area in which researchers have done evaluative studies of privatization is child support enforcement. Again, findings are mixed. One study by the Pioneer Institute for Public Policy Research, Inc. (1997), found that private firms performed more efficiently than government agencies in this arena. Specifically, the study found greater private sector efficiency in terms of developing and implementing information systems, employees' achievement of higher collection goals, and staff management (particularly, the dismissal of poor-performing employees and retention of better employees) (Pioneer Institute for Public Policy Research, 1997). In its study of fully privatized child support enforcement services in 15 states, USGAO (1996a), however, found more equivocal results. For-profits that provided child support enforcement services performed as well as, or in some cases, better than public programs on such indicators as locating noncustodial parents and collecting support. The results associated with cost-effectiveness, however, were not as clear (USGAO, 1996a).

The Arguments For and Against Contracting with For-Profit Entities. Some commentators emphasize the benefits associated with for-profit entities' assumption of services previously provided by public agencies. Hatry and Durman (1985), for example, wrote that difficulties with for-profits can be sufficiently minimized when the public agency subjects these providers to close scrutiny and has an understanding of the inherent problems that may arise when a contractor is profit-oriented. When the public agency "is capable of sophisticated administration" and "explicitly addresses service quality issues," they maintain that any issues related to quality can be readily addressed (Hatry & Durman, 1985, p. 42). In their opinion, "there is no inherent reason why for-profit firms could not compete for most, if not all, social service delivery activities" (p. 42).

Other experts are less convinced. Some critics of for-profit privatization efforts focus on the philosophical and ethical problems that are raised when public services are delivered by entities that are profit-oriented. Morgan and England (1988) maintained that for-profit privatization goes "hand in hand with the loss of cohesive community" (p. 982), Tobin (1983) contended that reliance on for-profits undermines public commitment to the availability of essential services, and USGAO (1997) expressed concern about the potential effect of profitmaking on clients' access to service, primarily in terms of providers' decisions to cream. Whitt and Yago (1985), in their study of for-profit assumption of public transportation services, observed that private dominance frequently leads to purely prof-it-seeking behavior, undermining the development of improved public services.

The documented abuses associated with a for-profit organization's provision of group care for the mentally retarded in Indiana illustrates the abuses that can occur. In that case, investigators found that the state and the for-profit provider had "agreed to a reimbursement rate for care of the retarded so low that it drove out of the market more conscientious and ethical community providers" (Kuttner, 2000, p. 4). The dangers associated with this type of arrangement are exacerbated when clients are relatively powerless. As in the case of group care for the mentally retarded, the individuals served are "hardly sovereign consumers," and given the diffusion of accountability, it is often difficult to determine "whom to blame" when problems develop (Kuttner, 2000, p. 4). Commenting on the abuses in that case and similar situations involving for-profit health care providers, Kuttner (2000) concluded, "this is the price of privatization coupled with budget austerity" (p. 4).

Gormley (1994–1995) took the view that a number of questions need to be addressed before dismissing the role that for-profit entities can and should play in the delivery of social services. Acknowledging that the for-profit and nonprofit sectors may "have different priorities and goals" (p. 229), he also asked to what extent differences in the level of external supports affect their performance. Raising the fact that in some industries, "we may need all the responsible providers we can get" (p. 229), he outlined four issues that should be explored with regard to for-profit entities assuming responsibility for public services:

- how for-profits would perform if they enjoyed the same tax benefits as nonprofits,

- how for-profits would perform if they could participate in government programs at the same level as nonprofits,

- how for-profits would perform if they had an equivalent level of volunteer support as not-for-profits, and

- what would happen to a service delivery area if for-profit providers "were to disappear."

Taking the position that for-profits are appropriate alternatives only under certain conditions, Melia (1997, p. 14) urged that for-profits be considered only for those programs in which the obstacles to efficient performance by the government (such as high overhead, inflexibility, inadequate technology, and the absence of performance incentives) outweigh the "handicaps" of these entities (profit motive and marketing costs). In his analysis of the cost-effectiveness of for-profits compared with government performance in three states, he found that depending on the program, the cost-effectiveness of for-profits ranged from 56% more effective to 37% less effective than the government. Melia (1997) concluded that one of two dynamics was taking place: either for-profit entities were not necessarily more cost-effective than governments, or, as he believed more likely, "a private company does not always pass those savings along to the taxpayers in the form of lower costs or better services" (p. 14).

Little has been written about the assumption of child welfare services by for-profit entities. Some of the arguments that have been made for and against private prison contracting, however, may apply equally to the provision of child welfare services by for-profit entities. Based on the work of the University of Connecticut (2000) on issues related to for-profit prisons, Table 1 lists the arguments that are made for and against the use of for-profit entities in providing public services.

Current Status of Contracting with For-Profits for the Provision of Child Welfare Services. Historically, few jurisdictions have privatized child welfare services through contracts with for-profit entities. USGAO (1997) found that the majority of privatized social services were provided by nonprofit entities. In its survey, USGAO (1997) found that the proportion of state and local budgets for private contractors allocated to for-profit organizations varied from as little as zero for child welfare services to as much as 100% for child support enforcement. The jurisdictions reported that the proportion of funding allocated to for-profits had not changed between 1990 and 1997.

In a subsequent report focused exclusively on child welfare services and use of managed care arrangements to serve children in foster care, USGAO (1998a) concluded that "for-profit managed care companies have not had a major role in implementing managed care in child welfare; only a few jurisdictions are using for-profit companies to administer and provide child welfare services" (p. 1). USGAO found that in two initiatives, for-profit entities were the lead agency and service provider; in five initiatives, for-profits provided services as part of a managed care network; in two initiatives, for-profits served as an administrative service provider; and in one case, a for-profit entity functioned as a managed care organization. In those communities in which for-profits were serving in some service provision role, USGAO found that the entities had provided services to children and families before the implementation of managed care.

In its 1998-1999 survey of states and counties that had or were planning privatization efforts, CWLA (1999) found that for-profits played a substantial role in the management of services in only 3 of the 47 reported managed care and/or privatization initiatives. CWLA, in fact, concluded that "public agency adminis-

Table 1

Arguments For and Against Contacting with For-Profit Entities

Performance Area	Pros	Cons
Cost	Discourages waste because careful spending enhances profits Counteracts the motivation of budget-based government agencies to grow in size and maximize budgets Makes true costs evident, allowing them to be analyzed, compared, and adjusted Avoids cumbersome and rigid government procurement processes	Is more expensive because it adds a profit margin to all costs Creates new costs associated with contracting—bidding, managing, and monitoring "Low balling" (low initial bids followed by unjustifiable cost increases in later contracts) may increase costs in long run May have higher initial margin costs than would be needed if government services were expanded
Quality	Creates an alternative and raises standards for the government as well as for the private sector Adds new expertise and skills Could hardly do worse than some current public efforts	May reduce quality because of pressures to cut economic corners May result in creaming, as providers serve the "best" and leave the "worst" unserved
Quantity	Allows quicker response to changing needs and to the correction of inaccurate predictions or faulty policies Helps limit the size of government	Creates incentives to lobby for laws and policies that serve the private provider rather than public interest Creates a type of underground government, which adds to the size of government

Table 1

Arguments For and Against Contacting with For-Profit Entities

Performance Area	Pros	Cons
Flexibility	Allows greater flexibility, promoting innovation and experimentation Reduces the level of bureaucracy involved in management decisions Reduces some of the political pressures that can interfere with good management Promotes specialization to deal with special needs populations	May limit flexibility if provider refuses to perform beyond contract without renegotiation Reduces the ability to coordinate with other relevant public agencies (i.e., police and courts)
Liability	May decrease government risks of liability through higher quality and insurance	May cost government more because of increased liability exposure May shift risk away from government, which is the best party to bear the risk

| Accountability | Increases accountability because market mechanisms are added to political process

Increases accountability because it is easier for the government to monitor a contractor than itself

Encourages broader interest and involvement of people outside government | Reduces accountability because private parties are not subject to the same political controls as the government

Diffuses responsibility, so the two parties can each blame the other

Reduces accountability due to difficulties in contract enforcement |

Source: University of Connecticut, 2000.

trators do not seem inclined to abandon their missions to for-profit organizations," and that, as a consequence, "the public sector and the nonprofit providers continue to be the dominant forces that are shaping managed care and privatization" (p. 6). In their 2000–2001 survey, McCullough and Schmitt (2002) found a slightly higher percentage of child welfare initiatives involved a for-profit entity, but the total remained less than 10%.

Nonetheless, concerns continue to be expressed about the increasing interest of for-profit entities in child welfare and the extent to which public agencies may ultimately be attracted to the resources, technology, and administrative expertise that for-profits appear to offer (Leadership 18 Group, 2000; Wulczyn & Orlebeke, 1998). The central concern may flow from the primary mission of for-profits, which is to maximize profits for the benefit of the shareholders. As opposed to nonprofits, which typically find alternative strategies to ensure that services can be continued when resources prove inadequate, for-profits are more likely to assess the financial viability of continuing to provide a service and make profit-based decisions accordingly (Leadership 18 Group, 2000). Accountability is likely to be framed in terms of financial benefit to shareholders, not the best interests of the clients who are served (Leadership 18 Group, 2000). This key difference between for-profits and nonprofits raises issues regarding the direct accountability of government-funded programs to the public and to the clients served by the program (Leadership 18 Group, 2000).

PART II

Child Welfare Privatization Initiatives: Six Case Studies

Many jurisdictions have developed new approaches to the design and delivery of child welfare services that incorporate aspects of privatization, managed care, performance-based contracting, and other features associated with these approaches. Six jurisdictions that have developed initiatives that fall broadly within the rubric of privatization are examined here. First, we explore the statewide initiative in Kansas, followed by a consideration of privatization (known as Community-Based Care) in Florida, where privatization has been mandated statewide and implemented on a county-by-county basis. Next, the book examines Missouri's Interdepartmental Initiative for Children with Severe Needs and Their Families, a more targeted initiative than the efforts in Kansas and Florida. The case study of the Creative Connections program follows. This initiative, developed by Hamilton County, Ohio agencies, resembles the Missouri effort in some ways (particularly in the population served), but its experience has differed from that of Missouri in many respects. The next case study is that of Michigan's Foster Care Permanency Initiative, a targeted effort in Wayne County that focuses on enhancing permanency outcomes for children in foster care. Finally, we examine Maine's Community Intervention Program. Unlike the other initiatives studied, it provides front-end services to families determined to be at moderate to low risk of child maltreatment. Because these jurisdictions provide a broadly diverse array of approaches, much can be learned from their experiences.

Kansas: Statewide Privatization of Family Preservation, Foster Care, and Adoption

The most well-known child welfare privatization initiative is the statewide effort in Kansas. In 1996, this effort privatized family preservation services, foster care, and adoption planning and services over the course of a single year. The Kansas privatization initiative has been evaluated extensively, both through independent third-party evaluators and by researchers whose findings have been widely reported. This case study examines the structure and implementation of the Kansas privatization initiative, the fiscal issues associated with the initiative, and the assessments that have been made of this effort in terms of its strengths and limitations.[1]

Implementation of Privatization

In 1996, the governor of Kansas initiated a statewide privatization of child welfare services. He proposed this strategy in response to a range of systemic problems that the Kansas Department of Social and Rehabilitative Services (SRS) had identified. SRS had recognized a number of systemic issues that signaled the need for major reform: an uncoordinated, crisis-oriented approach to service delivery; the fact that clients were subject to multiple assessments and the involvement of multiple staff; an evaluation of services that was process-based rather than out-

---

[1] In addition to the reports referenced in the document, telephone interviews were conducted with Lisa Shilkes, President, Foster Children of Johnson County, Inc. (a foster parent association); Nancy Peterson, foster parent; and Gary Brunk, Executive Director, Kansas Action for Children.

come-based; and reliance on multiple funding streams that often were at cross purposes and too categorical to effectively support clients in making needed changes (Kansas Action for Children, 1998). The privatization initiative was based on four guiding principles: private providers should be required to meet clearly defined program goals, quality and cost-effectiveness can be achieved through competition, a single case manager should oversee services to children and families through the process, and services should be equally available across the state (Craig et al., 1998).

The truly innovative aspect of the design of the privatization initiative was not the reliance on the private sector to provide child welfare services, as much of the child welfare system in Kansas was privatized in that sense before 1996. Instead, the radical feature was the development of a managed care approach to the delivery of child welfare services (Kansas Action for Children, 2001). Using managed care principles, Kansas designed its initiative with three major features:

- designation of lead agencies on a regional basis for family preservation and foster care services and on a statewide basis for adoption services;

- performance-based contracting, under which private contractors would be held to certain specified performance measures; and

- use of a case rate to cover the costs of all services needed by a child or family while being served through the family preservation, foster care, and adoption programs (Kansas Action for Children, 2001).

Between July 1996 and February 1997, after a relatively short planning phase that included public hearings and forums, Kansas put into place a competitive bidding process to select nonprofit contractors to serve as the lead agencies for the provision of three child welfare services: family preservation, adoption planning and services, and foster and group home care services. Kansas designed the bidding process to select contractors who would fully implement the privatized initiative on receipt of the contract. Kansas did not use any pilot programs to test the initiative's cost assumptions or evaluate the contractors' ability to deliver services under new case rates, nor did it use a pilot to test the service assumptions or the new performance-based standards (Kansas Action for Children, 1998). Likewise, no opportunities existed to develop mechanisms to ensure a cooperative relationship with the juvenile court system (Kansas Action for Children, 1998). One advocacy group, Kansas Action for Children (1998), commented that "in a sense, the children governed by each of the first-year privatization contracts all become test cases for the state" (p. 3).

In the initial round of contracting, five contracts for the delivery of family preservation and three contracts for the provision of foster care services were awarded in predefined geographical areas, and one contract was awarded for the delivery of adoption services throughout the entire state (Kansas Action for Children, 1998). Each contract specified a case rate and a payment structure based on the achievement of certain milestones, defined performance goals, and required contractors to accept all referrals that SRS made to them (Kansas Action for Children, 1998).

As a result of the contracting process, the nonprofit agencies undertook responsibility for all service delivery and all necessary day-to-day decisionmaking. SRS remained the funding source and continued to set and manage policies regarding the type and quality of services to be provided. Specifically, SRS retained responsibility for the following functions:

1. Case intake and assessment, including screening and investigation of child protection reports;

2. Family service delivery, including preventive services and other services that fell outside the contracts;

3. Management of cases referred to the contractors; and

4. Performance-based monitoring of service provision, and case and administrative reviews, to ensure compliance with SRS standards and the state's out-of-court settlement with the American Civil Liberties Union.

The experiences of the family preservation, foster care, and adoption contractors differed over the initial implementation period. In 2000, contracts in each of the three areas were rebid and resulted in changes in the contractors themselves, the payment structures (for foster care and adoption), and the performance measurement criteria (the standards, operational definitions, and calculation of the performance targets). These changes are discussed for each child welfare service area.

Privatization of Family Preservation

The first child welfare service to be privatized was family preservation. After 13 agencies bid to serve as the lead agency for family preservation services in one or more regions, Kansas chose 5 as lead agencies in July 1996 (Kaw Valley, Wyandotte Mental Health Center, Kansas Children's Service League, Saint Francis Academy, and DCCCA). After a one-year contract period, the five agencies received their second- and third-year contract renewals. On July 1, 2000, with the rebidding of the contracts for lead agencies, the number of family preservation service providers was reduced to two: St. Francis Academy maintained its contract as lead agency for one region, and DCCCA assumed lead agency status for an additional three regions (for a total of four regions in its contract).

Over time, the number of families served through the family preservation program has increased. Between July and December 2000, for example, the number of open family preservation cases increased by 21%, rising from 871 to 1,055 cases (James Bell Associates, 2001). It is estimated that family preservation contractors serve approximately 3,500 families per year (McCullough & Schmitt, 2002). Although there may be a number of reasons for the significant growth in the family preservation caseload, one explanation may lie in the efforts of SRS to reduce the number of children entering foster care by referring more families to family preservation services (James Bell Associates, 2001).

Privatization of Foster Care

In March 1997, SRS awarded contracts to three agencies (Kaw Valley Center, Kansas Children's Service League, and United Methodist Youthville) to oversee the provision of foster care and group care services in five geographic regions, with the expectation that between 740 and 1,070 families would be served per region (Poole, 2000). Under these contracts, contractors were required to:

- accept all referrals of children with the exception of juvenile offenders (who would remain under the responsibility of the youth authority);

- supervise and recruit foster parents;

- serve each referred child for a 12-month period following reunification with parents, and if a child required re-placement in foster care within the 12-month period, re-place the child under the initial case rate; and

- identify and pursue third-party funding for services that children and families needed.

In addition, the contracts provided that SRS could revoke the contract if the contractor experienced a greater than 5% incidence rate of child maltreatment by foster parents (Poole, 2000).

There appears to be consensus that the initial privatization of foster care was problematic, or, in the words of one commentator, "initially chaotic" (Snell, 2000, p. 6). The privatization of foster care elicited particular criticism in the media, with concerns repeatedly expressed that the privatization effort was "wrecking" foster care and driving away many providers and foster parents (Myers, 1997a, p. 8). Early criticism also surfaced from the juvenile court system, which had not been brought into aspects of the planning or implementation of privatization. At one legislative oversight committee hearing, juvenile judges, children's advocates, foster parents, and private contractors urged legislators to understand that privatization was "not working" (Myers, 1997a, p. 8).

A juvenile court judge reported a decline in the number of foster parents in her county from 60 to 22 homes during the eight-month period between March and October 1997. She attributed the decline to the complications of privatization and the lack of support that foster parents felt from the contracting agencies (Myers, 1997a). The SRS commissioner conceded that some participants in the newly privatized network were unclear as to "who was supposed to do what" (Myers, 1997b, p. 6).

Of particular concern was the speed at which foster care was privatized. SRS transferred the cases of 5,207 children in foster care to private providers in the first nine months of the privatization effort. In the first three months alone, SRS transferred the cases of 3,450 children to the contract agencies. Many of these children's records were not available on computer files, and in many instances, private providers had inadequate information and were required to reenter data on many children into their computer systems (Snell, 2000). This issue, now a historical artifact of the program, nonetheless appears to have had lingering effects, particularly in the relationships among SRS, private agencies, and community stakeholders.

Now, however, there appears to be a sense that foster care privatization is "going much more smoothly" (Snell, 2000, p. 6), with foster care contractors currently serving between 3,500 and 4,000 children at any point in time (McCullough & Schmitt, 2002). The outcomes that have been achieved reflect progress, although not to the extent that positive outcomes have been realized in the family preservation program (an issue discussed in greater detail later in this case study).

In July 2000, the foster care contracts were rebid, and five contractors were selected (the three previous contractors and two new contractors—The Farm and St. Francis Academy). In addition to changes in the fiscal methodology and performance standards, Kansas made other program changes. First, it made a modification in the previous practice of transferring a child's case from a foster care contractor to the adoption services contractor when the rights of one parent were terminated. Under the 2000 contract, children's cases are referred to the adoption contractor only when both parents' rights have been terminated. The benefit of this change is that foster care contractors may focus on reunification services and adoption contractors may focus on permanent adoptive placements. It raises questions, however, about the extent to which concurrent planning can be effectively implemented under such arrangement (an issue that continues to be assessed). Second, to address the problem of service gaps at the point of transfer from the foster care contractor to the adoption contractor, the contracts in effect as of July 2000 require the adoption contractor to hire service coordinators to negotiate case transitions from foster care. Third, the contracts establish maximum foster care caseloads of no more than 25 families (James Bell Associates, 2001). Fourth, foster care contractors must provide independent living services for youth age 16 or older in their care.

Privatization of Adoption

Unlike the regionally based contracts for family preservation and foster care, Kansas privatized adoption services through a statewide contract. Kansas awarded the first contract to Lutheran Social Services (LSS), the sole bidder, in October 1996. LSS established subcontracts with 12 adoption service providers across the state. LSS and its subcontractors assumed responsibility for recruiting and training of adoptive families, matching children and families, and providing postadoption support services for 18 months following placement (Poole, 2000). The contract estimated that SRS would initially transfer 1,000 children with adoption permanency plans to LSS and that an additional 325 to 425 children would be referred to LSS during the first year (Kansas Action for Children, 2001).

During the initial contract, LSS experienced significant financial difficulties, generally attributed to the inadequacy of the case rate. In summer 2000, LSS declared itself on the verge of bankruptcy, as it faced $9.2 million in debt and only $7.3 million in revenue (Miles, 2000; Ranney, 2000a). Only after an additional infusion of state funds was LSS able to repay its creditors (74 cents on the dollar) and rescind its plans to file for bankruptcy (Ranney, 2000a).

When the contract was rebid in July 2000, it was awarded to Kansas Children's Service League. The contract changed the fiscal methodology and, among other changes, set a maximum adoption caseload of 25 children. It required the contractor to plan for independent living services for youth age 16 or older (James Bell Associates, 2001).

Even with the contract changes, Kansas Children's Service League faced a number of challenges. Initially, social workers left their positions more quickly than they could be replaced; the number of children referred for adoption services, particularly children with special needs, continued to increase; and the number of agencies willing to subcontract with Kansas Children's Service League to provide adoption services dwindled (James Bell Associates, 2000; Ranney, 2000a). Nonetheless, adoption services have reported a number of positive outcomes, although with some regional variation. The Legislative Division of Post Audit (Legislature of Kansas, 2001) indicated that the number of finalized adoptions in Kansas had increased since privatization. The number of children freed for adoption, however, has continued to outpace the number of children whose adoptions have been finalized. In 2001, an estimated 1,100 children were waiting for placement with adoptive families, and 300 children were waiting for their adoptions to be finalized (James Bell Associates, 2001).

Fiscal Methodology

In the initial contracts, the fiscal methodology was a case rate. For the family preservation program, the established annual case rate covered all services provided to a family for a 12-month period. Although the state estimated that the average annual per-family cost of family preservation services was $3,500, the proposed contract case rate was set somewhat lower, at $3,464 (Craig et al., 1998). Contractors bid for service provision in five geographic regions, and Kansas awarded them a case rate that varied from $3,274 and $3,750 per family (Kansas Action for Children, 1998). Under the payment methodology, the initial case rate applied, and no additional funding was available if a family discharged from the program returned to the program within a 12-month period.

Under the new contracts effective July 1, 2000, case rates for family preservation services continue to vary by region, and range from $3,412 to $4,481 (McCullough & Schmitt, 2002). One-third of the case rate is paid at the time of referral. The lead agency is allowed to retain this sum even if the family does not use services. The remainder of the case rate is paid in two installments, at 45 and 90 days after referral. The case rate is paid in full when the family signs the case plan, regardless of whether they complete the plan (McCullough & Schmitt, 2002).

In the area of foster care, the case rate methodology proved to be far more problematic than in the family preservation program. SRS, in the first contracts with the foster care contractors, implemented a case rate that was to cover all foster care services to the child and family for the length of time the child was in care. The annual rate varied among the private contractors, ranging from $12,860 to $15,504 per child (Petr & Johnson, 1999). The contractor's individual case rates were based partially on their proposals to become the regional lead agency (Petr & Johnson, 1999). Although the expectation was that a case rate would create an incentive to move children out of foster care more quickly, it proved problematic as a result of several factors:

- The calculated case rates were not based on reliable cost data (NACA, 2000).

- The case rates applied to all foster care cases—both the old foster care cases that were transferred to contractors and the new referrals. No researcher assessed potential differences in the service needs of these two groups of children and families, which proved, in reality, to be significant (Snell, 2000).

- The funding necessary for start up was not built into the case rates (Snell, 2000).

- The case rates did not take into consideration court-ordered services, which in most cases were not included in the contracted case rate (Kansas Action for Children, 1998).

- The case rates did not take into consideration higher-than-anticipated referral rates or unexpected delays in discharge because of court scheduling problems and other issues (Kansas Action for Children, 1998).

Of particular relevance to anticipated rates of referral and caseload sizes was state legislation in 1997 (Senate Bill No. 615), which broadened the reach of child protective services through a more inclusive definition of "child in need of care" (Snell, 2000). As a result of this legislative change, foster care caseloads began to rise sharply, as the number of child maltreatment investigations increased and a larger percentage of children who were subject to such investigations entered foster care. Because the law also required courts to devote more time to adjudications of abuse and neglect, considerable delays existed in scheduling hearings to determine whether children could exit foster care (Snell, 2000).

As a result of high service demands by children and families who had long been in the foster care system, increased foster care case loads, and court delays, foster care contractors repeatedly experienced cost overruns in the first year of their contracts (Snell, 2000). Case rates fell substantially short of actual costs (Snell, 2000). As an example, United Methodist Youthville reported a monthly differential of $1,055 per child between the actual cost of providing services ($2,100 per month) and the case rate that it received ($1,045) (McLean, 1999b). By March 1999, Kansas Children's Service League had an operating deficit of $1 million; Kaw Valley Center had a deficit of $6.5 million; and United Methodist Youthville, which went into bankruptcy in June 2001 and subsequently reorganized under bankruptcy protection, had a $7.5 million deficit (McLean, 1999a;

Ranney, 2001b). The legislature made several efforts to address these issues. It transferred approximately $50 million from the federal welfare-to-work program to foster care (McLean, 1999a; Snell, 2000). It also adjusted the case rates in the second year of the foster care contracts to annual, per-child case rates between $14,740 ($1,228 per month) and $16,376 ($1,365 per month), depending on the region (Kansas Action for Children, 1998).

In February 2000, SRS abandoned the case rate approach for foster care services altogether and instituted a per-child, per-month rate payment system (Snell, 2000). This decision represented a return to the more traditional fee-setting structure and the elimination of what had been considered the most innovative aspect of the Kansas privatization initiative. In a statement to a legislative oversight committee explaining its decision to dismantle the case rate system, SRS observed:

> The financial review process created concerns regarding the viability of the case rate as the payment system for foster care. The primary concern was that the contractors did not have adequate control over when children returned home or moved to another permanency [arrangement] to manage their finances in such a payment system. Specifically, courts, SRS and others played a significant role in how soon a child could achieve their case plan goal. This left the contractors in a situation where their financial risk could not be appropriately balanced with their case responsibility. To resolve this concern, the basis for payment was modified to a per-child, per-month system. This new system will still require contractors to manage the placement of children and provision of services in an efficient manner but does not place them at risk for children who do not move through the system at a pre-planned pace. (Criswell, 2000, p. 4)

Supporters viewed the return to per-month payments as the solution to the "cash flow problems" (Ranney, 2000b, p. 6). Critics, however, suggested that the per-month methodology represented "a return to a perverse incentive structure that keeps children in foster care too long" (Snell, 2000, p. 7).

Under the contracts in effect as of July 1, 2000, foster care contractors receive a per-child, per-month rate that ranges from $1,958 to $2,381 depending on the region (McCullough & Schmitt, 2002). With the shift to a monthly rate (paid based on the number of children in care on the first of the month), contractors remain financially responsible (at risk) for children who reenter foster care within 12 months following reunification (McCullough & Schmitt, 2002).

As with foster care contractors, as the initial adoption contractor, LSS faced significant problems with the case rate, which was to cover the costs of all adoption placement services, mental health services, and other services such as day care (Poole, 2000). The contracted case rate was set initially at $13,556 for each child (although SRS had estimated a slightly higher average case rate of $13,756 per child) (Craig et al., 1998). LSS placed 10% of the children outside the case rate because of their medically fragile status or extraordinary medical needs (Poole, 2000). Under the terms of the first-year contract, LSS received one-half the case rate when the child was referred to an agency; 25% when the agency placed the child with an adoptive family; and 25% when the adoption was legally finalized (Belsie, 2000). It soon became clear, however, that the case rate was inadequate, particularly for children with significant special needs. Subsequently, the state revised the case rate upward (to $16,168 for each child in the agency's care), but financial problems continued to plague LSS (Ranney, 2000a).

Under the new adoption contract that took effect as of July 1, 2000, SRS changed the reimbursement methodology from a case rate to a monthly payment for each child ($1,426 monthly for each child), which ceases when the adoption is finalized (Ranney, 2000a). The lead agency remains financially responsible for children who return to adoption services within 18 months of their adoption (McCullough & Schmitt, 2002).

From a chronological perspective, it is interesting to note the fiscal methodologies that Kansas has used in an effort to meet the costs of privatization and protect providers from excessive cost overruns. The strategies include the following:

- **Shared Risk Corridor.** Initially, in connection with the established case rates, Kansas established a shared risk corridor that ranged between 90% and 110% of the case rate. Under this arrangement, if a lead agency's annual expenditures fell 90% below the case rate as aggregated for all children served, the difference in funds was returned to the state. However, if these same expenditures rose above 110%, the state would reimburse the difference to the lead agency.

- **Outside the Case Rate.** Because only one of the three foster care agencies remained within the shared risk corridor in the first year of the original contract, Kansas increased the case rates and designated certain service slots as outside the case rate. Each agency was allowed to designate its share of 150 children statewide for whom services would be reimbursed on a traditional fee-for-service basis (that is, outside the case rate). The designation of these service slots recognized the fact that certain children had specialized needs that could not be covered by the case rate. This approach, however, posed problems for agencies. They were forced to maintain separate accounting practices for children outside the case rate, and once designated, children could not be moved out of these slots nor could other children be assigned to those service slots.

■ **Enhanced Case Rate.** In the third year following privatization, the outside the case rate system was phased out, and the uniform case rate was reestablished for all children served under the foster care contracts, but at an enhanced rate. In 1999, the foster care case rate increased 14% and the adoption case rate increased 22% over 1997 rates.

■ **Per-Month, Per-Child Payment for Foster Care and Adoption Services.** Currently, foster care lead agencies are paid a per-child, per-month payment that varies across the five regions of the state. The monthly payment begins with referral and ends when the child returns home, ages out, or is referred to an adoption or other agency (such as the juvenile justice authority). The per-child, per-month payment does not place contractors at risk for children who do not move to permanency in a timely fashion. The statewide adoption contractor currently receives a monthly payment beginning with referral and ending when the adoptive placement is finalized or the child ages out of care or is referred elsewhere.

■ **Case Rate for Family Preservation Services.** The family preservation contract continues to use a case rate methodology, as it has since the program's inception in 1996.

Current Status of Privatization in Kansas

As of 2002, the privatization initiative in Kansas is composed of SRS and contractors for family preservation, foster care, and adoption. Table 2 provides a snapshot of the program put into place in 2000, compared with 1996 and 1997.

Key program and fiscal information (as of July 2000) is summarized for the family preservation, foster care, and adoption programs in Table 3.

Table 2

Privatized Child Welfare in Kansas

SRS	Family Preservation		Foster Care		Adoption	
	1996/1997	2000	1996/1997	2000	1996/1997	2000
Investigation child protective services	5 regions	5 regions	5 regions	5 regions	Statewide	Statewide
Family services case management	5 contractors: Kaw Valley Center Wyandotte Mental Health Center Kansas Children's Service League Saint Francis Academy DCCCA	2 contractors: DCCCA St. Francis Academy	3 contractors: Kaw Valley Center Kansas Children's Service League United Methodist Youthville	5 contractors: The Farm Kaw Valley Center Kansas Children's Service League Saint Francis Academy United Methodist Youthville	1 contractor: Lutheran Social Services	1 contractor: Kansas Children's Service League

Note: SRS = Kansas Department of Social and Rehabilitative Services.

Table 3

Program and Fiscal Features of Each Privatized Program

	Family Preservation	**Foster Care**	**Adoption**
Target population	Families in crisis	Children in need of care (CINC)	CINC with goals of adoption for whom both parents' rights have been terminated
Caseloads	No more than 10 cases per case manager (PCM)	No more than 25 families PCM	No more than 25 families PCM
Payment structure	Case rate	Per month, per child	Per month, per child
Payment amount	$3,412–$4,481	1,958–$2,381	$1,426
Specialized Services	None specified	Independent living services for youth 16 and older	Plan for independent living services for youth 16 and older
Aftercare responsibility	One year from referral, even if family moves to another service region	12 months from permanency (achievement of case plan goal)	18 months after finalization of adoption

Funding

The costs associated with privatization in Kansas appear to be substantially greater than nonprivatization. In 2001, the Legislative Division of Post Audit for the Kansas Legislature assessed the costs of the state's privatization of foster care and adoption (Legislature of Kansas, 2001). Although noting that the pre- and post-privatization costs could not be readily compared because the state had not tracked program-specific expenses when it provided foster care and adoption services, the audit concluded that the level of contractual payments to private providers was substantially greater during privatization. The audit compared costs for each of the service areas for FY 1996 and FY 2000 and found the following:

- With regard to payments for foster care services, in FY 1996 (pre-privatization), $63.6 million was expended (which excluded an unknown level of expenses for day care and mental health services but included an unknown level of expenses for the care of juvenile offenders in foster care). In FY 2000, a total of $87.6 million was expended (which included $11.4 million in estimated costs for day care and mental health services; excluded an estimated $8.6 million for the care of juvenile offenders; and included an unknown level of expenses for case management and other services formerly provided by the state agency staff).

- With regard to adoption services, there were no available data on the FY 1996 expenditures but a total of $21.8 million was expended on adoption service contracts in FY 2000.

- With regard to payments to families for adoption support, $4.9 million was paid in FY 1996 and $16.0 million in FY 2000 (Legislature of Kansas, 2001).

The audit concluded that in total, the state's expenditures on foster care and adoption increased by more than $100 million between 1996 and 2000 (Legislature of Kansas, 2001). In FY 2000, the budget for Kansas' statewide privatization initiative was $130 million, a figure that represented 90% of the total child welfare budget (McCullough & Schmitt, 2002).

Outcomes

In each of the contracts for family preservation, foster care, and adoption services, performance measures and standards were set in the initial contracts. With the new contracts in effect as of July 2000, significant changes were made in the outcomes for each program—in the standards, in their operational definitions, and in the calculation of performance targets.

Family Preservation

Table 4 provides the outcomes and performance standards for the family preservation program under the previous contracts and under the contracts in effect as of July 1, 2000.

The family preservation lead agencies have successfully achieved many of the outcomes outlined for family preservation services. As Table 5 indicates, the contractors met or exceeded standards on a statewide basis during the first three quarters of FY 2001 (the most recent data available at the time of this writing).

Foster Care

Table 6 provides the outcomes and performance standards for the foster care program under the previous contracts and under the contracts in effect as of July 2000.

The foster care contractors have achieved positive outcomes, although not to the same extent as the family preservation contractors. More success has been realized with regard to safety-related outcomes than permanency-related outcomes. The permanency outcome measure, "Children reunited with their families will not re-enter out-of-home custody within one year of return home," for example, has a performance target of 90%, but had an overall state performance rating of 85.57% in the first three quarters of FY 2001. During that same time period, the permanency outcome measure, "Children will be permanently placed within 180 days of referral (reunification, placement with relative, adoption)," with a performance target of 40%, had an overall state performance of 29.61%. The permanency outcome measure, "Children will be permanently placed within 365 days of referral (reunification, placement with relative, adoption)," with a performance target of 65%, had an overall state performance of 51.31% (James Bell Associates, 2001).

Kansas Action for Children (2001) observed that "the lack of success in meeting permanency standards is a significant weakness of the current [privatized] system since it goes to the heart of why the old system needed radical changes" (p. 5). Nonetheless, it is important to recognize that success has been noted in other areas. Table 7 provides data on foster care outcomes for the first three quarters of FY 2001.

Adoption

Table 8 provides the outcomes and performance standards for the adoption program. Generally, positive adoption outcomes have been achieved, although with some regional variation. Table 9 provides some of the outcomes for the first three quarters of FY 2001.

Assessment of Privatization in Kansas

Assessments of the privatization of child welfare services in Kansas have identified both strengths and challenges.

Table 4
Family Preservation

Previous Contracts	Current Contracts (as of 7/1/02)
Outcome 1. Contractor shall accept all SRS referrals.	**Outcome 1. Families referred will engage in program.**
97% of all families will be engaged in the treatment process.	Workers will engage 95% of all families in program services.
(Number of engaged families divided by number of referred families.)	(Number of families who had an initial case plan due during the month and who signed the plan divided by number of families who had an initial case plan during the month.)
Outcome 2. Children will be safe from abuse and/or neglect.	**No change in outcome title.**
90% of families will not have a substantiated report of abuse or neglect during program participation.	90% of all families will not have a substantiated report abuse or neglect within 90 days after referral.
(Number of engaged families with no substantiated abuse/neglect during program participation divided by number of engaged families.)	(Number of engaged families with no substantiated abuse/neglect within 90 days of referral divided by number of engaged families who were referred 90 days ago.)
80% of families successfully completing the program (no child removed from the home) will have no substantiated reports of abuse or neglect within six months of case closure.	80% of families will not have a substantiated report of abuse or neglect within one year of referral.
(Number of families successfully completing program with no substantiated abuse/neglect within six months of case closure divided by number of families successfully completing the program.)	(Number of engaged families with no substantiated abuse/neglect in one year divided by number of engaged families who were referred one year ago.)

Outcome 3. Children will not require out of home placement.

80% of families will not have a child placed outside the home during program participation.

(Number of engaged families who were not placed outside the home during program participation divided by number of engaged families.)

80% of families successfully completing the program (no child removed from the home) will not have a child placed outside the home within six months of case closure.

(Number of engaged families whose child was not placed outside the home within six months of case closure divided by number of families engaged.)

No change in outcome title.

90% of families will not have a child placed outside the home during the 90-day period following the referral.

(Number of families referred 90 days ago who had a child placed outside the home divided by number of families referred 90 days ago.)

80% of families will not have a child placed outside the home during the year after referral.

(Number of families referred one year ago and engaged in services who had a child placed outside the home divided by number of families referred one year ago and engaged in services.)

Outcome 4. Family members will be satisfied with services provided.

Participants (parents and youth ages 14 through 21 living in the home) will report 80% satisfaction measured by client satisfaction survey 30 days from start of the program.

(Number of satisfied participants divided by total number of respondents (each survey response is weighted.)

No change in outcome title.

80% of the participants (caregivers) will report satisfaction as measured by the client satisfaction survey 30 days after referral.

(Number of respondents whose survey indicates overall satisfaction divided by the total number of respondents.)

Note: Each outcome is followed by the performance standard and operational definition of the standard.
SRS = Social and Rehabilitative Services.

Table 5

Family Preservation Contractors' Rates of Meeting Standards 2000–2001 (in percentages)

Standard	Statewide Performance	Regional Performance
Workers engaged 95% of those referred	95%	95–96%
90% of children have no substantiated abuse and neglect within 90 days of referral	97%	94–98%
90% of children remain home within 90 days of referral	93%	90–96%
Of families, 80% are satisfied	89%	85–92%
Maximum of 10 cases per worker	9.2%	8.3–9.6%

Source: Adapted from McCullough & Schmitt (2002).

Strengths of the Kansas Privatization Initiative

- Consistent with the original guiding principles for privatization, a greater balance now exists in the level of services to children and families in rural and urban areas (Poole, 2000). Greater service equity has been especially notable in family preservation services (Gary Brunk, personal communication, February 1, 2002).

- Children now move through the child welfare system more quickly (Myers, 1997a).

- The number of adoptions of children in foster care has increased significantly (Myers, 1997a; McCullough & Schmitt, 2002).

- Program outcomes generally have been achieved at acceptable levels (Poole, 2000).

- Client perceptions of the new system generally have been positive (Kansas Action for Children, 2001), although James Bell Associates (2001) recommended that these results be viewed with caution because of low response rates on client surveys.

- Public agency costs have been reduced, as the number of full-time state employees in the child welfare program has decreased (Kansas Action for Children, 2001).

- Data are more comprehensively and accurately collected for purposes of program evaluation (Belsie, 2000; Poole, 2000).

Challenges Associated with the Privatization Effort

The Kansas privatization initiative also has been subject to criticism. Among the most frequently identified problems are:

1. Private contractors experienced significant cash flow difficulties as a result of the state's lack of understanding of what it costs to provide various child welfare services (Belsie, 2000).

2. Children may have moved through the child welfare system too quickly as a result of the pressures caused by the initial case rate financial methodology, with heightened risks of more children returning to foster care (Belsie, 2000).

3. Privatization created an additional layer of bureaucracy ("big contractors") between the state agency and local providers (Belsie, 2000; Kansas Action for Children, 2001).

4. Privatization developed separate contracts for family preservation, foster care, and adoption services, which have undermined the seamless coordination of services and opportunities for concurrent planning for children and families as they move through the system (James Bell Associates, 2000; Kansas Action for Children, 2001).

Table 6
Foster Care

Previous Contracts	Current Contracts (as of 7/1/02)
Outcome 1. Children are safe from maltreatment.	**No change in outcome title.**
98% of children in contractor's care will not experience confirmed abuse/neglect while in placement.	98% of children in out-of-home placement will not experience substantiated abuse/neglect while in placement.
(Number of open cases with no abuse/neglect divided by number of open cases.)	(Number of children in out-of-home placement with no substantiated abuse/neglect divided by number of children in out-of-home placement on the last day of the month.)
80% of children will not experience substantiated abuse/neglect within 12 months after reintegration.	80% of children will not experience substantiated abuse/neglect for 12 months following permanency.
(Number of children reintegrated with no substantiated abuse/neglect within 12 months of reintegration divided by number of children reintegrated 12 months ago.)	(Number of children returned home and who completed 12-month follow-up period with no abuse/neglect divided by number of children who returned home and who completed follow-up period of 12 months.)

Outcome 2. Children experience minimal number of placements.

70% of children referred to the contractor will have no more than three moves subsequent to referral.

(Number of children experiencing a fourth move divided by number of open cases (do not count return home as a move.)

65% of all children will be placed with at least one sibling.

(Average number of children with at least one sibling also in out-of-home placement who share placement with at least one sibling divided by average number of children meeting the criteria.)

Outcome 2. Workers will maximize well-being of children.

70% of children will have no more than four placement settings subsequent to referral.

(Number of children with open cases who experience fifth placement setting divided by total number of children with an open case on the last day of the month (moves do not necessarily include respite, hospitalizations, family visits, runaways, or observation/stabilization. Do not include reunification; include moves within facility/campus when there is a change in treatment program, such as level of care change.)

70% of all children will be placed with at least one sibling

(Number of children in out-of-home placement who have sibling also in out-of-home placement and are in placement with at least one sibling on the last day of the month divided by the number of children in out-of-home placement who have a sibling also in out-of-home placement.)

Table 6 Continued

Foster Care

Previous Contracts	Current Contracts (as of 7/1/02)
Outcome 3. Children maintain family, community, and cultural ties.	**These indicators are included under Outcome 2.**
70% of children are placed within their home or contiguous county.	70% of children referred after the implementation date are placed within their home county or a contiguous county.
(Average number of placed children who were in home/contiguous county divided by average number of children in out-of-home placement.)	(Number of children placed in their home or a contiguous county on the last day of the month divided by number of children in out-of-home placement on the last day of the month.)
75% of youth 16 and older released from custody have completed high school, have obtained a general equivalency diploma (GED), or are participating in an educational or job training program.	80% of youth aging out of the child welfare system will be prepared for transition to adult life as indicated by a score of 20 or more on the Preparation for Transition to Adult Life Checklist.
(Number of youth 16 or older released from custody who have completed high school, have obtained a GED, or are participating in an educational or job training program divided by number of youth age 16 or older released from custody.)	(Number of youth legally emancipated or aging out of the child welfare system who score 20 or higher divided by number of youth legally emancipated or aging out (includes youth 18+ and youth any age released from custody to live independently.)
No equivalent measure to 7/1/02 nongroup/noninstitutional placement standard.	85% of children in placement will be in non-group and noninstitutional placements.
	(Number of children in out-of-home placement in non-group/noninstitutional placements on the last day of the month divided by the number of children in out-of-home placement on the last day of the month.)

Outcome 3. Children move toward permanency in a timely manner.

40% of children placed in out-of-home care are returned to the family, achieve permanency, or are referred for adoption within six months of referral.

(Number of children who entered out-of-home placement six months ago and achieved outcome divided by number of children who entered out-of-home placement six months ago. (Return home is defined as return to parent, legal guardian, or living independently; permanency is defined as being released from custody unless the child goes into the custody of the juvenile justice agency or in the event of a child death while in custody; completed adoption means that there is a completed referral, both parents' rights have been terminated, and the case plan goal is adoption.)

Outcome 4. Children reunite with their families in a timely manner.

40% of children placed in out-of-home care are returned to the family or achieve permanency within six months of referral to the contractor.

(Number of children who entered out-of-home placement and returned home/achieved permanency within 180 days divided by number of children who entered out-of-home placement 180 days ago.)

Table 6 Continued
Foster Care

Previous Contracts	Current Contracts (as of 7/1/02)
65% of children achieve permanency within one year of referral to the contractor.	65% of children placed in out-of-home care are returned to the family, achieve permanency, or are referred to adoption within 12 months of referral to the contractor.
(Number of children who entered out-of-home placement and achieved permanency within one year of referral divided by number of children who entered out-of-home placement one year ago.)	(Number of children who entered out-of-home placement 12 months ago and returned to the family, achieved permanency, or have a completed referral for adoption within 12 months of referral divided by number of children who entered out-of-home placement 12 months ago. See above for definitions.)
90% of children who are reintegrated with their family do not reenter out-of-home custody within one year of return home.	90% of children who are reintegrated do not reenter out-of-home placement within one year of reintegration.
(Number of children reintegrated and did not reenter placement within one year divided by number of children reintegrated 12 months ago.)	(Number of children reintegrated and who did not reenter out-of-home placement within one year of reintegration divided by number of children released from custody 12 months ago.)

Outcome 5. Clients are satisfied with services.

80% of parents and youth (ages 14+) report satisfaction with services as measured by the Client Satisfaction Survey on case closure.

(Number of adult and youth clients indicating satisfaction divided by number of surveys returned.)

Outcome 4. Family members will be satisfied with the services provided.

80% of participants, including caregivers and youth ages 16-21, will report satisfaction as measured by the Client Satisfaction with Family Reunification Services Survey 90 days after referral or at case closure.

(Number of respondents whose survey score indicates over-all satisfaction divided by total number of respondents.)

Note: Each outcome is followed by the performance standard and operational definition of the standard.

5. Periodic rebidding of contracts (generally every three years) has resulted in turnovers in contractors and "institutionalization" of "a lack of system permanency" (Kansas Action for Children, 2001, p. 13).

6. The system of financial penalties and incentives related to outcome achievement is inadequate (Kansas Action for Children, 2001).

7. Delays in evaluations for children and families are a result of long waiting lists (Belsie, 2000, p. 5).

8. Support for and honest communication with foster parents is lacking (James Bell Associates, 2000, p. 139).

Foster parents express much concern about the role they have been allowed to play in privatization. Foster parents feel they were excluded completely from the privatization planning process, and, as a result, their trust in SRS and the private agencies has been undermined significantly. Foster parents also report that private agencies do not see themselves as accountable to foster parents. Finally, foster parents express concerns about the fragmentation of service as the children in their care move from contractors that provide foster care services to contractors that provide adoption services (Lisa Shikles, personal communication, April 22, 2002).

Lessons Learned

Kansas' experience in implementing statewide privatization of a full range of child welfare services (excluding only child protective services intake and investigations, basic family support, and oversight of case management related to permanency planning) can provide guidance for other communities considering a similar or more limited initiative.

Adequate Cost Data Are Essential if a Case Rate Approach Is Used. Most commentators agree that Kansas did not have complete or accurate information about its own costs in providing foster care and adoption services when it privatized child welfare services. As a result, it could not provide bidders with actual cost data (NACA, 2000; Snell, 2000). The case rates, which were not validated with actual cost data, required revision. In the case of foster care and adoption services, Kansas abandoned the case rate approach altogether in favor of the more traditional per-month fee for each child. As Kansas' experience suggests, the absence of historical cost data makes it extremely difficult to set case rates that appropriately reflect the cost of care and that adequately fund service provision.

It Should Not Be Expected that Privatization Will Control Costs.
Although privatization typically is seen as providing the opportunity to streamline child welfare services and save money or, at least, control costs (Craig et al.,
1998), in most cases, it has not resulted in decreases in the cost of foster care and
adoption services (Ranney, 2000b). In Kansas, a report by the consulting firm
Deloitte and Touche (as cited in James Bell Associates, 2001, p. 138), issued in
April 1999, identified two reasons that costs were considerably higher under privatization than was anticipated:

- Significant start-up costs were related to staffing, larger than
  expected numbers of referrals, difficulties associated with information systems development, and the need for each provider to
  develop services that appropriately met the needs of referral
  clients.

- The monthly cost of providing care proved to be much higher
  than expected: 65% higher than originally estimated for foster
  care and 13.5% higher for adoption.

It appears that the costs associated with the privatization of foster care substantially exceeded expectations. From 1996 to 2000, the foster care contractors
received $178.5 million in case rate payments, $8.4 million for services to children outside the case rate, and $98.7 million for other "risk share payments"
(defined by the state as "legitimate, unforseen, and unknown costs due to lack of
data" [Kansas Action for Children, 2001, p. 11]. In spite of this infusion of
resources, several agencies teetered on the verge of bankruptcy. Problems were also
evident in the privatization of adoption. The state had to invest additional
resources to prevent LSS from going into bankruptcy. In total, LSS, as the adoption lead agency, received $37.4 million in case rate payments, $6.97 million for
children outside the case rate, and $24.4 million for other risk share payments
(Kansas Action for Children, 2001). These data suggest that privatized services,
particularly when provided under expectations of higher quality, cost more, not
less, than services provided by public systems.

Rapid Implementation of Major System Change Is Not Well-Advised.
Organizations such as the Reason Public Policy Institute (2000b) have com-
mended Kansas for the fast pace of its implementation of privatization and have,
in fact, urged other systems to "phase in the privatization over several months."
Others, however, have viewed the state's rapid implementation as a key factor in
some of the more negative outcomes that it experienced. Kansas Action for
Children (2001, p. 12), for example, identified a number of problems associated
with the very short timeframe for implementation of privatization: a shortage of

Table 7

Foster Care Contractors' Rates of Meeting Standards 2000–2001 (in percentages)

Standard	Statewide Performance	Regional Performance
98% of children have no substantiated abuse or neglect.	99	99–100
Placement within home or contiguous counties: 70%	71	64–80
85% placed in nongroup/noninstitutional setting	85	81–89
70% placed with siblings	67	61–75
40% achieve permanent placement within 6 months	25	10–34
80% satisfied	55 (adults) 57 (youth)	43–73 (adults) 50–67 (youth)

Source: McCullough & Schmitt (2000).

available, trained professional staff to assume responsibility for the transferred cases; the lack of fully developed service options; "miscues" in the development of information systems; tensions in the relationships among providers and other professionals; extensive communication breakdowns; and high stress on children, families, and direct service workers. in In November 1997, SRS acknowledged that it should have transferred foster care and adoption cases over longer periods of time (Poole, 2000). Officials indicated that six months (as opposed to three months for foster care cases and overnight for adoption cases) would have been a more appropriate time period for case transfer and would have caused fewer problems in the transition (Poole, 2000).

Two particularly negative effects of the rapid transition were difficulty in recruiting and training professional staff and foster parents in such a short period of time and difficulty in adequately communicating with all stakeholders as major changes were made. The effect of the short implementation period has continued in the form of tension in the relationships between SRS employees and private agency staff, particularly with respect to case management. Recent efforts to develop and clarify public-private staff relationships have included the involve-ment of external facilitators in several SRS area offices (James Bell Associates, 2001).

At the same time, the rapid pace of implementation undermined effective rela-tionships among SRS, the private sector, the juvenile courts, and the advocacy community. Although the Reason Public Policy Institute (2000b) maintained that a strong collaboration in Kansas resulted in a high level of support from providers, the courts, and the advocacy community, other observers, including SRS itself, identified significant problems in this regard. Because of the short timeframe, it was extremely difficult to educate foster parents and advocates about privatization (Craig et al., 1998) or to appropriately involve juvenile courts in planning and implementing the initiative (USGAO, 1998b). SRS acknowledged that the lack of judicial involvement was a serious oversight for a variety of reasons but, partic-ularly, because courts (not private agencies) determine when a child may leave the foster care system (USGAO, 1998b).

Appropriate Outcome and Performance Measures Should Be Reexamined and Strengthened Based on Service Provision Experience. A critical issue in any privatization effort is how a program selects and defines outcomes and per-formance targets. Assuming that the selected outcomes are valid indicators of good outcomes, it is essential that each outcome be clearly defined from the out-set. In Kansas, early questions arose in this regard, particularly in the context of possible skewed reporting because of definitional ambiguity. For example, one outcome related to the number of foster care placements. The outcome did not clearly specify what constituted a placement. Subsequently, it was discovered that some providers excluded emergency placements of less than 30 days from the child's placement count, whereas other providers counted such placements (Myers, 1997b). The disparate approaches not only created difficulties in com-paring performance but fed an already tense environment. Some attributed mis-counts to uncertainty as to what actually constituted a placement, but others viewed it as a tactic to establish favorable compliance rates with the state (Myers, 1997b).

Early on, some also raised issues about the appropriateness of the outcome measures in light of children's and families' experiences and outcomes (Kansas Action for Children, 1998). Given the serious needs of most children in foster care for mental health services, for example, some criticized the fact that no out-come measure addressed the extent to which programs identified or addressed a child's mental health needs, whether the child's mental health status improved, or whether the placement was appropriate in light of the child's mental health needs

Table 8
Adoption

Previous Contracts	Current Contracts (as of 7/1/02)
Outcome 1. Children shall be placed for adoption in a timely manner.	**No change in outcome title.**
55% of children shall be placed with adoptive families within 180 days of the referral for adoption.	55% of children shall be placed with adoptive families within 180 days of the receipt of the referral for adoption.
(Number of children referred for 180 days who have been placed divided by number of children referred for 180 days.)	(Number of children referred for six months and who have been placed prior to the sixth month divided by number of children referred six months ago.)
70% of children will be placed with adoptive families within 365 days of the receipt of the referral for adoption.	
(Number of children referred for 365 days who have been placed divided by number of children referred for 365 days.)	
Outcome 2. Children shall have permanent homes through the adoption process.	No change in outcome title.
90% of adoptive placements shall be finalized within 12 months of the placement date.	No change
(Number of children placed for 12 months whose adoptions have been finalized divided by number of children placed for 12 months or longer.)	

Outcome 3. Adoptive family members shall be satisfied with adoption services.

No change in outcome title.

90% of families (parents and youth ages 14 older living in the home) shall report satisfaction with the adoption process at the time the adoption is finalized.

No change

(Number of respondents whose survey indicates overall satisfaction divided by number of responses.)

Outcome 4. Siblings shall be kept together.

No change in outcome title.

65% of children will be placed with at least one sibling.

No change in standard.

(Number of children who at the time of adoptive placement had a sibling also referred for adoption and were placed in the same adoptive placement divided by number of children who at the time of placement had a sibling referred for adoption.)

(Number of children in prefinalization adoptive placement who have a sibling also referred and who are placed in the adoptive placement with at least one other sibling divided by the number of children in prefinalization adoptive placements who have a sibling also referred for adoptive placement.)

Outcome 5. Children shall remain in the same foster care placement pending adoption.

No change in outcome title.

90% of all children placed for adoption shall experience no more than two moves from the point in time parental rights are terminated until the adoption is finalized.

90% of all children in an open case shall experience no more than three placement settings subsequent to referral.

(Number of children whose adoptions have been finalized and who experienced fewer than three moves (not counting the adoptive placement) divided by number of children whose adoptions have been finalized.)

(Number of children with open cases in prefinalization who experience their fourth placement setting after referral divided by number of children with open cases in prefinalization on the last day of the month.)

Table 8. Continued

Adoption

Previous Contracts	Current Contracts (as of 7/1/02)
Outcome 6. Children are safe from maltreatment.	**No change**
95% of children in the care and supervision of the contractor will not experience substantiated abuse/neglect prior to finalization	98% of children in the care and supervision of the contractor will not experience substantiated abuse or neglect prior to finalization.
No operational definition.	(Number of children for whom a case was open (excluding those whose adoptions were finalized prior to the program year) and no substantiated abuse/neglect since referral divided by number of children for whom a case was open in the report period. Substantiations are reported in the month the substantiation was made for an incident that occurred during the time the child was under the care and supervisor of the contractor.)
No equivalent outcome.	**Outcome 7. Children are placed in the least restrictive setting.**
	85% of children referred but not in an adoptive placement will be placed in a nongroup or noninstitutional placement.
	(Number of children in nonadoptive placements who are in a nongroup/noninstitutional placement divided by the number of children in nonadoptive placements.)

Table 9

Adoption Contractor's Rates of Meeting Standards 2000–2001 (in percentages)

Standard	Statewide Performance	Regional Performance
98% of children have no substantiated abuse or neglect	99	99-100
85% placed in nongroup/noninstitutional setting	81	78-86
55% placed with adoptive family within six months of referral	17	6-41
90% satisfied	72 (adults)	NA

Source: McCullough & Schmitt (2002).

(Ranney, 2001a).

Despite these criticisms, however, it is important to note that Kansas used the opportunity provided at the time of contract rebidding in 2000 to reexamine the original outcomes and performance standards and improve the clarity of the outcomes, the operational definitions of key concepts, and the performance targets. As Tables 4, 6, and 8 indicate, the outcomes, definitions, and performance targets were considerably enhanced, based on a four-year history of private service provision. When very limited data are available at the outset of an initiative, it is likely that difficulties will exist in establishing appropriate outcomes and performance targets. This situation—which Kansas confronted and which led to many criticisms of the initial efforts—heightens the importance of establishing baseline data and revising outcomes and performance targets. The efforts reflected in the contracts that took effect in July 2000 provide a strong example of how researchers can use data collected over time to improve outcomes and performance measures.

Florida: Community-Based Care

Privatization of child welfare services in Florida began in 1996, when the state legislature required the Department of Children and Families (DCF) to establish pilot programs in which community-based agencies would provide child welfare services through contracts with DCF. DCF subsequently established four privatization pilots. Following the implementation of these pilot programs, in 1998, the state legislature mandated statewide privatization of child welfare services. Over time, the term *privatization* came to be replaced with the Community-Based Care program ("Community-Based Care," 2001). Currently, Florida uses *community-based care* to refer to the development and implementation of a system of care in which private providers, acting in collaboration with community stakeholders, provide child welfare services; flexibility exists in how groups provide services; and efficiency is expected in all aspects of service provision, particularly in relation to fiscal management (Florida State University, 2001). Included within the concept of Community-Based Care are a child-centered orientation and an expectation that individualized services will be provided to meet families' needs through a wraparound approach (that is, a community-based approach that incorporates formal and informal services; Bruns, Buchard, & Yor, 1995). This case study of Community-Based Care in Florida is presented in three parts. First is a discussion of the overall planning and implementation of community-based care at the state level, where decisions have been made about the overall design of the initiative. Second is a discussion of the implementation of Community-Based Care in Sarasota County, which, among all Florida counties, has been involved in the development of Community-Based Care for the longest period of time. Although Sarasota County is the focus of this examination of Community-Based Care, it is important to note that Florida counties have had highly varied experiences in planning for and implementing Community-Based Care. As a result, it is not possible to present a uniform picture of the implementation of the program statewide. The experience of Sarasota County is described as illustration, with references to other Florida counties, where possible, on certain issues, but it is not intended to reflect Florida's initiative overall, given the diversity among counties in their approaches to and experiences with Community-Based Care.[2] The third part of this case study identifies some of the overarching issues in the implementation of Florida's Community-Based Care initiative and examines some of the perspectives on the successes and challenges of this effort.[3]

Part I: State-Level Planning and Implementation Efforts

The implementation of Community-Based Care in Florida began with the state legislature's interest in privatizing child welfare services and its mandate to test strategies through a pilot project involving four counties. Following that experience, the legislature mandated statewide privatization, and DCF initiated a planning process that was dictated, in large part, by the statute itself. The planning and implementation process at the state level addressed a range of issues:

- development of guiding principles through community-based activities,

- determination of the fiscal methodologies that would be used in the privatization initiative,

- clarification of the role of lead agencies,

- delineation of a process through which lead agencies would be selected for the implementation of privatization in each county,

- assessment of county readiness to privatize,

---

[2] See, for example, the experiences of Lake, Sumter, Pinellas, Pasco, and Palm Beach Counties in developing and implementing Community-Based Care (Florida Department of Children and Families, 2000b; Office of Program Policy Analysis and Government Accountability, 2001; Krueger, 2002). In the case of each of these counties, unique factors have affected the planning, implementation, and eventual success or lack of success of the community-based care initiative.

[3] In addition to the written resources cited in this study, researchers obtained information through interviews with David Overstreet, Deputy Director, and Theresa Leslie, Community-Based Care, Florida State Department of Children and Families; and Lee Johnson, Vice President, YMCA Children, Youth, and Family Services, Sarasota County, Florida.

- development of community alliances (a component of privatization that was mandated by the state legislature in 2000), and

- determination of outcome measures (in a very preliminary manner).

These activities established a framework for the implementation of what generally has become known in Florida as Community-Based Care.

The Privatization Pilot Project

Following the legislature's mandate in 1996, DCF implemented a pilot program during fiscal year 1996–1997 to privatize child welfare services in Duval, Manatee, Lake, Sumter, and Sarasota Counties. The most comprehensive and successful effort took place in Sarasota County. Evaluations of the pilot programs in the four counties revealed that when compared to DCF's own performance on a range of indicators, some pilot programs had achieved more positive outcomes. It was found, for example, that in two of the pilot counties:

- Children more frequently had weekly contact with their caseworkers,

- The average number of children placed in each foster home was lower,

- Caseload sizes were lower,

- The average number of placements per child was lower,

- Fewer changes in caseworkers occurred per case, and

- Foster parents rated the new system as highly effective (Florida DCF, 1999).

In addition, in Sarasota County, the average length of stay in foster care was reduced to 10.3 months, substantially lower than the standard of 18 months that had been set for the project (Florida DCF, 1999; Office of Program Policy Analysis and Government Accountability [OPPAGA], 2001). Nonetheless, with the exception of Sarasota County, the pilot counties either exceeded the standard for length of stay or were unable to report data in this regard (OPPAGA, 2001).

Legislatively Mandated Statewide Privatization

Based on its assessment of the successes of the pilot privatization effort, the Florida legislature in 1998 enacted HB 3217, sweeping legislation that mandated the privatization of child welfare services across the entire state. Defining privatization as "contract[ing] with competent, community-based agencies" (Florida Statute §409.1671), the legislature directed that foster care and "related services" be privatized on a statewide basis over a three-year period beginning in 2000, to be completed by the end of 2002 (Florida Statute §409.1671).[4] The services designated as subject to privatization were: foster care, therapeutic foster care, residential group care, residential treatment, permanent foster care, and the related services of family preservation, independent living, emergency shelter, foster care supervision, case management, postplacement supervision, and family reunification.

Under the new privatization structure (which continues to shape Community-Based Care), only private, community-based agencies are eligible to serve as lead agencies (public agencies and for-profit businesses are excluded). Lead agencies assume some of the management and operational responsibilities previously held by the DCF district service offices. Specifically, lead agencies are responsible for planning, administering, and delivering client services; ensuring that child welfare services are provided in accordance with state and federal law; and coordinating with other agencies (public or private) that provide services to children and families (OPPAGA, 2001). Lead agencies are permitted the latitude to provide services directly or to contract for services from other agencies. Private agencies are required to bid through a competitive process to serve as lead agency.

Although not an aspect of privatization, the law also mandated the transfer of child protective services investigations to the sheriff's department in Pinellas, Pasco, Manatee, and Broward Counties by the end of FY 1999–2000 (Florida Statute §39.3065). The law gave the sheriffs of these counties three options with regard to their new responsibilities: They could conduct child maltreatment investigations themselves, they could subcontract with other law enforcement officials, or they could subcontract with "properly trained employees of private agencies." Under the law, if a sheriff opts to subcontract with private agencies, those agencies are allowed to investigate neglect cases only (the sheriff's department is required to retain responsibility for investigation of abuse cases). The law also stated that during the first year of implementation, DCF was to remain responsible for quality assurance and for the performance of all child protection investigations. The pilot project that placed responsibility for protective service investigations with sheriff departments expanded in 2000, when the legislature authorized DCF to enter into grant agreements with sheriffs in other counties to assume responsibility for child protection investigations. As of summer 2002, only

---

[4] The Florida legislative subsequently amended the statute to require that the full transfer of foster care and related services be completed statewide by December 31, 2004.

Seminole County had entered into such an agreement (Kearney, 2002).

Not part of privatization, but nevertheless of interest because of its coincidence with the privatization mandate, the law required the transfer of child welfare legal services to the state attorney or the Office of the Attorney General in Sarasota, Pinellas, Pasco, Broward, and Manatee Counties. The law stated that the transfer of child welfare services was to occur "as determined as reasonably feasible...after the privatization of associated programs and child protective services investigations has occurred" (Florida Statute §409.1671[a][1]).

The Planning Process

In response to the legislative mandate, in 1999, DCF began to implement a framework for statewide privatization of child welfare services. Florida DCF (1999) viewed this effort as "the most comprehensive reform effort undertaken anywhere in the nation" (p. 3). Although DCF approached the task with determination, others expressed concern that a clear vision for child welfare privatization on a statewide basis had not been articulated and that the effort was not the result of "thought-through statewide policy" (Krueger, 2001, p. 1D).

Despite concerns on the part of commentators outside DCF, the department moved forward, as mandated, with statewide privatization. The first step, as the law required, was the development of a privatization plan "with local community participation, including but not limited to input from community-based providers that are currently under contract with the department to furnish community based foster care and related services" (Florida Statute §409.1671). The planning process involved focus groups and community forums across the state "to promote [DCF's] dialogue with community members and stakeholders" (Florida DCF, 1999, p. 5). Participants included foster parents, children and youth already in foster care, community-based agency representatives, clergy, and other community representatives.

Among the tasks in this process was the development of guiding principles for child welfare privatization. These guiding principles, developed collaboratively by DCF staff and community providers (David Overstreet and Theresa Leslie, personal communication, September 4, 2002), are listed in Table 10. These principles (with their focus on safety and permanency, community involvement and responsibility, accountability, and collaboration and communication) are consistent with the legislative directive related to the purpose of privatization ("to increase the level of safety, security, and stability of children who are or become the responsibility of the state" (Florida Statute §409.1671) and the legislature's intent that child welfare services be strengthened through communities' direct involvement ("It is further the Legislature's intent to encourage communities and other stakeholders in the well-being of children to participate in assuring that children are safe and well-nurtured," Florida Statute §409.1671).

Financial Aspects of Community-Based Care

As part of its implementation plan and as required by statute[5], DCF developed a fiscal analysis and methodology for the implementation of Community-Based Care. DCF also sought approval for a Title IV-E waiver from the federal government to implement specific aspects of its privatization initiative.

The Planning Process and Implementation Plan: Financial Issues

After discussions with community representatives regarding the fiscal aspects of Community-Based Care, DCF concluded that "the only way to sustain a truly comprehensive and effective service delivery system was through increased funding flexibility coupled with a reimbursement system that rewards performance measured by the safety and permanency of children" (Florida DCF 1999, p. 7). In accordance with statutory requirements regarding the fiscal methodology for privatization, DCF addressed a number of financial issues in its implementation plan: current child welfare funding mechanisms; a plan to transfer funds to lead agencies for services, administrative costs, and capital equipment; workload transfer; and the financial methodologies that the department would use in implementing Community-Based Care.

> 1. **Current Funding Sources and the Current Resource Allocation and Management Model.** DCF identified Title IV-E as the most significant source of federal funding for child welfare services, and Medicaid as a source of substantial funding for specialized, therapeutic services for children in foster care. The DCF implementation plan emphasized that using its current methodology, fiscal "inequities and perverse disincentives in the system" resulted in greater allocations to districts within the state that had higher placement rates and longer lengths of stay in foster care. In its plan, DCF stated that the allocation formula would be changed to apportion funding on the basis of other criteria, specifically through the use of a computer model that would reallocate funds "to more equitably distribute funds, reward districts with

---

[5] The Florida statute required that the plan include a method for the "transfer of funds appropriate and budgeted for all services and programs that have been incorporated into the project" (Florida Statute §409.1671[1][a]).

Table 10

Guiding Principles for the Florida Community-Based Care Initiative

1. The care of children and assistance to their families must be a community responsibility involving partners such as foster parents, the school system, courts, law enforcement, the faith community, other community organizations, and Florida.

2. The system of care will be child-safety focused, family-centered, respectful of individual needs, outcomes-based, and directed toward achievement of timely permanency.

3. Families in the system will receive flexible, responsive, relationship-based services from competent staff who maintain frequent contact.

4. The care system must use an inclusive planning process. System changes will be phased-in and targeted to produce improved outcomes through efficient resource management.

5. The local provider network is the foundation for an orderly transition of child welfare services from the public to the private sector.

6. Integrity is the core value of the privatized system, creating a sense of normalcy for children through communication and developing trust relationships with stakeholders in the child welfare system.

7. Relationships among clients and providers of services are paramount in fostering a cooperative community voice regarding protection of children.

8. Adequate resources will be required to address the myriad issues in child protection. Each community must mobilize resources from various sources.

9. Accountability will be required at all levels to ensure treatment consistency using data-driven, objective, outcomes-based measures.

10. All stakeholders will be brought together to develop a common planning and implementation process for Community-Based Care.

Source: Adapted from Florida Department of Children and Families 1999.

better performance related to permanency, and encourage all districts to better manage available funding" (Florida DCF, 1999, p. 16).

2. **Transfer of Funds for Services to Lead Agencies.** As required by statute, DCF confirmed in its implementation plan that it would conduct a three-year historical analysis of all expenditures for foster care and related services for each community as it became ready to transition to Community-Based Care and provide services under a lead agency. DCF stated that it would develop a standard formula for each district to determine the funding needed by the lead agency to meet its monitoring and contract management responsibilities. DCF (1999) would develop an "advance payment type of contract utilizing a cost reimbursement process" and make start-up and transition funds available to permit lead agencies "to hire staff, establish a community stakeholder group, develop a community plan, submit a Financial and Service Plan, and initiate a process to transition staff from the Department to the lead agency" (p. 16).

3. **Transfer of Funds for Administrative Costs and Transfer of Capital Equipment to Lead Agencies.** DCF also outlined its plan to transfer funds to assist lead agencies with administrative costs as well as capital equipment (computers, office furniture, and other items). The implementation plan stated that a formula would be established under which DCF would transfer administrative and management resources (including capital equipment) to the lead agency in each district based on a calculation of the pro-rata share of public agency positions eliminated as a result of privatization. Although the plan indicated that DCF would consider the use of a statewide administrative services organization to perform all administrative and management functions for lead agencies statewide, thereby reducing costs and duplication, the state has not done this (Charlotte McCullough, personal communication, January 25, 2002). At the same time, DCF has not implemented the

transfer of funds to assist lead agencies with administrative costs (Lee Johnson, personal communication, August 14, 2002).

Although it did not initially provide assistance to lead agencies for start up, DCF later addressed issues related to lead agencies' start-up costs in connection with Community-Based Care. After the initial implementation period, DCF provided lead agencies with transition funding to facilitate capacity building and start up (McCullough & Schmitt, 2002). With regard to the start-up needs of lead agencies that assume responsibility for Community-Based Care in the future, DCF developed partnerships with children's services councils and local public agencies through a Temporary Assistance to Needy Families grant program (McCullough & Schmitt, 2002). In addition, in FY 1998–1999, at the urging of DCF, the state legislature approved a 25% budget increase to provide requisite funds for expanding local provider capacity so that an infrastructure could be established for Community-Based Care (McCullough & Schmitt, 2002).

4. **Transfer of Expected Workload.** In its fiscal methodology, DCF further indicated that a formula for workload transfer would be developed, based on the most recent three-year caseload data in each community. DCF stated that it would provide technical assistance on workload issues to each community during the Community-Based Care planning phase.

5. **A Future Cost and Risk Prediction Model.** Finally, the implementation plan described the use of risk-modeling technologies to "test various methodologies to forecast and manage system costs" (Flordia DCF, 1999, p. 19). DCF stated its interest in moving from "a fixed 'global' budget to a case-rate method of budgeting and payment" (Florida DCF, 1999, p. 19). DCF, however, has retained a "global budget transfer" methodology, in which lead agencies assume almost full risk for the cost of all child welfare services and supports needed by enrolled children

and families ("Community-Based Care," 2001). DCF contracts with lead agencies for a fixed dollar amount that approximates the appropriation that the DCF district office previously received to provide foster care and related services (McCullough & Schmitt, 2002). DCF expects lead agencies to access other funding sources, such as Medicaid ("Community-Based Care," 2001), and to maximize local funding resources to expand services.

Florida's Title IV-E Waiver

As an additional aspect of DCF's fiscal planning, the agency submitted for approval a federal waiver to allow Florida greater flexibility in its use of Title IV-E funding. The proposal (in line with references in the implementation plan to "a case-rate method of budgeting and payment" (Florida DCF, 1999, p. 19) had three financial components:

- Allocation of financial risk through a fixed contract amount to a lead agency to cover all services for all children and families referred,

- Use of additional incentives for outstanding performance through financial bonuses and penalties linked to performance for lead agencies and/or network providers, and

- Coordination and case management of child welfare services with Medicaid-funded behavioral health services for children and families.

USDHHS approved the waiver in September 1999 for implementation beginning between July and December 2000. The approved waiver targeted children in 10 counties for whom there were substantiated reports of abuse and neglect and who required child welfare services beyond protective service investigations. The project allowed the flexible use of Title IV-E funds for the provision of services through locally controlled, nonprofit, community-based systems of care. Consistent with the overall privatization initiative, Florida stated that it would contract in each county with lead agencies that would assume responsibility for all service needs of children from the time of referral until they were discharged from the child welfare system. Lead agencies would receive a fixed amount to cover the costs of all services for a broad population of children for a fixed period of time, thereby assuming full financial risk. Florida indicated in its waiver application that it would develop a catastrophic risk plan to protect itself from risks associated with lead agencies' bankruptcy or breach or termination of their contracts with the state.

The evaluation component of the waiver program involved the use of matched experimental groups (the 10 selected counties) and comparison groups (13 counties). In proposing such a methodology, Florida acknowledged that the statewide implementation of privatization might affect the status of the comparison counties and that a reassessment of this evaluation plan might be necessary as these counties became fully privatized. The outcomes on which the state proposed to evaluate the project were improved access to services, reduced lengths of stay in out-of-home care, reduced reentry into out-of-home care, improved client satisfaction ratings, and reduced variability in service delivery across sites (USDHHS, 1999).

In October 2000, the DCF commissioner testified to Congress that although the waiver program was to have been initiated between July and December 2000, Florida had not yet begun to implement the waiver program (Kearny, 2000). She stated that the current waiver program posed "barriers to optimal performance" that had negatively affected the state's ability to implement its waiver program, although the nature of these barriers was not made clear. Florida subsequently determined that it would not implement the waiver and, instead, would rely on funding through TANF to defray state costs associated with foster care room and board (Charlotte McCullough, personal communication, January 25, 2002).

The Budget for Community-Based Care

In 1998, the first year of implementation, the total budget for Community-Based Care (as determined by the level of funding committed to lead agencies implementing it statewide) was $15 million (Florida DCF, 2002d; McCullough & Schmitt, 2002). In 2002, DCF reported a Community-Based Care budget of approximately $54 million for FY 2001–2002 and projected increasing budgets over the next three fiscal years ($187 million for FY 2002–2003, $438 million for FY 2003–2004, and $469 million for FY 2004–2005) (David Overstreet, personal communication, August 26, 2002). It also projected that on full implementation of Community-Based Care, between 10% and 15% of the total child welfare budget for the state would be retained by DCF for child protective services intake and investigations and quality assurance activities (McCullough & Schmitt, 2002). The remainder of the child welfare budget—estimated by DCF to be between $250 and $300 million each year—would be transferred to the lead agencies for Community-Based Care (McCullough & Schmitt, 2002).

The Planning Process and Implementation Plan: Data Systems

In the implementation plan, DCF emphasized the importance of "data systems to keep track of children and families at risk" (Florida DCF, 1999, p. 19). The plan characterized Florida's delays in building its data system capacity through the

Statewide Adoption and Child Welfare Information System (SACWIS), which federal law requires each state to implement, in a positive light, characterizing the situation as "a fortunate opportunity to now build the system to accommodate what will undoubtedly need to be an Internet accessible system" (Florida DCF, 1999, p. 19). In the plan, DCF stated that SACWIS would be "key" to integrating the necessary data to manage Community-Based Care. Private providers were not involved, however, in the planning of the data management systems (Lee Johnson, personal communication, August 14, 2002), a factor which appears to have had a significant effect on the successful integration of various information systems.

Despite early optimism, DCF has encountered ongoing problems in implementing a comprehensive and reliable information management system and creating a monitoring infrastructure to ensure appropriate implementation of Community-Based Care. As of mid-2002, Home Safenet, the state's information system, had been in development for 11 years (its original expected completion date was 1998); had risen in cost from the original estimate of $32 million to an estimated cost of $230 million to complete the system; was operational only for case management services; and was considered by some to be inordinately slow and cumbersome ("Child Welfare Database," 2001; Kestin, 2002a). Phases of the information system other than case management are not expected to be operational until 2005 at the earliest ("Child Welfare Database," 2001; Mahlburg, 2002).

Nonetheless, DCF has mandated that all Community-Based Care lead agencies use Home Safenet[6] as the data management system. In September 2002, DCF reported that two improvements had been made in the use of the Home Safenet system: (1) Community-Based Care lead agencies could directly access the data that they themselves provide (eliminating the need for a lead agency to request that DCF retrieve and analyze the data that the lead agency itself had provided); and (2) through the "Unity One" system, lead agencies could access a client's information in Home Safenet, and in the mental health, substance abuse, and Medicaid data systems through a single portal (David Overstreet and Theresa Leslie, personal communication, September 4, 2002).

---

[6] The effect of this mandate has been intensified further by requirements in all lead agency contracts that case management staff, not data entry staff, enter all data (Charlotte McCullough, personal communication, September 10, 2002).

The Role of Lead Agencies

As part of the planning process, DCF attempted to clarify the specific roles and responsibilities of lead agencies (as well as the ongoing roles and responsibilities of DCF) and the process by which lead agencies would be selected. The statute provided some guidance on the responsibilities of the lead agencies by specifying their qualifications (Florida Statute §409.1671[b]). DCF, however, developed a more detailed framework of the roles and responsibilities, both for lead agencies (whether they provided foster care and related services on their own or through subcontracts with other agencies in the defined geographical area) and for DCF itself. Table 11 provides a summary of the initial DCF framework of Community-Based Care roles and responsibilities. These, however, have evolved over time (Lee Johnson, personal communication, August 14, 2002), and may not, in reality, be as clearly delegated as the table would suggest.

Regardless of any evolution in specific responsibilities, however, the lead agency is charged with providing or overseeing the provision of all child welfare services other than child maltreatment investigations (the core services specified in Table 12) and stimulating development of services for children and families that have not been provided through traditional approaches. The agency also creates relationships with other systems to ensure children's and families' access to behavioral health and other services.

The Selection of Lead Agencies

Although DCF initially considered a request for proposals (RFP) process to select lead agencies, in an effort to streamline the competitive process, it ultimately implemented a process called "invitation to negotiate" (ITN), which involves a written solicitation for competitive procurement, in which potential lead agencies have the opportunity to describe their qualifications and offer a creative and innovative approach to community-based services in their community (Florida DCF, 1999). According to OPPAGA (2001), DCF opts to use ITN as the form of competitive procurement:

> When a Request for Proposals or Invitation to Bid will not
> provide the solution the Department desires; the qualifica-
> tions of the provider or the terms of the working relationship
> required to achieve the goal of the contract is more critical to
> the success of the program than the price; or single source
> procurement might otherwise be the only available method.
> (p. 49)

Table 11

Roles and Responsibilities of the Lead Agencies and DCF in Community-Based Care

Type of Responsibility	Responsibilities of Lead Agency	Responsibilities of DCF
Child abuse and neglect investigations		Continue to operate the Florida Abuse Hotline
		Continue to operate child protective services investigations unless there is an agreement with a sheriff's department
Child Welfare Legal Services		Continue to operate child welfare legal services unless there is an agreement with the Attorney General's office or state attorney
Delivery of Child Welfare and Related Services	Organize and manage continuum of needed services for abused children and their families by creating a comprehensive provider network that includes child abuse and neglect prevention activities	Provide financial and service utilization data to all prospective lead agencies for the bid process
	Handle intake and referrals to network providers in collaboration with DCF and courts	Assist with the development of community partnerships and collaboration, including selection of the lead agency
		Negotiate contract with lead agency
		Maintain licensing responsibilities of foster homes and child care facilities

Finances	Manage capped amount of contract and address cost overruns	Provide federal claiming activities and reports
	Maximize additional resources and other services to expand services and leverage resources available through the contract	Assist the lead agency in maximizing and documenting federal funds
Accountability	Profile clients and providers and monitor resource use	
	Establish a quality assurance system	
	Gather and report information to DCF as required to support evaluation and reporting	
	Collect data and analyze information in coordination with DCF	
	Establish grievance and appeal procedures for all stakeholders	
Training	Train and recruit providers	Provide training and technical assistance to lead agency staff and community providers
Community outreach	Engage law enforcement, child protection teams, state attorneys, and the judiciary in the community partnership to protect children	

Source: Adapted from Florida DCF, 1999, p. 11; also based on personal communication with David Overstreet and Theresa Leslie, September 4, 2002.

Table 12

Community-Based Care: Core Services

Adoption Recruitment

Adoption Services and Postadoption Subsidies and Support

Assessment and Diagnosis

Case Management for Child Protection and Behavioral Health Issues

Court-Related Services

Crisis Services

Emergency Shelter

Family Foster Home Recruitment and Care

Home-Based Family Preservation and Support Services

Independent Living

Kinship Care

Permanency Planning

Residential Group Care and Treatment

Respite Care

Therapeutic Foster Care

Transportation and Other Support

DCF chose the ITN approach because "it provides the Department, community and applicants with the best opportunity to work together to develop a comprehensive and locally supported system of care for child protection services" (OPPAGA, 2001, p. 79).

DCF describes the ITN process as involving the following steps:

■ The DCF district administrator releases an ITN notice and holds a bidders' conference.

■ The DCF district administrator appoints a qualifications review committee.

■ The qualifications review committee (composed of community and DCF representatives) conducts a two-stage review:

(1) The committee reviews all responses to the ITN to determine each applicant's general capacity to serve as a lead agency (a standardized process throughout the state).

(2) Once one or more qualified applicants have been identified, the committee reviews each applicant's "system of care design," ranked on both standardized criteria and community-specific needs and interests.

- The DCF secretary approves the final selection of the lead agency for the community.

- A contract negotiation team (composed of local and state-level DCF staff) hold contract negotiations sessions with the highest ranked applicant (which are open to the public).

- A transition contract is negotiated, based on the lead agency's service plan and the fiscal resources that DCF has available. The transition contract usually has a term of six to nine months to allow the lead agency to develop a service delivery and management plan and build the needed infrastructure.

- The lead agency and DCF sign a standard operation contract (which may vary in length from one to five years) (Florida DCF, 1999; OPPAGA, 2001).

In reality, these steps are not implemented uniformly in each community. As one example, contracts may not be negotiated through face-to-face negotiation teams.

As part of the lead agency selection process, DCF uses a community-based care readiness assessment (based on accreditation standards) to assist it in determining the readiness of an organization to assume lead agency responsibility (Florida DCF, n.d.). The assessment focuses on the organization's readiness in eight areas: (1) its purpose and relationship to the community, (2) quality assurance and improvement, (3) organizational stability, (4) management of human resources, (5) quality of the service environment, (6) financial and risk management, (7) management information systems, and (8) "system of care," in which the organization specifies its model for providing services and its capacity to comply with state and federal laws and regulations (Florida DCF, 2002b). The organization's specific expertise in child welfare is not solicited, although it may be a factor that is considered in the evaluation of an applicant's proposed system of care.

There is considerable focus on issues related to financial stability and management. The community-based care readiness assessment requires that an organization either have the following in place prior to beginning operation as a lead agency or have systems in place shortly thereafter:

- security bonds, liability insurance, and performance bonds;[7]

- existing resources to ensure at least 60 days of agency operation;

- a long-term business plan (if not at the time that operation as the lead agency begins, within 90 days);

- an accounting system that collects costs by cost centers that will eventually allow the provider to evaluate costs by recipient and predict cost patterns; and

- a risk management program with components that address the unique factors required by managed care.

The community-based care readiness assessment is the state's key tool in determining a lead agency's readiness to enroll and serve children and families. Only on a determination of readiness does DCF sign the final contract with the lead agency (McCullough & Schmitt, 2002).

Phased-In Implementation of Community-Based Care

During the planning phase, DCF determined that implementation of Community-Based Care would take place county by county (as opposed to a full-scale statewide implementation, as was the case in Kansas). DCF developed a time frame for phasing in Community-Based Care, beginning with the counties that already had converted to privatization as part of the original pilot project. After its initial review of the ability of the state's 67 counties to implement Community-Based Care, DCF determined that 7 counties likely would not be able to implement a privatized system within the legislatively mandated period. As required by statute, DCF identified the reasons for these counties' likely inability to privatize within the required time frame:

- community sentiment that child welfare services are a state, not county, responsibility;

- the rural nature of some counties that posed transportation issues and other challenges to the implementation of privatization;

- the absence of a qualified community-based organization to serve as lead agency and concerns that an outside agency would not understand the community;

---

[7] Florida law requires that lead agencies obtain a minimum of $1 million per claim or $3 million per incident in general liability insurance coverage (Florida Statute §409.1671[1][f]).

■ the historical lack of financial support for children's services in the county; and

■ a perception that the current system was working effectively and did not need to be changed.

The law further required DCF to delineate "the efforts that should be made to remediate the obstacles" to privatization in these counties and authorized the use of "alternatives to total privatization, such as public-private partnerships" (Florida Statute §409.1671[1][a]). In line with this statutory directive, DCF indicated that "efforts to establish public-private partnerships" would be made to take "initial steps towards community-based services" in those counties that lacked interest in or the ability to privatize their child welfare services (Florida DCF, 1999, p. 15).

Given that 4 counties already were privatized as a result of the pilot program (although 2 of these four counties, Lake and Sumter, subsequently were deprivatized when problems developed with the lead agencies) and seven were not ready for privatization, DCF scheduled the remaining 56 counties to privatize on a phased-in basis, with the state's newly-created Community-Based Care Office coordinating efforts. DCF scheduled 5 counties for full-scale implementation in 2000, 20 counties (some of which were grouped together to implement multi-county systems of care) in 2001, and 31 counties (some of which were grouped together) in 2002 (Florida DCF, 1999).

The phase-in, however, did not occur on schedule. In March 2001, OPPAGA reported that 46% of the 63 counties (29 counties) had not yet privatized. Given the start-up time required for implementation of Community-Based Care, OPPAGA (2001) predicted that the remaining 29 counties could not bring all foster care and related services under the responsibility of a lead agency by the original deadline of January 1, 2003. OPPAGA identified three major challenges to implementation of privatization: (1) Many providers were reluctant to assume the financial risk that lead agency status entailed; (2) to become a lead agency, many providers would be required to significantly expand their capabilities, as they did not offer a full continuum of child welfare services; and (3) many communities were resistant to a transition to a lead agency model, either because the community had very limited resources or it was currently providing high quality, well-managed services under the public system and wished to retain that model.

Nonetheless, in August 2002, DCF reported that 61 of Florida's 67 counties were in some stage of privatization: 5 counties were fully privatized (Sarasota, Manatee, Pasco, Pinellas, and DeSoto), 7 counties were in early stages of phasing-in privatization, 7 counties had start-up contracts with community-based lead agencies,[8] and 42 counties had released ITNs (Florida DCF, 2002a). Florida DCF (2002a) estimated that approximately 99,000 children were being served through Community-Based Care in these counties. In August 2002, DCF also reported that the seven counties originally determined to be not ready for privatization were "moving toward privatization" (David Overstreet, personal communication, August 23, 2002). Among these counties was DeSoto County, where the Sarasota County YMCA assumed lead agency responsibilities and developed a Community-Based Care system that responds to the unique needs of DeSoto County. DCF currently projects that it will complete statewide implementation of Community-Based Care by the new statutory completion date of December 31, 2004 (David Overstreet, personal communication, August 23, 2002).

A New Planning Requirement: Community Alliances

In 2000, the Florida legislature, with the support of DCF, added "community alliances" as a mandatory component of Community-Based Care in each county or group of counties (Florida DCF, 2000a). The law requires that each county implementing Community-Based Care put into place:

> [A] Community Alliance of the stakeholders, community
> leaders, client representatives, and funders of human servic-
> es...to provide a focal point for community participation and
> governance of community based services. An Alliance may
> cover more than one county when such arrangement is deter-
> mined to provide for more effective representation. The
> Community Alliance shall represent the diversity of the com-
> munity. (Florida Statute §20.196[a])

DCF describes the role of community alliances "as providing the central point for broad-based community input and collaboration" (Florida DCF, 2000a, p. ii). The alliances are integral to the "overarching strategy to build partnerships in the community which significantly impact the outcomes, quality, effectiveness, and efficiency of services in the community" (Florida DCF, 2000a, p. iii). Community alliances are collaborative partnerships that strategically plan systems of care specifically tailored to meet the needs of families in each community (Florida DCF, 2000c).

Under the new statutory requirements, district DCF offices are charged with forming alliances in their areas (OPPAGA, 2001). The initial membership of each

---

[8] In Hillsborough County, the lead agency entered into a limited, nonrisk contract to provide certain specified services to 50 cases. This "mini-pilot" is designed to test the proposed
system of care before the lead agency enters into a full service contract.

alliance must include the DCF district administrator and representatives from county government, the school district, the county United Way, the county sheriff's office, the county circuit court, and the county children's board, if one exists (Florida Statute §20.196[d]). Community alliances may create work groups that include community stakeholders who are not members of the alliances (such as local providers, DCF staff, advocacy groups, and consumers) to address specific community issues (Florida DCF, 2002c). Work groups, for example, may focus on such issues as access to behavioral health services (David Overstreet and Theresa Leslie, personal communication, September 4, 2002).

Community alliances are charged by statute with a range of responsibilities: Joint planning for resource utilization in the community, including resources appropriated to the department and any funds that local funding sources choose to provide; needs assessment and establishment of community priorities for service delivery; determining community outcome goals to supplement state-required outcomes; serving as a catalyst for community resource development; providing for community education and advocacy on issues related to delivery of services; and promoting prevention and early intervention services. (Florida Statute §20.196[b])

As of this writing, there were 33 community alliances serving the 67 Florida counties (Florida DCF, 2002c).

Preliminary Statewide Outcome Measures

During the planning phase, DCF established eight core outcome measures (listed in Table 13) to monitor the effectiveness of Community-Based Care. These outcomes formed the basis of the model contract initially negotiated with lead agencies, and they functioned as one component of DCF's performance-based budgeting with the Florida legislature (Florida DCF, 2000b). DCF, however, expressed caution from the outset about the use of these outcome measures. In the 1999–2000 evaluation of Community-Based Care, DCF stated that "because of a lack of national historical data to support what is and is not best practice in child welfare, it is difficult to pre-determine, unequivocally, what are important to monitor" (2000b, p. 22).

As counties have developed and implemented Community-Based Care initiatives, each lead agency has defined in its contract the outcomes and indicators to be used in its individual initiative (Florida DCF, 2000b; McCullough & Schmitt, 2002). Performance assessments in Sarasota County, for example, reflect outcomes that diverge to some extent from the proposed statewide indicators. In its most recent ITN, the department outlined general outcomes for its Community-Based Care initiative: children's safety and protection from abuse and neglect,

Table 13

Florida Privatization

Preliminary Outcome

- The percentage of children served who will not be abused or neglected during the provision of services.

- The percentage of children served who will have no findings of child maltreatment within one year of case closure.

- The percentage of all families who will be satisfied with the care they receive.

- The percentage of children legally available for adoption who are adopted.

- The percentage of children returning to foster care within one year of case closure.

- The percentage of children satisfied with their foster care placement, as recorded on the exit interview form.

- The percentage of children who exited out-of-home care by the 12th month from the date of removal from their parents' custody.

- The number and percentage of protective service cases with case plans requiring substance abuse treatment that are referred for treatment and who subsequently receive treatment.

Source: Florida Department of Children and Families, 2000, p. 4.

timely permanency and stability in children's living arrangements, improved child functioning and well-being, and increased com-munity ownership of the child protection system (McCullough & Schmitt, 2002). Considerable variability exists, however, in how the specific outcomes are defined in each contract.

Part II: Implementation of Community-Based Care in Sarasota County

This section of this case study focuses on the experiences of Sarasota County in the implementation of Community-Based Care. Sarasota County was an original pilot county for the privatization initiative, and the county has sustained its privatization effort. As a result, its experience can provide valuable information not only for other counties in Florida but for communities outside the state that are considering initiatives similar to Community-Based Care. When relevant, the analysis makes comparisons to the experiences of other counties, including Broward County, where Community-Based Care is in the planning and early implementation stages. The implementation of Community-Based Care in Florida has varied significantly from one county to another, and no one county's experience with Community-Based Care can be considered definitive.

Sarasota County[9] was the first county in Florida to fully implement Community-Based Care. After being designated as one of the counties for the legislatively mandated privatization pilot project in 1996, Sarasota County began the planning process with a meeting of local stakeholders, including representatives from the county commission, the school system, the county's juvenile justice program, the courts, law enforcement, the county department of health, the medical community, social services agencies, and family advocates (Florida DCF, 2000a). This group evolved into the Sarasota County Coalition for Families and Children Stakeholders Advisory Committee, which assumed responsibility for the implementation of child welfare privatization in the county. The coalition developed a formal set of operating principles and began a process of financial and programmatic development to support a community-based care system in the county (Florida DCF, 2000a, Attachment K-21; OPPAGA, 2001). The coalition in Sarasota County, in fact, provided the model for the 2000 state legislation that mandated community alliances in each county that implemented Community-

---

[9] The placement of Sarasota County in Florida's system of child welfare districts has changed over time and, thus, references to the organizational status of the county vary. At the time of the child welfare privatization pilot project, Sarasota County comprised District 8. In 2000, the Florida legislature required the Department of Children and Families to establish a prototype region for the purpose of developing detailed protocols and procedures for the department's transition from its current 15-district structure to a new 7-district structure. The prototype district, now known as the SunCoast Region, is composed of six counties: Sarasota, DeSoto, Pasco, Pinellas, Hillsborough, and Manatee counties (Auditor General, 2001; Office of Program Policy Analysis and Government Accountability, 2001).

Based Care (Florida DCF, 2000a, Attachment B-3).[10]

Implementation of the Pilot Project

The pilot project in Sarasota County began in January 1997. DCF began a phased-in transfer of responsibilities for the coordination of child welfare services in Sarasota County to the coalition, which shortly thereafter contracted with the YMCA Children, Youth and Families Services, Inc. to serve as lead agency ("Community-Based Care," 2001). YMCA began to develop a broad network of service providers.[11] Throughout 1997, YMCA assumed responsibility for a growing number of child welfare services, beginning with adoption, licensing, recruitment, and contracting services in January of that year; adding foster care placements in March; and then incorporating voluntary and protective family services under its Community-Based Care program in June (Markowitz, 2000).

The pilot program in Sarasota County was highly successful. Opinion differs as to the reasons for the remarkably greater success in Sarasota County than in the other pilot counties. OPPAGA (2001) attributed Sarasota County's success to such factors as the high per capita income of county residents (Sarasota County is among the wealthiest of Florida counties), the local community's commitment of time and money to the effort, and the fact that Sarasota County has the lowest percentage of children of all Florida counties and, therefore, had lower caseloads.[12]

---

[10] Broward County, for example, formed a community alliance, the Broward Child and Family Leadership Association (CFLA), to oversee the implementation of Community-Based Care. Many members of CFLA were drawn from the Broward Child Welfare Initiative (BCWI), the original planning body for Community-Based Care in Broward County and an entity that has continued to function in Broward County along with CFLA (Charlotte McCullough, personal communication, January 17, 2002). In 2001, CFLA notified the Department of Children and Families of the county's readiness to move forward with privatization, and Broward County initiated the ITN process.

[11] The provider network in Sarasota County initially included the Child Development Center, Family Counseling Center, First Step, LifeLink Child and Family Services, Child Protection Center, Foster Parent Association, Westcoast Access to Children's Health, Sarasota Memorial Hospital, Coastal Recovery Center, Foster America, Sarasota School District, Big Brothers/Big Sisters, and Sarasota County Government. As of August 2002, the network included the same providers, with the exception of LifeLink Child and Family Services and Big Brothers/Big Sisters.

DCF, however, disagrees, maintaining that Sarasota County's "success...cannot be directly tied to the relative wealth of the community or the percent of children of all Florida counties" (OPPAGA, 2001, p. 77). Instead, DCF attributes Sarasota County's success to "community support and commitment to invest time in the program," which it maintains can be replicated in any Florida county, and its low caseloads to its determination to "reduce duplication, leverage federal funding, and implement a coordinated system of care" (2001, p. 77).

YMCA attributed (Lee Johnson, personal communication, August 14, 2002) the success of Sarasota County to strong leadership, particularly that of Carl Weinrich, President of the YMCA; to a historical tradition of community involvement with children socially, politically, and economically; and to the model that was used to implement privatization. YMCA also pointed to strong community involvement, including the county's community-based leadership group (which, as noted earlier, served as the model for the subsequent legislative requirement for community alliances in all Community-Based Care efforts).[13] Although YMCA noted that there are certain unique aspects of the Sarasota County experience, it also emphasized that the Sarasota County model of Community-Based Care has been replicated successfully in Manatee and DeSoto Counties.

It should be noted that despite the overall success of the initial pilot project, the coalition in Sarasota County experienced some difficulties in implementing privatization. As one example, DCF district staff and coalition staff were not successful in developing and maintaining an effective working relationship. The tensions resulted in DCF's decision to move contract management from the DCF District 8 office (Sarasota County) to the DCF District 6 office (Manatee County).

OPAAGA (2001) also pointed to Sarasota County's heightened need for technical assistance regarding cost allocation methodologies and requirements related to federal funding. DCF maintained that OPAAGA incorrectly interpreted the need for assistance as problematic. DCF viewed the county's needs in this area as "a natural result of the significant expansion of scope and responsibilities that community-based agencies must manage as they move into the child protection

---

[12] In 2000, for example, Sarasota had a child population of 53,170 (compared to 178,359 in Pinellas County and 69,966 in Pasco County). The percentage of children in poverty in Sarasota County was 15.3%, compared with 19.4% in Pinellas County and 21.8% in Pasco County (University of South Florida, 2002).

[13] The Sarasota County community alliance has undertaken a number of innovative activities since full implementation of community-based care, including, for example, the creation of a legislative advocacy committee to coordinate strategies with the local legislative delegation (Florida Department of Children and Families, 2002c).

service delivery system leadership role" (OPAAGA, 2001, p. 77). DCF noted that lead agencies needed assistance in understanding the use of Medicaid-funded targeted case management services for children who were not eligible for Title IV-E assistance and in understanding how to use local funds, instead of state revenues, as the match for federal Title IV-E funds for eligible children (David Overstreet, personal communication, August 23, 2002).

The University of South Florida (USF) took yet another view of the lead agencies' need for technical assistance with regard to federal funding requirements and cost allocations methodologies. USF (2002, p. 25) noted that Community-Based Care brought about significant changes in prior practice, in which DCF undertook the responsibility of allocating and reconciling expenditures to appropriate budget categories and state and federal funding streams. As USF noted, Community-Based Care lead agencies are "given a lump sum of money and have to make decisions about the services needed, what funding sources can be used to fund them, and how to allocate these expenses to budget categories to meet state and federal guidelines" (p. 25). The extreme learning curve "that lead agencies needed to master the complexity of federal financing requirements" was, according to USF, "greatly underestimated" by all concerned (p. 25). Technical assistance was, in fact, critical to enabling lead agencies to negotiate the complexities of the new financing system and their responsibilities for ensuring adequate financial support for all aspects of their newly designed systems of care.

Full Implementation of Community-Based Care

After the pilot project concluded and statewide privatization was mandated in 1998, YMCA continued to function as lead agency in Sarasota County, assuming responsibilities for other child welfare services, including the adoption subsidy program. By 2000, all child welfare services provided after the initial investigation for child maltreatment had come under the responsibility of YMCA. In 1999, YMCA became the lead agency for Manatee County (OPPAGA, 2001). In 2001, it became the lead agency for DeSoto County (Lee Johnson, personal communication, August 14, 2002). The programs at that point became known as the Partnership for Safe Children and was implemented with five Manatees County–based partners. Because YMCA currently serves as lead agency for Community-Based Care in three counties, some lead agency functions are integrated for the three counties, and some functions are met in ways that are unique to each county. Table 14 provides a comparison of structural and functional components for the three counties' Community-Based Care programs.

Although some may view YMCA as a nontraditional provider of child welfare services, YMCA views provision of community-based social services as highly con-

Table 14

YMCA: Sarasota, Manatee and DeSoto County Structural and Program Components

Component	Program Comparison
Administrative and Financial	Same administrative staff provide account ing and other financial services; audit and financial reports are combined
Advisory Council	Separate councils
Case Management	Separate case managers in each county location; case records maintained separately at each location
Services	Similar in all locations
Service Providers	Service networks and partners are separate; all counties use same providers of services for children from birth to age 5
Planning and Outcomes	Similar outcome measures used
Protective Services Investigations	DCF conducts investigations in Sarasota County and DeSoto County; the Sheriff's Department conducts investigations in Manatee County
Child Welfare Legal Services	DCF provides legal services in Sarasota County and DeSoto County; the Attorney General provides legal services in Manatee County

Source: Adapted from Florida State University, 2001; Lee Johnson, personal communication, August 14, 2002.
Note: DCF = Department of Children and Family Services.

sistent with its history and tradition. In assessing its role as lead agency in Sarasota County, YMCA points (Lee Johnson, personal communication, August 14, 2002) to its longstanding presence in the community and its community orientation as the particular strengths that it has brought to its role of lead agency. Other counties, however, have not used well-established service providers as their lead agencies. Some counties, by contrast, have selected entirely new entities created specifically to serve as lead agencies for Community-Based Care. In Palm Beach County, for example, two existing service providers, Children's Home Society and the Children's Place at Home Safe, joined together to create Child and Family Connections (Cooper, 2002). Broward County selected Community Based

Solutions, a new entity formed by Family Central, Inc. (a nonprofit agency that provides child care for 50,000 children and families in Broward and Miami-Dade Counties), to negotiate a transition contract as lead agency (Community Based Solutions Proposal, 2001; "Privatization's Big Test," 2002).[14]

As Sarasota County moved into full implementation of Community-Based Care in 1999, the coalition built on the infrastructure that had been developed during the pilot project. Consistent with the general framework that DCF already had in place, it crafted a mission statement and a set of principles to guide the county's Community-Based Care program. The mission statement, which continues to guide community-based care in Sarasota County, reads:

> This coalition of community based agencies provides compre-
> hensive services to children and families needing services due
> to abuse and/or neglect through a collaborative effort that
> unites our resources, holds all parties accountable to specific
> standards of care, evaluates performance and distribution of
> resources based upon specific and measurable outcomes,
> holds permanency of the child's living arrangement and the
> continuity of relationships for the child as the primary goals,
> and provides these services through an inclusive and informa-
> tive relationship with the community and with the state.
> (Florida DCF, 2000b, p. 18)

The coalition also developed principles for its Community-Based Care initiative (see Table 15).[15]

Having crafted a mission statement and guiding principles as the framework for the county's system of Community-Based Care, the coalition oversaw the development of a continuum of services to be provided through a community partnership of agencies under YMCA. The Sarasota County model of service delivery is an "80% peer lead agency" model (Lee Johnson, personal communication, August 14, 2002). Because it provides only 20% of Community-Based Care

---

[14] Differences among lead agencies also are evident in the roles that lead agencies have opted to take in implementing Community-Based Care. YMCA, for example, has generally viewed its role as leader/advocate and has contracted out most services. Family Continuity Programs, the lead agency in Pinellas and Pasco Counties, by contrast, has continued to provide case management services directly and, consequently, has maintained a service leadership role (University of South Florida, 2002).

[15] Similar principles govern Community-Based Care in Manatee and DeSoto Counties where YMCA is also lead agency, but with slight variations reflecting unique considerations in each county.

Table 15

Sarasota County Principles for Community Partnership for Comprehensive Services

Principle

■ Services will be provided with the safety and best interest of the child as our first consideration.

■ Foster care adoption and protective services is a community effort and issue. We shall involve the community through a Stakeholders Advisory Committee, the involvement of volunteers, the solicitation of donations, and annual participation in the evaluation of services.

■ This system of care will be held accountable for the provision of high quality care in the most efficient manner.

■ We shall establish internal standards of care for each service being provided. There will be a continuous quality improvement system throughout the continuum of care. Measurable outcomes will be established. There will be an annual independent audit of the entire system. There will be competency based training for foster parents and staff.

■ All resources will be used in the most efficient method to reach the stated outcomes with families receiving services expected to contribute, whenever feasible.

■ We believe the State of Florida, the school system, the courts, law enforcement, foster parents, local governments, churches, the child and family, local businesses and foundations as well as other community organizations are critical partners in attaining successful outcomes.

■ Services will be delivered through a rapid response and attentive approach. No family or child receiving services will go more than a week without direct contact (phone contact or face to face visit) unless a decision to reduce services is made by a formal staffing process or court order.

■ This system of services will develop concurrent planning that assures strategies for service and permanency regardless of the turns a particular family may take over the course of their involvement with this Coalition.

■ There will be a "single point of entry" approach that assures the children and families consistency of treatment, reduction of duplication of services and efforts, a match of children and their alternative care provider to allow for a successful placement, and establishment of a plan of service based upon a comprehensive assessment.

■ There will be an individualized case plan developed for each child and family receiving services, including input from the child and family, which will direct the course of intervention throughout the time of service.

Source: Florida Department of Children and Families, 2000b.

Table 16

Sarasota County Community-Based Care Continuum of Care

Service	Service Characteristic
Parent Training and Support Groups	Provided, as needed, to all families receiving services and to foster families. Includes active parenting, nurturing, single parents, parents of teens, dads only, and children's foster care.
Outpatient Individual, Family, and Group Counseling	Available to all children and families receiving services and foster families. Includes treatment specific to the needs of children and families. Services are provided by an assigned master's-level counselor who shares responsibilities with the case manager.
Healthy Families Sarasota	Available to children and families who present a specific need or situation, in which this type of intervention is determined to be the most effective strategy based on a thorough assessment. Service is home-based for families with new-borns and can continue until child reaches age 5.
Developmental Day Treatment Services	The program provides services when assessment indicates that this is an effective strategy to resolving identified issues. Services may be school or facility based. Services are Medicaid reimbursable.
Case Management	Available to all children and their families that are provided services. Direct support is provided by a bachelor's-level professional who assists the child and family to ensure services are obtained, appointments are met, and necessary documentation is completed. Services include case plan development, coordination of communication and staffing, court appearances, case record responsibility, and work directly with all individuals involved.

Children's Outpatient Psychiatric Services	Available to all children and families determined to need such services.
In-Home Family Preservation Services	Available to all families with the goal of reunification and to intact families to prevent removal of the child from the home.
Comprehensive Assessment	Provided to each child and family eligible for services. Service involves determination of the type of placement and the specific home or facility that is the best match, based on the child's immediate needs and long-term plans; and an individualized case plan that sets specific goals for the family and child with estimated time lines. Concurrent planning also may begin at this point.
Out-of-Home Placement	Available to all children needing such service. All placement facilities are licensed and staffed by trained individuals demonstrating competency in providing out-of-home care. Placements include foster homes, group homes, residential treatment facilities, relatives' homes, independent living, and psychiatric care facilities.
Reunification/Postplacement Services	Available to all children who are being reunited with their birthfamilies. Services include in-home intensive counseling services, outpatient counseling services, parent education and support services, and recreational services.
Adoption Services	Provided to children who are freed for adoption. Services include assessment of child's needs, preparation of adoptive home, legal document preparation, and postadoptive services. Concurrent planning ensures that it will not be necessary to "start from scratch" if reunification is not successful.

Table 17

Broward County: Community Based Solutions' Services

- Services to Victims of Child Abuse and Their Families in Their Own Homes
- Services to Children in Out-of-Home Settings
- Services to Children with Adoption as Their Permanency Goals
- Permanency Planning and Services to Support Reunification
- Kinship Care Services
- Independent Living Services
- Child Abuse Prevention and Early Intervention to Prevent Escalation of Problems Leading to Child Abuse or Neglect
- Crisis Intervention
- Discharge Planning and Aftercare Support
- Access to Behavioral Health Services (and Funds to Support Access) for Parents of Children in Care or at Risk of Placement
- Access to Nontraditional, Individualized Services

---

services in the county, YMCA relies on the development of partnerships with other community service providers and a broad-based provider network to offer the range of services that form the service continuum (Lee Johnson, personal communication, August 14, 2002). The network provides these services to children and families referred from the DCF child protective services unit, by court order, or under other circumstances outlined in the contract between YMCA and DCF (Florida State University, 2001).

Table 16 provides the current key service components of the service continuum in Sarasota County and the characteristics of the services, including eligible populations. YMCA stresses that as a result of its continuous quality improvement process, ongoing evaluation of services and the partners with whom YMCA needs to work is required. It is anticipated that both the services provided and the partners will change as the needs of children and families change and the service environment evolves. Two areas in which YMCA anticipates further service development, for example, are early childhood development (given the growing knowledge base regarding early brain development) and services to adolescents (whose needs are becoming increasingly complex). To facilitate assessments of needed services and appropriate partnerships, YMCA holds monthly meetings with all partners to discuss programmatic, policy, and budgetary issues. Each year, it holds

Table 18

Sarasota County Outcomes and Performance Measure

Outcome	Performance Measure
Percentage of children served who are not abused or neglected during the provision of services	97
Percentage of children who have no findings of child maltreatment within one year of case closure	95
Percentage of clients who are satisfied with the services received	95
Percentage of children who are adopted within 12 months of becoming available for adoption	90
Percentage of children reunified with their families who return to foster care within one year of case closure	0
Average number of face-to-face contacts per month with each child served	4 per month
Caseload per case manager	No more than 15
Overall average length of stay in out-of-home care	Reunification: 12 months Adoption: 30 months Overall: 18 months

a planning retreat, which involves all principal partners in assessing the program's strengths, opportunities, weaknesses, and challenges.

By comparison, the proposed Community-Based Care system in Broward County uses a wraparound model of services funded through a variety of federal, state, and local sources, as well as fee-for-service arrangements. Table 17 provides the services that the lead agency, Community Based Solutions, has proposed to make available through a provider network in Broward County.

It is noteworthy that DCF reported that lead agencies have struggled most with the assumption of responsibility for out-of-home placement services (David Overstreet and Theresa Leslie, personal communication, September 4, 2002). DCF noted that the transition of this service component of Community-Based Care from the public to the private sector rarely has been smooth (David

Table 19

Comparison of Community-Based Care (CBC) and Non-CBC Counties

Outcome	Key Finding
Percentage of children exiting foster care within 11 months of entry	Increased for CBC counties, except Pasco. Increased for non-CBC counties.
Percentage of children reentering foster care within 11 months after discharge	Increased slightly for CBC counties, except Manatee and Sarasota counties. Increased for non-CBC counties.
Percentage of recurrence of maltreatment	Increased for all CBC and non-CBC counties, but lower rates for CBC counties versus non-CBC counties.
Percentage of children returned to parents and legal guardians after exiting care	Increased for all CBC counties, except Pasco. Increased for all non-CBC counties.
Average expenditures per child served	FY 95-96 and FY 99-00: Slightly increased in CBC and non-CBC sites.
Average expenditures per child/day	FY 00-01: Decreased in CBC sites and increased in non-CBC sites.
Average expenditures per total child population	Pinellas and Pasco had lower average expenditures than non-CBC sites. Sarasota and Manatee had similar average expenditures to non-CBC sites.

Overstreet and Theresa Leslie, personal communication, September 4, 2002). It is not clear, however, whether difficulties relate to the nature of the service itself, the extent to which lead agencies have expertise and experience in providing this child welfare service, and/or the extent to which community placement resources are available or must be further developed.

Outcomes Measures

Sarasota County has developed a number of substantive and process outcomes and performance measures that integrate, but also expand on, the preliminary outcomes developed by DCF early in its planning process. Table 18 outlines the key outcomes and performance measures currently used in Sarasota County.

YMCA also has developed a methodology for collecting relevant data from key stakeholders: (a) an annual parent and community survey to build a baseline for

Table 20

Selected Program Performance Measures

Performance Measure	Sarasota County		Manatee (comparison data)	
	Annual Objective	Average/Percentage	Average Objective	Average/Percentage
Percentage of children safe from abuse during foster care	97	98.3	97	96.1
Percentage of children safe from abuse for one year following case closure	95	93.1	95	96.1
Number of children returning to care after reunification within one year of case closure	0	10 children/5 families	0	0
Face-to-face contacts	4/month	79% seen four times a month; 17% not applicable	4/month	Not available
Caseload	15	23/29	20	29.1/35.5
Average length of stay (in months)				
Return home	12	9.2	12	19.4
Adoption	30	30	30	49.9
Overall	18	20.5	18	30.6
Total number of adoptions annually	31	2	56	8

Table 21

Program Data on Number of Placements and Permanency Goals for Sarasota and Manatee Counties by Data Source—June, 2001

Performance Measure	Sarasota County CIS Data (n = 1,776)	Manatee County CIS Data (n = 1,339)	Sarasota County Program Data File (n = 660)	Manatee County Program File Data (n = 836)
Placements				
Percentage of children with two or fewer placements			68.9	64.9
Mean number of placements			2.7	2.8
Median number of placements			1.0	2.0
Permanency Goals (in percentages)				
Reunification	25.2	30.6	37.8	40.7
Adoption	7.0	10.3	10.5	9.1
Long-term foster care	1.5	2.9	3.5	5.8
Long-term relative care			0	4.6
Independent living	2.0	1.1	3.8	0.0
Permanent commitment with foster parents			0	0.4
Termination of parental rights		0	0	
Not specified	64.3	54.9		

Source: Florida State University, 2001

Table 22

Comparative Data on Selected Child Safety and Permanency Indicators—June 2001

Child Safety Measure	Sarasota County	Manatee County	Statewide
Percentage of children not abused or neglected while receiving services[a]			
4/99–3/00	91.81	94.90	93.49
4/00–6/00	98.29	96.10	98.09
7/00–9/00	97.55	95.89	98.09
Percentage of children who have no findings of maltreatment within one year of case closure			
7/97–6/98	88.68	NA	90.28
7/98–6/99	92.50	100	90.11
7/99–9/99	93.10	NA	89.82
10/99–12/99	98.28	78.57	90.05
Percentage of children reunited with family who did not return to foster care within one year of reunification			
7/97–6/98	100	NA	96.82
7/98–6/99	100	NA	95.21
7/99–9/99		NA	98.16
10/99–12/99	100	81.82	96.39

[a] Because data collection procedures in Florida record child abuse and neglect as of the date of the report rather than the date the maltreatment occurred (which in some cases, may be prior to services), caution must be taken in interpreting these data (David Overstreet, personal communication, August 23, 2002).

future outcome measures, (b) annual interviews with children on each placement change, and (c) an annual survey of foster parents (Florida DCF, 2000a, Attachment A-3).

Since Sarasota County developed its outcome measures, a number of reports have been issued that assess these outcomes and other indicators of program performance. The following discussion addresses findings from the federal compliance review, a study by USF, and a series of studies by Florida State University.

Federal Compliance Review, Summer 2000.[16] In summer 2000, DCF conducted an internal federal funding compliance review that examined 72 indicators (including indicators in the areas of safety, permanency, and child well-being). YMCA scored at least 90% on 29 indicators, with highly positive outcomes found on timeliness of judicial reviews, preservation of family and community connections for children, development of case plans, communication with providers, and appropriate arrangements for services. The review identified several areas, however, that needed improvement: identification of the educational and dental needs of clients, documentation of extenuating circumstances for extending case plans, and monthly face-to-face contact with children in their foster homes (OPPAGA, 2001).

Evaluation by USF. In 2002, USF released the results of its evaluation of Community-Based Care in Manatee, Sarasota, Pinellas, and Pasco Counties. This study compared Community-Based Care counties with non–Community-Based Care counties. In general, results were somewhat mixed but, overall, the "performance of [Community-Based Care] counties...is better than in comparison counties" (USF, 2002, p. 58). Table 19 presents the key findings on five key factors: timing of foster care exit, foster care reentry, recurrence of maltreatment, reunification rates, and program expenditures.

Studies by Florida State University. Florida State University (2001) conducted a number of studies of outcomes associated with Community-Based Care in Sarasota County and other counties. Because of its longer history with privatization, more comprehensive data were available from Sarasota County (as was true

---

[16] Since this federal compliance review, the Department of Children and Families has begun to conduct quality services reviews using the Federal Child and Family Service Reviews criteria in seven districts, with the expectation of completing reviews in all districts by the end of 2002 (David Overstreet, personal communication, August 23, 2002; University of South Florida, 2002).

Table 23

Case Review Findings (2000-2001) in Sarasota and Manatee Counties

Area of Inquiry	Findings
Children for whom concurrent planning had been implemented	37%
Placements	
Type of initial placement	
Foster care	40%
Emergency shelter	19%
Highest number of placements for a child served through Community-Based Care	11
Average length of time per placement	8.63 months[a]
Children with only one placement	33%
Children with five or more placements	17.5%
Safety While Receiving Services	
Number of children with reports of abuse or neglect while receiving services	12% (7 children)
Number of reports verified or found to have "some indicators"	57% (4 children)
Permanency Goal	
Maintain/strengthen family	25%
Reunification	21%
Adoption	21%

[a] Sarasota = 6.56 months; Manatee = 11.13 months.

of Manatee County in a number of areas). One study focused on Sarasota County's performance on the key outcomes established for the county (see Table 18).[17] Table 20 provides performance outcomes for Sarasota County as of September 2000, as well as comparison data for Manatee County, where YMCA is also lead agency. These data suggest that Sarasota County has met the majority of its performance objectives.

---

[17] The study did not report client satisfaction levels.

Table 24

Survival Analysis in Sarasota County: Average Length of Time in Out-of-Home Care

Population	Length of Time in Care (in months)
All Children in Care	8.3
By Race and Gender	
Minority males	12.5
White males	7.3
Minority females	9.0
White females	7.6
Minority children (both genders)	11.0
White children (both genders)	7.5
By Permanency Goal	
Reunification	5.4
Adoption	19.3
Independent living	20.5
Long-term foster care	27.0
Long-term relative care	11.8

Source: Adapted from Florida State University, 2001.

In addition, YMCA reported significant improvements in caseload sizes since September 2000 (Lee Johnson, personal communication, August 14, 2002). Average caseloads as of June 2002 were 13.8 children in Sarasota County, 19.2 children in Manatee County, and 18.7 children in DeSoto County (Lee Johnson, personal communication, August 14, 2002).

Florida State University also reviewed data from two sources: the client information data file maintained by the Florida DCF, and the program database maintained by the YMCA Children, Youth and Family Services (Florida DCF, 2001a). This analysis focused on the number of placements that children averaged and the permanency goals for children in the Sarasota County Community-Based Care program. The results of this analysis are provided in Table 21, along with comparison data from Manatee County. It is important to note that the state's data (from the client information data file) and the data from YMCA's database (when both sources provide data) do not coincide, making it difficult to assess either county's performance in these areas.

Table 25

Preliminary Outcomes Proposed by Community Based Solutions for Broward County Community-Based Care

Outcome	Outcome Measure
Reduce recurrence of child abuse and neglect	Decreased percentage of children in out-of-home care who are reentries.
Reduce abuse and neglect in foster care	Percentage of all children in foster care who were subject to substantiated or indicated maltreatment by foster parent or facility staff.
Increase permanency for children in foster care	Reduced median length of time children exiting foster care have been in placement. Reduced median length of time children continuing in care have been in placement.
	Increased percentage of children who exit out-of-home care to permanency compared with all children who exit out-of-home care.
Reduce time to reunification without increasing reentry rates	Of all the children who were reunited with their caregivers at the time of discharge from foster care, what percenaget were reunified within the following time periods? Less than 12 months, 12–24 months, 24–36 months, 36–48 month
Reduce time in foster care to adoption	What percentage exited care to a finalized adoption within 12 months of placement or at 12–24 months, 24–36 months, 36–48 months, or 48 months or more?
Increase placement stability	A reduction in the mean number of placements experienced by children in an episode of out-of-home care.
Reduce placements of young children in group homes or institutions	Percentage of children younger than 12 placed in congregate settings.
Promote most appropriate, least restrictive placements	Reduced percentage of children in high cost placements (treatment of foster careand purchase-of-service care) without compromise to care requirements.
	Increased percentage of children placed in a family setting without compromising care requirements.

Source: Adapted from Community Based Solutions Proposal, 2001.

Florida State University also analyzed data on child safety indicators over the course of time. Table 22 provides the results of this analysis in Sarasota County, with comparative data from Manatee County and statewide. The table suggests that when compared with statewide data, data for Sarasota County are comparable.

From December 2000 through March 2001, Florida State University (2001) reviewed case records of children served by the Community-Based Care programs in the two counties (30 children in Sarasota County and 27 children in Manatee County). The average child's age was between 8 and 9 years (8.81 in Sarasota County and 8.4 in Manatee County). A somewhat larger proportion of children in Manatee County (50%) than in Sarasota County (43.3%) was black. Florida State University reported findings for the combined population of children in the two counties ($n = 57$). Table 23 provides some of the key findings from this case record review: the percentages of children with different permanency goals; the extent to which concurrent planning was being used; the type, number, and average length of children's placements; and children's safety while in foster care. Because the researchers combined data and did not provide statewide data for comparative purposes, it is difficult to assess Sarasota County's performance on these factors, other than in relation to length of care, which is approximately 40% shorter in Sarasota County than in Manatee County (reflecting the longer operation of the program in Sarasota County).

In addition, Florida State University (2001) conducted a survival or event history analysis to examine length of time in out-of-home care for the entire population of children in foster care in Sarasota County and for certain subgroups of children in that county's foster care program. Table 24 provides some key findings regarding average length of time in out-of-home care for all children in the county's foster care system and by race, gender, and permanency goal.

As a point of comparison, Community Based Solutions, the proposed lead agency in Broward County, takes a different approach to outcomes for its Community-Based Care program. It proposed outcomes that are consistent with federal mandates under the Adoption and Safe Families Act of 1997 and with existing state mandates. These outcomes, which the agency will further discuss with DCF, are listed in Table 25.

Fiscal Analyses

The budget for Community-Based Care in Sarasota County proved elusive. YMCA reported that for 2002, the combined budget for Community-Based Care in Sarasota, Manatee, and DeSoto Counties was $16.1 million[18] (Lee Johnson,

---

[18] This amount includes a legislative earmark of $1.2 million for a special pilot project for "hard to serve" children.

Table 26

Fiscal Data for YMCA: Sarasota County

	FY 1999	FY 2000
Average revenue per child	$4,592.36	$6,827.30
Average expenses per child in foster care program[a]	$5,097.17	$6,562.46
Profit/loss per child	$504.81 loss per child	$264.84 per child in excess of expenses

Source: Florida State University, 2001.

[a] The reported FY 1996 cost to the Department of Children and Families when it provided foster care directly was $7,553.64 per child.

personal communication, August 14, 2002). The Reason Public Policy Institute (2001) reported that Community-Based Care in Sarasota County costs about $4.5 million each year, with DCF providing approximately $3 million (the level of funding previously provided by DCF to the district) and the balance obtained from Medicaid and community donations. The difficulty in precisely determining the budget for the county's Community-Based Care program may result in part from changes in the budgeting process over time. Previously, the level of funding for any county's Community-Based Care initiative was based on the historical pattern of budget allocation to the DCF district office in which the county was based. Currently, the budgeting process is being revised to rely on a methodology that allocates available state dollars on a statewide basis. According to YMCA, even with the shift in the state's budget methodology, it is expected that Community-Based Care initiatives will seek funding from additional sources to enhance the Community-Based Care financial base (Lee Johnson, personal communication, August 14, 2002). YMCA itself historically has used a diversified funding base, a factor it sees as a key strength of its initiative.

In 2001, Florida State University reported an analysis of fiscal data for the Sarasota County Community-Based Care program, comparing average revenue and expenses per child. Table 26 provides some of the data generated through this analysis. These data suggest that Community-Based Care in Sarasota County has been able to realize a revenue-expense balance.

Assessment of the Implementation of Community-Based Care in Sarasota County

The implementation of Community-Based Care in Sarasota County has been generally successful. Between March 1, 1997, and December 18, 2000, the program served a total of 3,251 children (Florida State University, 2001). Indicators, in general, suggest positive outcomes.

Earlier in the initiative, researchers identified certain areas as requiring greater attention to ensure the successful implementation of Community-Based Care. Markowitz (2000), for example, called for improvements in six areas: (1) development of management information systems to provide ongoing, time-sensitive contract management; (2) greater clarity regarding the roles of all parties in the use of information systems; (3) assessment of how to manage the risk of an increased caseload; (4) clearly defined outcome goals for the Community-Based Care initiative; (5) clearer articulation of the role of DCF (both locally and at the central office), including the role of DCF in quality assurance; and (6) assessment of the appropriate level of DCF monitoring to ensure efficient use of time and data.

In 2002, YMCA (Lee Johnson, personal communication, August 14, 2002) reported that improvements had been made in each of these areas of concern, with progress evident in its management information systems, risk management approaches, definition and measurement of outcomes, and monitoring. YMCA noted that as a result of a variety of factors (including changes in state law and increasing caseloads), the Community-Based Care program experienced negative finances in the early years of the initiative. The financial status has now stabilized, and in contrast to some communities in Florida, Sarasota County has experienced what is described as "a gentle decline" in caseload size (Lee Johnson, personal communication, August 14, 2002). YMCA attributed this trend to a strong team effort as embodied in the Community-Based Care partnership and development of a comprehensive and effective array of preventive and early intervention services.

Based on its experience in implementing Community-Based Care in Sarasota County, YMCA identified (Lee Johnson, personal communication, August 14, 2002) seven key factors as critical to the success of its privatization initiative:

1. the choice of a model of service delivery that the community supports and that it will continue to support as challenges arise;

2. strong executive leadership;

3. the involvement of as many partners in the initiative as feasible (partners provide additional insights into community needs and can serve as checks and balances);

4. a strong financial contingency plan at the outset, which

fully anticipates fiscal losses;

5. a strong working relationship between the public and private sectors, with mechanisms in place for prompt and effective problem-solving;

6. a well-developed and well-functioning database; and

7. mechanisms that ensure "that you know what you are doing every day."

Part III. General Issues Related to Florida's Community-Based Care Initiative

An overall assessment of Florida's Community-Based Care initiative reveals both strengths and ongoing challenges.

Strengths of Community-Based Care

Those involved with the Florida Community-Based Care initiative highlight five strengths of the program: the pace at which the transition to Community-Based Care has proceeded, involvement of community stakeholders from the outset, use of a one-year planning and transition process prior to lead agencies' service delivery, flexibility in meeting community needs, and development of a statewide Community-Based Care leadership forum.

1. Carefully-Timed Pace. Those who have implemented Community-Based Care believe strongly that it is imperative that public-to-private transitions be made slowly and carefully. State leaders and lead agencies have supported a "go slow" approach that ensures that local service providers and communities are ready to implement Community-Based Care (Child Protection Report, 2002). The Florida legislature initially mandated that child welfare services be fully privatized by January 1, 2003, but it subsequently extended the deadline to December 31, 2004 (Florida Statute §409.1671). DCF's close, continuing work with the legislature provided legislators with an appreciation for a "healthy readiness period" and a definition of success grounded in "good projects" rather than short time frames (David Overstreet, personal communication, August 23, 2002). Although it is apparent that the transition to Community-Based Care went more smoothly in some communities than others, there appears to be unanimous support for a slower pace that provides opportunities to build community support.

2. Community Involvement. Those who have implemented Community-Based

Care in Florida focus on the importance of involving all community stakeholders. The critical role of community involvement was an important lesson taken from the experiences of the counties that participated in the pilot project. DCF integrated the concept of community involvement into the initial Community-Based Care planning process, into its design of the competitive procurement process for securing a lead agency, and into its implementation of community alliances. It strongly advocates direct communication with stakeholders on the issues that are most meaningful to communities and the full engagement of community leaders in the development of any initiative that responds to local concerns (USF, 2002).

3. One-Year Transition to Service Delivery. Key to the success of Community-Based Care, according to many participants, has been the use of a readiness assessment process and the provision of a six- to nine-month planning period prior to a lead agency assuming responsibility for service delivery. The Community-Based Care Readiness Assessment outlines the roles and responsibilities of DCF and the lead agency during the transition period, and, as a result, provides a way to determine the extent to which the necessary infrastructure for Community-Based Care has been developed in the community. The use of a transition period also has been associated with a smoother transition of staff. The transition period permitted extensive staff training staff regarding Community-Based Care; appropriate transition of professional staff formerly in DCF positions to positions with the lead agency; assumption of new roles by public agency staff, such as quality assurance; and provision of needed technical assistance to lead agencies (David Overstreet, personal communication, September 4, 2002).

4. Flexibility to Ensure that Community Needs Are Met. DCF (David Overstreet, personal communication, August 23, 2002) noted that Community-Based Care has been successful because of the flexibility permitted in the program design in each community. For example, many of the rural counties that were initially unready for privatization have been able to move toward Community-Based Care in large part because of flexible arrangements with lead agencies. Out-of-county lead agencies have been able to successfully assume responsibility for Community-Based Care implementation in rural counties because they have the flexibility to design systems of care that recognize the needs, interests, and "flavor" of the community. This approach has allayed concerns that a program would be intrusively imposed on the community (David Overstreet, personal communication, August 23, 2002).

5. Development of a Statewide Community-Based Care Leadership Forum.

One component of Community-Based Care in Florida is a statewide leadership forum convened by DCF. Still in the early stages of development, the forum brings together executive directors of lead agencies and DCF district administrators on a quarterly basis. They discuss emerging issues and policy changes, share lessons learned, and resolve conflicting views of the roles and responsibilities of DCF, lead agencies, and members of provider networks (USF, 2002). USF highlighted the need to continue to develop and strengthen the forum as "an ideal vehicle" for resolving Community-Based Care issues (p. 72). (DCF David Overstreet and Theresa Leslie, personal communication, September 4, 2002) also reported that as an additional facet of the state's efforts to bring Community-Based Care stakeholders together, it held one statewide conference (January 2001) and will hold a second in February 2003. The state views these efforts as key to problem solving, planning, and moving forward in a timely way (David Overstreet and Theresa Leslie, personal communication, September 4, 2002).

Challenges in Community-Based Care

A review of several reports issued since the inception of the initiative and interviews with key informants suggests that a number of issues remain. Among the problems identified are the fiscal structure of the initiative; financial risk issues; DCF's monitoring capability; the development of appropriate, consistent outcomes to assess the overall success of Community-Based Care; the adequacy of state funding; the need for more effective contracting procedures; and the adequacy of management information systems.

1. **The Fiscal Structure for Community-Based Care.** The current fiscal structure of Community-Based Care poses serious issues in connection with the ability of lead agencies to project the financial effect of the program. Lead agencies develop their system of care plans without clear budget data from DCF, their ultimate budgets do not include the administrative costs that DCF incurred prior to transfer of child welfare services to the lead agency, lead agencies typically are not told what the approved budget for the program will be until the point of actual transfer of service responsibility, and cost reimbursement is often significantly delayed because the payment mechanism is tied to the DCF data system (Charlotte McCullough, personal communication, September 10, 2002). These structural issues have resulted in an unpredictable environment for lead agencies that is further undermined by inadequate cash flow (Charlotte McCullough, personal communication, September 10, 2002).

2. **Management of Financial Risk.** Issues related to financial risk in connection

with community-based care surfaced initially when caseloads in Florida dramatically rose from 1999 to 2000, just as DCF was embarking on its planning process for statewide privatization. Between December 1999 and March 2000, Florida experienced an 18% increase in the number of child protective services investigations, and between January 1999 and March 2000, the number of children entering foster care increased 13% (Florida DCF, 2000b). The rise in the number of foster care entries is attributable to new Florida legislation, the Kayla McKean Child Protection Act (a law inspired by a young child who died despite repeated reports to child protection authorities). This law subjects social workers to possible criminal prosecution if they fail to remove a child from parental custody and the child is later abused (Snell, 2000).

In her evaluation of Community-Based Care, Markowitz (2000) highlighted the need to address risk management in relation to increased caseloads, particularly when precipitated by factors outside the control of lead agencies. As has been the case in other jurisdictions using fixed-sum contracts, Florida has had to face the financial implications of caseload growth and other fiscal uncertainties under such contracts. This has resulted in the reluctance of some agencies to assume the role of lead agency (OPPAGA, 2001). In one case, for example, a private agency, Devereaux Florida, entered into a transition contract to become lead agency in Pasco and Pinellas Counties, but then terminated its contract after its national board of directors became concerned about the level of financial risk involved (OPPAGA, 2001).

In response to concerns on the part of providers about the financial risk involved in assuming the role of lead agency, in 2000, the Florida legislature established a risk pool of $4.5 million to offset extreme growth in caseloads beyond the lead agency's control ("Community-Based Care," 2001). These funds may be used to provide case rates for all referrals above the thresholds established in contracts with lead agencies (McCullough & Schmitt, 2002). This approach is critical to ensuring that lead agencies have some protection against risks associated with unpredictable volume. Nonetheless, some view the $4.5 million as "woefully inadequate," as a statewide risk pool at this funding level could easily be used by a single large district to offset financial losses as a result of unanticipated caseload increases (Charlotte McCullough, personal communication, January 25, 2002). DCF reported that no lead agency has sought access to the risk pool (David Overstreet, personal communication, August 23, 2002), but it is also not clear how lead agencies can access the pool nor how much they can expect to receive if their caseloads grow dramatically.

Although other options were proposed in response to concerns about excessive levels of financial risk,[19] the legislative option endorsed was that DCF develop a proposal for a statewide shared earnings program to address the risk lead agencies face as a result of unanticipated caseload growth or significant changes in "client mixes or services eligible for federal reimbursement" (Florida Statute §409.1671[7]). At minimum, the proposal to be developed by DCF "must allow for use of federal earnings received from child welfare programs, which earnings are determined by the department to be in excess of the amount in the General Appropriations Act, to be used for specific purposes" (Florida Statute §409.1671[7]). Among the appropriate purposes specified by the statute for use of shared earnings are: significant changes in the number or composition of clients eligible to receive services; significant changes in the availability of federal funds; shortfalls in state funds available for services; "scheduled or unanticipated, but necessary, advances to providers or other cash-flow issues"; and continuity of care in the event of lead agency failure, discontinuance of service, or financial misconduct (Florida Statute §409.1671[7]). The DCF final proposal was to be submitted to the legislative budget committee for formal adoption by December 31, 2002. It is not yet possible to assess the extent to which this approach may resolve issues related to financial risk.

3. The Development of Strong, Ongoing Monitoring Capacity. Florida law requires, as part of the Community-Based Care initiative, that DCF "have a comprehensive monitoring infrastructure that ensures that State funds are appropriately used and that contractor performance meets state standards and assists in achieving program objectives and outcomes" (Florida Statute §409.1671). DCF is required by law to

> adopt written policies and procedures for monitoring the
> contract for delivery of services by lead community-based
> providers...[that] at a minimum, address the evaluation of fiscal accountability and program operations, including provider
> achievement of performance standards, provider monitoring
> of subcontractors, and timely follow-up of corrective actions
> for significant monitoring findings related to providers and
> subcontractors. (§409.1671[2][a])

---

[19] These options included: (a) the development of risk corridors to limit the liability of lead agencies within a capitated allocation methodology, such as making additional resources available if expenditures exceed 5% of the total contract amount as a result of increased caseloads and in the absence of indicators of poor performance; (b) the development of stop-loss measures when children require care at a significantly higher cost than anticipated under the contract; (c) the development of an emergency resource pool in the event of unanticipated crisis in communities; and (d) ongoing funding to support transitional costs for counties (Florida Department of Children and Families, 1999).

Table 27

Elements of Monitoring Infrastructure

- Clear assignment of responsibility and lines of authority regarding monitoring.
- Sufficient staff for contract negotiations, contract management, and contract monitoring functions.
- Monitoring instruments specific to Community-Based Care.
- Requirements regarding adequate documentation of all monitoring activities and the maintenance of all documentation for a specified period of time.
- Independent reviews of case files and other program documentation maintained by Community-Based Care providers.
- Guidelines for a minimum number of applicable cases that should be reviewed to draw conclusions about performance criteria.
- Collection and validation of data used for evaluating achievement of performance measures.
- Requirements that personnel attest to any conflict of interest with the Community-Based Care provider at each monitoring engagement.
- Written monitoring reports that include the response of the Community-Based Care provider.
- Requirement that Community-Based Care providers submit written corrective action plans to the department for determination of appropriateness.
- Minimum qualifications and training for monitoring personnel.
- A quality assurance process for review of monitoring.

In response, DCF created a Community-Based Care Office within its Office of Mission Support and Performance to focus on alliance building and support, reorganization of services, ITN support, assessment of lead agency readiness and transition to Community-Based Care, quality assurance activities, and community capacity building (Florida DCF, 2001c).

In September 2001, Florida's Auditor General (2001) issued the results of an operational audit that assessed DCF's performance in monitoring Community-Based Care providers of child welfare services. The audit focused on DCF policies, procedures, and implementation plans, with a primary emphasis on the quality of DCF monitoring in Sarasota and Manatee Counties, where Community-Based Care has been in the place the longest. Four key deficiencies were identified:

- **The Absence of a Comprehensive Monitoring System.** The Auditor General (2001) found that DCF had not adapted its program monitoring policies and procedures to address the unique features of community-based care and had relied on the federal compliance review in lieu of traditional program monitoring. The Auditor General recommended that DCF implement "a coordinated monitoring infrastructure to address the unique relationship" (p. 3) between DCF and Community-Based Care providers and outlined a number of monitoring infrastructure elements that DCF should integrate into its monitoring system (see Table 27).

DCF reported that in response to these recommendations, it is implementing a quality service review system that will assess substantive outcomes as well as the procedural issues identified in the Auditor General's report (David Overstreet, personal communication, August 23, 2002).

■ **Inadequate Evaluations of Community-Based Care Providers' Achievement of Performance Measures.** The Auditor General also found insufficient monitoring with regard to outcomes contractual requirements. Specifically, DCF had not monitored the extent to which Sarasota and Manatee Counties had achieved the five performance measures outlined in their contracts from October 1999 through September 2000.[20] YMCA reported, however, that outcome monitoring has improved as it has expanded and redefined outcomes and performance measures and strengthened data collection· (Lee Johnson, personal communication, August 17, 2000) .

■ **Lack of Follow-Up on Significant Deficiencies Noted During Monitoring.** Of specific concern to the Auditor General were DCF's failures to require written corrective action plans for all significant deficiencies that it identified through monitoring. In addition, it was found that DCF did not appropriately follow-up when the corrective action response by the Community-

---

[20] Those outcomes were: (1) 95% of the clients were satisfied with the services received, (2) 90% of the children legally available for adoption were adopted during the 12-month period ending June 30, 2000, (3) 97% of the children served were not abused or neglected during the provision of services, (4) 91% of the children served had no findings of child maltreatment within one year of case closure, and (5) 3% or less of the children who reunited with their families returned to foster care within one year of case closure.

Based Care provider seemed inadequate.

■ **Inadequate Policies Regarding DCF Oversight of the Lead Agency's Monitoring of Subcontractors.** Initially, to provide lead agencies with flexibility, DCF did not set forth detailed requirements regarding lead agencies' monitoring of subcontractors. DCF, instead, contractually required that lead agencies develop written procedures to monitor subcontractors at least annually, engage in quarterly quality improvement activities, and provide technical assistance, as needed. The Auditor General found that DCF had not complied fully, even with these conditions. With regard to YMCA's program monitoring activities in Sarasota and Manatee Counties, the Auditor General found that DCF had not conducted an independent review of the lead agency's monitoring of its subcontractors, had not adequately followed-up on fiscal and personnel issues that had been identified in connection with the subcontractors' performance, and had not required that YMCA notify DCF of serious deficiencies in subcontractors' performance. In this connection, DCF reports (David Overstreet, personal communication, August 23, 2002) that it now includes language in lead agency contracts that requires DCF's prior approval of subcontractors, DCF review and approval of lead agencies' subcontracting procedures, and periodic sampling by DCF of subcontractors' performance, including DCF monitoring to ensure that any subcontractor has not performed poorly in another Community-Based Care program.

In findings similar to the Auditor General's, OPPAGA (2001) highlighted the need for improvement in DCF's monitoring system. OPPAGA noted that DCF primarily focused on contract compliance issues and did not routinely assess service quality. DCF program management attributed its monitoring difficulties to two factors: the limited number of staff with necessary expertise to monitor performance and the need to assign staff to other responsibilities, particularly to protective services investigations. DCF program management reported to OPPAGA (2001) that in June 2000, as a result of extremely high staff turnover in child protection investigations, there 48,541 investigations open statewide and staff had been reassigned from other program areas to bring these investigations to a close. Some anticipate that as a result of recent developments—including the recommendations of the Governor's Blue Ribbon Panel on Child Protection following the disappearance of Rilya Wilson, a child in foster care who had been missing for more than 16 months before her disappearance was discovered—there may be an impetus for significant improvements in DCF monitoring systems ("More Reforms," 2002).

At the same time, at least two reports have focused on the duplicative and overlapping auditing and program monitoring functions that have characterized Community-Based Care[21] (Stitt, Olsen, & Certo, 2001; USF, 2002). All stakeholders, including DCF, identified this issue. DCF established a work group to streamline monitoring activities (including efforts to coordinate concurrent Title IV-E, mental health, and quality assurance evaluations) (David Overstreet, personal communication, September 4, 2002; USF, 2002). Currently, multiple entities conduct auditing and monitoring on three issues: lead agencies' financial viability and compliance with federal and state fiscal rules, compliance with terms of the contract, and compliance with performance standards related to child safety and permanence (USF, 2002). USF recommended that a process be initiated to set priorities and maintains a focus on program issues (p. 73).

4. The Need to Develop Consistent, Well-Defined Core Outcomes to Measure All Initiatives. DCF has not developed uniform outcome measures to be used in each Community-Based Care initiative. The outcomes that Sarasota and Manatee Counties monitor and report, for example, are not necessarily used in contracts with potential lead agencies in other counties. In a recent comparison of four Community-Based Care contracts with lead agencies, one contract had 47 outcome measures, one contract had 9 measures, and two contracts had 7 measures (Charlotte McCullough, personal communication, September 10, 2002). In fact, no CBC contract expressly states how the program will assess success in terms of outcome achievement (Charlotte McCullough, personal communication, September 10, 2002).

DCF reported that it continues to struggle with the appropriate balance between using consistently defined statewide measures that allow comparisons and community-specific measures that reflect local concerns and interests (David Overstreet, personal communication, August 23, 2002). In fact, consensus has yet to be reached on using federally defined outcomes assessed as part of the Child and Family Services Reviews.[22] As the USF (2002) noted, the tension between the dual objectives of local flexibility and standardization statewide is one that "is likely to become more problematic as CBC is implemented statewide" (p. x).

---

[21] Community-Based Care programs are monitored and evaluated by local, state, and federal agencies; by child welfare, mental health, and Medicaid authorities; and by university-based and independent evaluators. One lead agency reported for example, that it was subject to more than 15 quality assurance audits by DCF in the first year of its contract (Charlotte McCullough, personal communication, September 10, 2002).

[22] The federal outcomes with performance measures are: reduction in the reoccurrence of child abuse and/or neglect, reduction in the incidence of child abuse and neglect in foster care, increase in permanency for children in foster care, reduced time to reunification without increasing reentry into foster care, reduced time to adoption, and increased placement stability (U.S. Department of Health and Human Services, 2000).

At the same time, to the extent that programs have developed outcomes and performance targets, the outcomes generally have not been validated with historical data. The one exception may be Sarasota County, because of its longstanding history of Community-Based Care. Without such historical data, and in the absence of a decision to rely on the federal outcomes and performance measures, the current system of diverse outcomes and performance measures remains questionable. Lack of uniformity in outcome selection and definition and the absence of historical data to promote the development of valid measures are likely to continue to pose barriers to assessment of the effectiveness of Community-Based Care overall.

5. The Adequacy of State Funding. Of concern is whether the state will adequately fund Community-Based Care over the long term (Neary, 2002). Advocates express concern that the Florida legislature will not authorize funding at a level sufficient to support privatization statewide (Neary, 2002). The Governor's Blue Ribbon Panel on Child Protection (2002) emphasized the importance of adequate funding for Community-Based Care. Recognizing that "Community-Based Care costs more, not less, than the services now provided via DCF," the panel urged that "along with great promise, Community-Based Care carries great peril unless it is funded and supervised adequately" (p. 14). Since 1998, the legislature has authorized a 50% increase in child welfare funding (approximately $400 million) (Child Protection Report, 2002). The question remains, however, whether this level is sufficient, and when funding reaches a sufficient level, will it be sustained?

One specific issue related the adequacy of state funding is the extent to which an appropriate level of resources has been and will be available in the future to provide lead agencies with start-up resources. Lead agencies largely are expected to mobilize the resources required to create the infrastructure for Community-Based Care. For example, Broward County's ITN required any lead agency applicant to describe "the commitment your organization plans to make to start up and administer services." Community Based Solutions (CBS) estimated that the transition to Community-Based Care (including staffing, building leases, software and equipment purchases, and other initial operating expenses) would be approximately $2 million dollars. CBS described two key strategies for financing its start-up: (1) It reported that one of Broward County's state representatives had earmarked $825,000 of tobacco funds for the county's transition to Community-Based Care; and (2) it stated that it planned to avail itself of Florida law that allows local children's councils and other local government entities to make contributions to a local lead agency and have it matched two-to-one up to $2 million from TANF (provided that a minimum of $825,000 is contributed locally).[23]

CBS and DCF have agreed to work with the Broward County Children's Services Council to obtain $1 million in local funds, to draw $2 million from TANF. Anticipating that the $1 million contribution by the Children's Services Council and the $825,000 from the Florida legislature would cover the majority of transition expenses, CBS will request the remainder from the United Way of Broward County, with a plan to make a formal request for $200,000 of the United Way on notification that CBS' bid had been accepted, and from the partnership between the Broward Child Welfare Initiative and the Child and Family Leadership Association.

The issue of adequate financial support for start-up is important, and it is addressed quite differently from one Florida county to another. The resolution of this issue seems to rely on a host of factors, including the level of political commitment and influence in the jurisdiction, the relative wealth of the community, and the overall level of community support for the effort.

6. More Effective Contracting Procedures and a Standardized Contract. The very diverse nature of the contracting process DCF has implemented for Community-Based Care, although sensitive to different community needs and interests, has nonetheless created a high degree of uncertainty. Observers stress the need for a more standardized contracting process with common elements across the state. Similarly, the negotiation process also has led to frustrations for lead agencies, particularly when face-to-face negotiations with local DCF staff are used initially but last minute changes are made by state DCF staff and the lead agency is simply informed of these changes. Workers have expressed frustrations about the contracts themselves, which are highly diverse and lack uniformity in the definitions of the roles and responsibilities of DCF and the lead agency (Charlotte McCullough, personal communication, September 10, 2002).

The issues related to the contracting process play out in the broader context of concerns about the relationship between DCF and lead agencies (USF, 2002). As USF sums up the key question that confronts Community-Based Care in this area, "Are the lead agencies simply an extension of DCF, or are DCF and the lead agencies business (or service) partners?" (p. 30). The principal role of the lead agency has remained unclear—is it a partner in partnership with the state or an independent contractor accountable under contractual terms (USF, 2002)? Although DCF prefers to characterize Community-Based Care as a negotiated

---

[23] The Department for Children and Families (DCF) reported that the Temporary Assistance for Needy Families matching grant program has the express purpose of providing transition support for infrastructure development to Community-Based Care lead agencies. DCF has developed five matching grant programs, including Broward County's (David Overstreet, personal communication, August 23, 2002).

partnership between the state and the lead agency (as opposed to a strict contractual relationship), continuing indicators exist that lead agencies may be perceived as extensions of the public agency rather than as independently governed, private agencies.

7. Management Information Systems to Support Community-Based Care. As described earlier, Home Safenet, the state's planned management information system, has not proven to be a fully functional system that supports Community-Based Care data collection and reporting. Among the elements USF (2002) has recommended to strengthen the current data system are the development of an interface between the lead agencies' data systems and the DCF system or, at minimum, an agreement between DCF and lead agencies regarding the data needed, a specified data format, and acceptance of electronic data submission. Although some improvements have been made in the area, serious data management issues remain (Kestin, 2002a, 2002b).

Missouri: The Interdepartmental Initiative for Children with Severe Needs and Their Families[24]

The Missouri Interdepartmental Initiative for Children with Severe Needs and Their Families focuses on a targeted group of Missouri children with serious emotional problems. The initiative, developed by two state agencies, is being implemented by the Missouri Alliance for Children and Families, a company formed by child welfare service providers to bid for the contract to implement the initiative. This case study examines the formation of the Missouri Alliance for Children and Families, the development and implementation of the Interdepartmental Initiative for Children with Severe Needs and their Families, and the key issues that Missouri, the initiative, and the Missouri Alliance face as the initial contract comes to a close and plans are made to rebid the contract in 2003.

The Creation of the Missouri Alliance for Children and Families

In 1997, service providers formed the Missouri Alliance for Children and Families as a limited liability, for-profit corporation to enhance the service delivery system for children who receive public social services in Missouri. The founders were concerned that children with serious emotional disturbances needed services other than residential treatment, that practice was developing in the direction of community-based services and away from reliance on residential care, and that

---

[24] The sources for this case study included reports issued by the Interdepartmental Initiative for Children with Severe Needs and their Families and interviews with Richard Matt, President and Chief Executive Officer of the Missouri Alliance for Children and Families; Kathleen Buescher, Chairman of the Board of Directors of the Missouri Alliance; and Keith Krueger, Director of the Missouri Interdepartmental Initiative for Children with Severe Needs and their Families.

residential treatment providers needed to expand their services into new areas to meet the needs of children and families and remain viable providers. The Missouri Alliance was created to provide intensive, community-based, family-centered services in place of traditional, institution-based behavior modification and individual therapy programs (the only generally available options) and to demonstrate that children with serious disturbances could achieve significantly better outcomes as a result of a community-based approach.

The owners and chief executives of major private social service agencies in the state joined together to form the alliance. Eight of the nine founders were associated with some of the largest residential treatment agencies in Missouri (Boys and Girls Town of Missouri, Butterfield Youth Services, Cornerstones of Care, Edgewood Children's Services, Evangelical Children's Home, General Protestant Children's Home, Missouri Baptist Children's Home, and Presbyterian Children's Services). The other organization was Provident Counseling, Inc., a mental health services provider with experience in managed care networks. The providers came together in a highly collaborative manner, motivated by both an interest in developing new ways of providing services to children and families beyond the traditional residential models that characterized most programs, and by their awareness that the state planned to develop a new initiative that would use managed care principles to serve ch ildren in residential settings, an initiative that conceivably could be implemented by a managed care organization based outside of Missouri.

Each of the founding organizations contributed significant capital funding (approximately $90,000 each). In addition, the founders secured a $500,000 credit line. The Missouri Alliance began operation in October 1997 with an executive director who was supported by a small staff, and its first office opened in St. Louis. A second office was later opened in Jefferson City. During its first year of operation, the Missouri Alliance focused on developing an administrative infrastructure so that it could bid on the interdepartmental initiative the founders knew the state would announce shortly.

The Interdepartmental Initiative for Children with Severe Needs and Their Families

Missouri developed the Interdepartmental Initiative for Children with Severe Needs and their Families to address the needs of children with serious emotional disturbances and their families. The initiative had its beginnings when the directors of the Missouri Department of Mental Health (Roy Wilson) and the Missouri Department of Social Services (Gary Stangler) became interested in developing services that children with serious emotional disturbances and their families could access without having to meet categorical program eligibility requirements. They approached the Robert Wood Johnson Foundation for seed money to initiate the program.

The history of residential treatment utilization in Missouri illustrates the reasons that both the Department of Social Services and the Department of Mental Health viewed this type of program with such interest. Most children in Missouri enter residential treatment through the public child welfare system, known as the Division of Family Services (based in the Department of Social Services). In contrast to other state agencies (such as the Department of Mental Health), which have no mandate to provide residential treatment for children, the Division of Family Services is required to ensure that children in its care and custody who need residential care receive it. As a consequence, children served through the Division of Family Services historically have obtained residential treatment when they required this service, whereas families who attempt to obtain residential treatment for children through the Department of Mental Health have faced long waiting lists. Many families, in desperation, have turned to the child welfare system and relinquished custody so that their children could be placed in a residential facility. Until 2002, Missouri law did not permit voluntary placements of children and, as a result, families had to be determined to be abusive or neglectful for their children to enter foster care and qualify for residential treatment.[25] Although there are many residential treatment facilities in Missouri and the vast majority of children are placed in-state, residential treatment beds consistently have been filled by children referred by the Division of Family Services.

Over the past decade, the number of Missouri children in child welfare custody in residential care has grown significantly. These children typically have remained in highly restrictive settings for long periods of time. High caseloads, the demands of child maltreatment investigations, and the need to manage the care of children in family foster care have made it difficult for child welfare caseworkers to focus on plans to move children in residential care to less restrictive settings. At the same time, caseworkers have found it difficult to dispute the recommendations of residential care providers that children need long-term involvement in residential treatment programs even when the careworkers believe that children could be served appropriately in the community. The lack of resources to support

---

[25] In 2002, Missouri law was amended, giving courts the right to order mental health care without parental relinquishment of custody (Hoover, 2002). Although courts may now order mental health services, the Department of Mental Health may decline to provide services because of inadequate resources (Richard Matt, personal communication, September 30, 2002).

successful community placements further intensifies the difficulties associated with moving children to less restrictive settings.

The directors of the Departments of Social Services and Mental Health believed that with the commitment of both agencies' resources, it would be possible to reduce the number of children entering foster care (particularly the number of children whose families seek foster care so that their children can obtain residential treatment) and decrease the number of children in residential care (by making it possible for children to be moved from residential care to community-based settings). They anticipated that a shift from residential to community-based care would result in significantly improved outcomes for children and families. Furthermore, they believed that with the reduced use of expensive residential treatment, significant resources could be allocated for the development of community-based alternatives. With these goals in mind, they proposed a program with three key features: flexible funding, the use of minimal eligibility requirements, and guaranteed resources to divert children from the most restrictive and expensive components of the service delivery system to community-based alternatives. Ultimately called the Interdepartmental Initiative for Children with Severe Needs and their Families, the program initially was funded with support from the Robert Wood Johnson Foundation and pooled funding of state dollars from social services and mental health.

Participating in the initiative were three divisions of the Department of Social Services: the Division of Family Services, the child welfare program that, in the mid-1990s, spent between $60 and $70 million annually on residential services for children; the Division of Youth Services (DYS), the juvenile justice program that serves the majority of the children in its care through its own facilities and only periodically refers children to privately operated residential facilities; and the Division of Medical Services, the state's Medicaid agency. Within the Department of Mental Health, three divisions participated in the initiative—the Division of Comprehensive Psychiatric Services, the Division of Mental Retardation and Developmental Disabilities, and the Division of Alcohol and Drug Abuse.

Initial Steps: Development of the Case Rate and the Request for Proposals (RFP)

As an initial step in implementing the initiative, Missouri established a case rate for each child served through the program. The case rate, once established, was funded through a pooling of resources from the participating agencies, with each agency contributing a specified percentage.

To establish the case rate, Missouri identified all children who had been in residential or inpatient care in 1996 and who resided in the state's central or eastern regions (the geographic areas covered by the initiative), for a total of 1,635 children. It then calculated each child's cost of care by reviewing all historical expenditures for each child from all state agencies involved in the child's care during that year, including Medicaid, with the only exclusions being services provided through the Medicaid Home and Community Based Waiver or through a Department of Mental Health intermediate care center for mentally retarded individuals.

Missouri grouped the 1,635 children according to total expenditures, based on increments of $10,000. Of the identified children, 77% had total expenditures less than $30,000; 19.2% had total expenditures between $30,000 and $60,000; 2.2% had total expenditures between $60,000 and $100,000; and 1.3% had total expenditures in excess of $100,000. The median total expenditures for the children were calculated at both the 75th percentile ($16,468.36) and the 100th percentile ($29,331.21). The state then focused on the 1,000 children whose care was most expensive and calculated an average monthly cost for these children. Finally, Missouri established a fixed monthly, per-child case rate to serve as the rate at which contractors would be paid for each child served through the initiative. Some have criticized these data as an inadequate basis for determining the case rate. The state, however, points out that these data reflect actual expenditures and the extent to which the state has resources to invest in the initiative.

Certain service and other costs were withheld from or deducted prior to calculation of the case rate. First, the calculation did not include the costs of case management services provided by the Division of Family Services, as it was assumed that the contractors for the initiative would be able to reduce service costs sufficiently to pay for case management out of the total payment they received. Second, the state deducted from the total an amount in excess of $1 million to fund a separate contract with a technical service organization (TSO) for the initiative (described later). Missouri anticipated that this amount would ensure that a TSO could provide technical assistance to the initiative's contractors and take responsibility for all monitoring and oversight functions (the state did not wish to retain these functions). Finally, the state subtracted a sum that would constitute a "risk pool" for the initiative. Ultimately, the case rate was set at $3,199 per child, per month. The state anticipated that as the initiative was implemented, the case rate would be reduced in each succeeding year as the agency achieved greater efficiency. This expectation, however, has not been realized. The case rate for the second and third years of the initiative, in fact, was increased to $3,329 per month, suggesting that it was unreasonable to expect case rate reductions so early in the program's implementation.

Missouri released the initiative's RFP in June 1998, with an original due date

Table 28

Eligibility Criteria for the Initiative

1. The child is between the ages of 4 and 18 (a child in state custody who enters custody prior to age 18 may continue treatment beyond age 18 in accordance with the goals in the child's plan of care).

2. The child's family lives in either the eastern region (St. Louis and a 3-county area) or the central region (a 17-county area).

3. The child is currently in or at serious risk of a long-term residential placement.

4. The child has serious behavioral health needs as measured by the the Childhood Severity of Psychiatric Illness (CSPI).[a]

[a] Developed by John Lyons at Northwestern University, Chicago, CSPI is an assessment tool that the Missouri Division of Family Services uses to evaluate children's eligibility for Medicaid-funded residential treatment services. The initiative uses it at the time of the child's enrollment and periodically throughout the child's enrollment in the program. Although the Missouri Alliance collects data on this measure, it has not, as yet, analyzed aggregate scores.

of July 8, 1998. Because many questions arose that required clarification and the issuance of additional guidance, the due date was changed to July 22, 1998, and then again to August 12, 1998. The highly detailed RFP described the initiative as one that would "integrate funding to support comprehensive, integrated Plans of Care for children with severe behavioral health needs and their families, implemented under a single, unified care management process." The term of the award was set at 40 months (an anticipated 4-month start up period and a 36-month service period). The intent was that when the initiative was fully implemented, four contractors would serve 1,000 children. RFP required that each contractor have the capacity to serve 150 to 400 children and accept 6 to 16 newly enrolled children each month.

A number of agencies expressed interest in submitting proposals, but in the end, they declined to do so, concluding that the case rate was too low in light of the target population's extremely high level of needs. In the end, only the Missouri Alliance submitted a proposal. The state was concerned about the organization's ability to implement the initiative, given its new business status, the fact that it had no direct service staff, and its need to build a service infrastructure within a financial framework that limited the entity to only 15% of the funding for administrative costs. Nonetheless, after a number of discussions between the state, represented by the Departments of Social Services and Mental Health, and the Missouri Alliance, the contract was awarded in October 1998.

The Contract: Key Programmatic Provisions

Consistent with the RFP, the contract with the Missouri Alliance specified a fourth-month start-up period after the award of the contract, with referrals to begin in the fifth month. The lengthy contract (which essentially tracked the RFP but also included a number of revisions and clarifications as well as deletions) included the following provisions, among others.

Target Population. The state defined the initiative's target population as "children and families with disruption in their family lives likely to result in long term residential care." The children to be enrolled were to represent "a mixture of children in long-term residential care who can move to community living with intensive supports and children at risk for placement in long-term residential care whose home environment can be preserved through a community-based Plan of Care." The contract, which duplicated the provisions of the RFP, specified the eligibility criteria that children and families must meet. These criteria, which do not include that a child be in state custody at the time of referral, are set forth in Table 28.

Despite the fact that the Missouri Alliance was the only entity with which the state contracted for the initiative, the contract specified that it was expected that 1,000 children ultimately would be enrolled in the program. Under its contract, the Missouri Alliance agreed to serve 150 to 400 children and their families after full implementation. It would build the caseload through a process in which each of the participating divisions (two in the Department of Social Services and three in the Department of Mental Health) would incrementally enroll 40 children per month, with the incremental enrollment being accelerated or decelerated depending on the Missouri Alliance's ability to manage a growing caseload effectively.

Locally Organized Systems of Services and Supports. The contract required the Missouri Alliance, designated as a care management organization (CMO), to develop and manage a locally organized, family-focused system of services and supports for children and families at risk. The guiding principles outlined for this system were public-private partnerships, consumer and community empowerment, cultural competence, community and neighborhood resource development, and outcome-based care management.

Structural Components of the Initiative. The contract also established an "organized system of care" composed of a hierarchy of planning and oversight entities, some of which came into being following the award of the contract and some of which did not. The contract designated the following entities as having certain planning and oversight responsibilities:

- Interdepartmental Policy Authority (IPA): Designed to represent the participating departments and oversee funding, planning, and contract oversight, IPA was to be appointed by the state. Although representatives of the Departments of Social Services and Mental Health met often prior to and during the implementation of the initiative, no formal IPA evolved.

- Child and Family Advisory Committee: Described as a body that would assist IPA in all aspects of policy development and operations oversight, IPA never formed this committee because IPA did not emerge as a formal policymaking body for the initiative.

- Interdepartmental Management Team (IMT): To be created by IPA, IMT was a mechanism to bring together the participating departments for the purposes of funding, planning, and administration of the contracts with the Missouri Alliance as the CMO and with the entity designated as the TSO. The state formed IMT with principal functions of oversight of the day-to-day activities of the initiative and policymaking. IMT also has served as the body that hears appeals from the decisions of the interagency teams.

- Interagency Teams: Interagency teams were formed as entities at the operational level with authority to review and screen referrals of children and continuation of services for eligible children and families. The state created one team for each of the two designated geographical regions. The teams assign children and families to the CMO, address problems related to service provision, and approve ongoing services and disenrollment of children from the initiative.

- Family Support Teams: The state required and the alliance established a family support team for each child to assess the child's and family's needs, oversee development of the child's individualized plan of care, approve all services authorized and purchased through the plan, and assure compliance with the plan. Family support teams are composed of a representative of the referring state agency division, a staff member of the Missouri Alliance (who serves as facilitator), the child's parent (when applicable), a representative from the child's placement setting (a staff member of the residential facility or the child's foster parent), and other individuals important to the child and family, such as a counselor, school official, or the child's juvenile officer.

Table 29

Responsibilities of the Care Management Organization (CMO)

Key Responsibilities

■ Recruit, develop, and contract for a comprehensive array of community-based providers and resources.

■ Design and implement comprehensive, individualized care management processes to support the family support teams.

■ Authorize and reimburse services delivered under the plan of care.

■ Provide all care required under each child's plan of care within the case rate resources paid, in total, to the CMO.

■ Provide disenrollment planning and transition management for all children and families.

■ Gather and organize all information required by the interdepartmental policy authority (IPA) or technical service organization for quality management and performance oversight.

■ Manage child and family satisfaction at all levels of the care management process (including installation of a grievance and appeal process approved by the IPA).

■ Recruit and train all care managers.

■ Establish a continuous quality improvement system for all resource development, child and family services, and care management processes, subject to IPA approval.

Responsibilities of the CMO. As a CMO, the Missouri Alliance was contractually required to assume responsibility for a range of functions. These responsibilities are set out in Table 29.

No Reject, No Eject Policy. Under the contract, the Missouri Alliance must accept any child referred by an interagency team. A child may not be disenrolled unless all plan of care objectives are met, and the interagency team approves disenrollment.

Care Managers. The contract required that the Missouri Alliance meet extremely specific requirements regarding the professional credentials of care managers, which are related both to professional education and experience. It further specified a caseload of no more than 10 children and their families per care manager.

Child and Family Participation. The Missouri Alliance must involve children and families and ensure their satisfaction at all levels of the care management process, including the design and implementation of plans of care.

The Contract: Key Financial Provisions

In addition to establishing the initial case rate of $3,199 per child, per month, the contract contained a range of other financial provisions.

Payment of the Case Rate. The contract stipulated that the alliance was to be paid the case rate at the beginning of each month. No other form of financial reimbursement was available to the Missouri Alliance, as the case rate was expected to cover the costs of all services with the exception of physical health care. The Missouri Alliance had to refund the pro rata share of the case rate paid for any child who was disenrolled or who otherwise ceased receiving services from the initiative prior to the end of the month for which the case rate was paid.

Direct Client Services. The contract required the Missouri Alliance to spend 85% of the total contract compensation on "direct client treatment services." The TSO monitored its performance in this area.

Penalties and Incentive Payments. The contract established financial penalties in the event that a child required an out-of-home placement within 120 days after he or she had been disenrolled from the initiative. The interagency team determined whether an out-of-home placement occurred that triggered the penalty. In the event that a child required an out-of-home placement, the Missouri Alliance had to pay the costs of such care, up to an amount equal to two monthly case rates (approximately $6,600).

The contract further established an incentive payment when a child successfully disenrolled from the program and remained stable postdisenrollment. The Missouri Alliance was eligible for an incentive payment when a child continued to satisfy disenrollment criteria for 120 days after disenrollment. That payment was equal to one-half the child's monthly case rate (or approximately $1,600, or less than one-quarter of the penalty rate). The Missouri Alliance allocates $250 of any incentive payment to the care manager for the child in recognition of effective casework. The Missouri Alliance reports that 90% of the children disenrolled into a community setting have remained in those settings at the end of 120 days and, as a result, have qualified the Missouri Alliance for an incentive payment.

Per Diem Charges to the CMO. The contract charged the Missouri Alliance if, after a child is enrolled in the initiative, the child is placed in a treatment facility or program maintained by the Department of Social Services or the Department of Mental Health. The contract stipulated per diem inpatient care "charge backs" of $400 per day for care in a Department of Mental Health inpatient facility, $205 per day for residential secure care through the DYS, and $180 per day for care in a Department of Mental Health residential facility. Charge backs also were stipulated for Department of Mental Health outpatient services, such as physician care, therapy, and treatment family home care. The state deducted charge backs from the case rates prior to payment.

Risk Pool. The contract also indicated that the state would fund a risk pool to partially reimburse the Missouri Alliance for extraordinary treatment costs for children. The level of reimbursement varied by contract year. In the first year, the alliance could request risk pool funds for children whose actual expenses exceeded $32,700 in the first six-month authorization period (reimbursement of 75% of the actual expenses in excess of that figure would be provided, but no more than $52,300 per child). In the second year, the alliance could request risk pool funds for children whose actual expenses exceeded $39,250 in the first six-month authorization period (reimbursement of 50% of the actual expenses in excess of that figure would be provided, but no more than $52,300 per child). In the third year, the contract allowed the alliance to request risk pool funds for children whose actual expenses exceeded $39,250 in the first six-month period (reimbursement of 40% of the actual expenses in excess of that figure would be provided, but no more than $52,300 per child).

The contract made clear that the risk pool would be limited to a finite amount each year, with unused funds from each year rolling over to the next year. It was anticipated that unused funds would exist at the end of the final year of the contract. In such circumstances, at least one-half of the unused funds was to be returned to the state, with the remainder of the unused funds distributed to the Missouri Alliance, and other CMOs if applicable, to compensate them for any unreimbursed treatment costs. The contract further stipulated that once the risk pool was exhausted in any one year, no further risk payments would be made that year.

The Start-Up Phase

Between October 1998 and March 1999 (when it received its first referral of a child), the Missouri Alliance focused on building its infrastructure and capacity to comply with its obligations. It hired care managers, trained staff, and began to build a network of service providers. Although it was intended that the program would implement a wraparound model and offer a continuum of services that allowed children to step down from residential care to community-based settings, primarily through family foster care, observers agree that the initial service-building efforts did not result in substantial progress. The development of the network of providers more closely resembled the construction of an array of services and the purchasing of programs in which children would be enrolled. The strongest component of the array initially was residential care as provided by the Missouri Alliance's founders (which, principally, were residential treatment agencies with existing contracts with the state for such services). Far less developed as components of the service array were treatment foster care and other community-based alternatives. The Missouri Alliance struggled to add these basic services to the array of services, although at the time, the state placed greater emphasis on the importance of developing new services that went beyond the traditional service alternatives. Paralleling the difficulties it encountered in developing a provider network that could offer a wide array of services was the alliance's difficulty in clearly defining the role of care managers. Care managers came to be viewed essentially as coordinators of units of services for children and not as providers of hands-on management of children's care with the involvement of their families and informal support systems.

During the start-up phase, the state and the Missouri Alliance engaged in a number of discussions regarding the number of children to be served. The contract provided that the Missouri Alliance would serve 150 to 400 children. In the negotiations, the state and the Missouri Alliance agreed that the alliance would build its caseload from zero to 150 children over a period of time but then would close referrals at some point in the third year of the contract so that the caseload would shrink to zero by the time the contract ended. Although this plan was not implemented, it is noteworthy that both parties initially believed that the Missouri Alliance could fully staff and implement a program and then complete-ly cease serving clients at the end of the three-year period, at which time, the con-tract would be rebid. It was apparently assumed at the outset of the program that referred children could be fully stabilized in least-restrictive placements within six months and that, on closing referrals, the population served could be reduced to zero. Those assumptions, as discussed later, did not prove to be correct.

Technical Service Organization (TSO)

As the RFP for the CMOs made clear, the state planned from the outset to enter into a separate contract with a TSO to provide financial and information man-agement for the four CMOs that would implement the program. It was expected that the TSO would develop and maintain a central database for performance and outcome data, a financial management system, and a quality management system. The TSO was also to provide technical assistance regarding provider/resource development, communication planning and implementation, and quality project management.

In contrast to the CMO contract, there were multiple bidders on the TSO contract, including Value Options, which was awarded the contract in late 1998. At the time that the contract was awarded, it was evident that the role of the TSO as initially envisioned had changed, as there were not to be four contractors for which the TSO would develop an integrated management information system, monitor performance and outcomes, and provide technical assistance. Because the Missouri Alliance was the only contractor for the initiative, it was obvious that the TSO's responsibilities would be far more limited, although the contract fee remained as initially stated and the state provided start-up funding for the TSO, although that was not the case for the CMO. Operationally, the TSO's responsibilities were further reduced. As the Missouri Alliance began to implement its CMO contract, it made the decision to develop its own management information system, and it declined to accept the system offered by Value Options. The Missouri Alliance also determined that it did not wish to avail itself of Value Options' technical assistance. The role of Value Options became primarily focused on monitoring and reporting on the CMO's performance and achievement of the outcomes specified under its contract—the five key domains of safety, school, community, family, and health/mental health/substance abuse.

As required under the contracts of both the Missouri Alliance and Value Options, the TSO was to conduct a readiness assessment before the Missouri Alliance could begin receiving referrals. After the four-month start-up period, Value Options conducted a readiness assessment and determined that the Missouri Alliance had failed each readiness requirement. Value Options developed and implemented a corrective action plan with the alliance, conducted a second readiness assessment, and after extensive discussions, provided the state with a positive assessment that allowed the Missouri Alliance to begin receiving referrals of children.

The Initial Period of Service Provision

In March 1999, the Missouri Alliance received its first referrals and began providing services to children and their families. By October 1999, six months into the provision of services, it was apparent that the organization was struggling to implement the initiative as contractually required and, particularly, within the approved budget. By October 1999, the alliance had incurred losses in an amount of approximately $1.5 million. The founders decided to seek new leadership, and the CEO of one of the founding organizations, Boys and Girls Town of Missouri, assumed responsibility as interim president and CEO of the alliance.

An analysis of the organization's financial status revealed that the case rate was far too low in relation to the cost of care for the majority of enrolled children, although the cost data used were recognized as far from adequate. Although the contract provided for access to a risk pool in the event that the expenses for an individual child exceeded a specified amount, no mechanism had been created to trigger such payments. The Missouri Alliance, consequently, had not tapped the risk pool as the contract permitted. In 1999, the Missouri Alliance requested and the state agreed to allow a cash payment of approximately $500,000. In January 2000, the state allowed the Missouri Alliance to borrow an additional $338,974 (referred to as a "realignment payment"), which the alliance repaid through monthly deductions of $22,599 from its monthly contract payment until the realignment was offset. The alliance was extended funds again in August 2001 when, as a result of a significant reduction in the number of referrals, the Missouri Alliance required financial assistance to cover costs. In February 2002, the funds associated with the envisioned risk pool were completely exhausted.

When the interim president and CEO of the Missouri Alliance accepted a state cabinet level position in January 2000, the organization began a search for a permanent executive director. At the time, Richard Matt, then child welfare director for the Missouri Division of Family Services for 10 years, was eligible for retirement. He was committed to the initiative as a result of his work in supporting the program, and he joined the Missouri Alliance as president and CEO in April 2000. At that point, the organization was already serving 150 children and was continuing to accept referrals without clear guidelines to govern caseload growth.

Mr. Matt immediately identified a number of challenges that were confronting the initiative:

- Although the staff of care managers was a strong one, the alliance was adding too many care managers too quickly. It could not adequately train and supervise them, given the rapid pace of growth. Matt advised the founders that it was necessary to slow the rate of referrals or stop referrals for some period of time. In June 2000, the Missouri Alliance and the state agreed to suspend any new referrals for a period of three months to allow the alliance to assess its organizational needs and strengthen its processes. In October 2000, the alliance accepted referrals on a replacement-only basis, and shortly thereafter, the census began to grow once again. By April 2001, the alliance was serving 240 children. As of April 2002, the initiative was serving 279 children, its largest census since inception.

- No information was readily available under the cost reporting system to determine per-child costs, identify which children had service costs at or below the case rate, or identify which children had service costs significantly above the case rate.

- The documentation system focused too much on process, in large part owing to the TSO's extensive documentation requirements and quarterly site visits, during which the TSO reviewed case records and conducted interviews. The review process lacked a social work focus on the implementation of plans of care, permanency, or achievement of child and family outcomes.

- The Missouri Alliance had not embraced a true wraparound approach, particularly in terms of recognizing and supporting informal support systems for children and families that would be available to them after they left the program. The staff needed training in the wraparound approach as they worked with other professionals, particularly professionals from the residential facilities in which children were placed.

- The alliance did not pay enough attention to permanency outcomes for children. Although the initiative's philosophy endorsed community-based placements for children, assessments tended to focus on children's mental health problems rather than on the factors that might support their placements in less-restrictive settings. Of the 150 children enrolled in the initiative in April 2000, 75% were in residential settings and not a single child was placed with a foster family.

- The case rate was too low to cover the costs of many children's care. As one of his first steps, Matt negotiated a case management fee for children referred by the Division of Family Services, which, as discussed earlier, was not included in the original calculation of the case rate. Effective July 1, 2000, the state added a case management monthly fee of $226 to the rate for children referred by the Division of Family Services, bringing the case rate to $3,555. The Department of Mental Health did not add a case management fee, as it believed that this cost was already built into the case rate.

Services to Children and Families

Eligible Children

As required by contract, the only children enrolled in the initiative have been children who meet referral criteria, are referred by a participating division of the Department of Social Services or the Department of Mental Health, and are approved for enrollment by an interagency team. Thus far, the majority of enrolled children have extensive and severe needs. Typically, their histories have included years in out-of-home placement settings, multiple placements in foster homes and residential facilities with no reported successful outcomes from those interventions, and the absence of any meaningful connection between the youth and their families or communities. Their prognoses in terms of maintaining family-like living arrangements, gaining independence, and making a future contribution to society typically have been quite dismal at the time of referral.

Between March 1999, when the initiative first accepted referrals, and June 2002, the initiative served more than 600 children. Almost 80% of the children were in a residential setting at the time of referral; the remaining 20% were in crisis and at immediate risk of a residential care placement. Most of the children enrolled in the initiative were referred by the Department of Social Services. Of the 242 enrolled children on December 1, 2001, 74% had been referred by the had been referred by a participating division of the Department of Mental Health.

Service Provision

The process of referral, service provision, and termination of services is as follows:

- A participating division of the Department of Social Services or Department of Mental Health makes a referral to the interagency team (one for Central Missouri and one for Eastern Missouri).

- The interagency team meets to review the referral. The Missouri Alliance is not permitted to be present.

- The interagency team authorizes referral to the initiative and the provision of services for a period of six months.

- The Missouri Alliance accepts the referral under the "no reject" requirement.

- A care manager is assigned for the child within 24 hours of the child's enrollment.

- The care manager makes the first contact with the family within 48 hours of the child's enrollment.

- A family support team is convened by the care manager for purposes of assessment and service planning. The team's first meeting is held within 14 days of enrollment.

- The family support team oversees development of the child's plan of care and makes decision about child's placement. The team must develop and approve the plan within 14 days of enrollment.

- The family support team meets at least every 30 days to review the child's progress, and as the six-month service authorization period draws to a close, makes a recommendation to the interagency team as to whether the child should remain enrolled in the initiative.

- The interagency team makes a decision as to whether the child should remain enrolled for another six months or should be disenrolled or discharged.

- If the Missouri Alliance disagrees with the decision of the interagency team, it may appeal the decision to IMT.

In contrast to the service delivery approach that characterized the early implementation of the initiative, the program currently uses a wraparound philosophy that supports the incorporation of both professionally provided services and informal supports for children and families, such as extended family, friends, neighbors, and community. The current array of services incorporates three major service types: 24-hour inpatient services, family home care, and treatment and support services. Table 30 provides, for each of these three major service types, the array of community-based services and resources that are available to enrolled children and families.

With regard to family involvement, the Interdepartmental Initiative principally has involved families through the family support teams. The Missouri Alliance reports that it is extremely rare that no family member is involved with a family support team. In most instances, a birthparent, member of the extended family, or member of a child's "new" family participates (Richard Matt, personal communication, September 30, 2002). Although initially attempted, a family advisory committee was not successfully implemented (Richard Matt, personal communication, September 30, 2002).

The areas on which the Missouri Alliance has focused its service development efforts have been family foster care, family support services, and redirection of residential beds. To further the availability of family foster care services through the initiative, the Missouri Alliance developed a specialized foster care program that it administers directly (the alliance is licensed as a child placement agency). The alliance recruits and trains its own foster parents, who are required to complete both the Missouri-mandated STARS (Specialized Training Assessment Resources and Support/Skills) training program (which, under the Missouri Alliance program, foster parents complete in five, as opposed to nine, weeks) and an additional 27-hour curriculum on behavioral interventions designed as career training

Table 30

Array of Services Provided by the Initiative

Type of Service	Specific Services Required
24-Hour Facility Care	Inpatient psychiatric evaluation and treatment
	Residential treatment
	Sex offender intensive residential treatment
	Sex abuse victim intensive residential treatment
	Adolescent mother and child residential treatment
	Family-focused residential treatment
	Residential alcohol and drug abuse treatment
	Group home care
	Independent supported living
	Crisis/respite bed
Family Home Care	Family foster care
	Behavioral foster care
	Specialized family foster care
	Individualized care payment
	Kinship/relative care
	In-home respite care
Treatment and Support	Initial psychiatric evaluation
	Medication monitoring
	Assessment services
	Psychological consultation
	Individual therapy
	Family therapy
	Group therapy
	Specialized sex abuse therapy
	Alcohol/drug abuse therapy
	Intensive in-home services
	Day care
	Day treatment
	Crisis response
	Family support group
	Adoption services
	Educational services
	Case management
	Child and family support services
	Transportation
	Emergency transportation
	Family assistance

for specialized foster parents. As of February 2002, the alliance had 20 licensed foster families it directly supervised. In addition to its own foster families, the alliance is allowed to use foster families licensed by the Division of Family Services and the Department of Mental Health (60 to 70 families). Because these homes are used by state agencies for non–initiative enrolled children, however, the Missouri Alliance is not assured of the availability of those families for initiative children, an issue that prompted the decision to license the alliance's own foster families. Finally, a few foster family placements are available to the initiative through two of its providers, Missouri Baptist and Boys and Girls Town. The Missouri Alliance has viewed the expansion of family foster care services as essential to the successful transition of children from long-term residential care to community-based settings, particularly when birthfamilies are no longer actively involved in their children's lives. Its plan is to triple the number of foster families that it directly recruits, trains, and licenses.

One of the principal new wraparound services developed by the initiative has been family support services. This service combines a range of family supports to strengthen family functioning and maximize the safety of children in their homes. Family support services are provided through contracts with outside providers and by Missouri Alliance staff. The alliance is assessing whether the staff model or the contract model is the stronger approach. Family support services include mentoring children, performing behavioral interventions, tutoring, accompanying children to school and remaining with the child through the day to assist the child in regulating his or her behavior, and providing parent aid services such as mentoring, modeling, and hands-on assistance with parenting issues. The Missouri Alliance has considered this service as an area of particular strength.

Finally, the Missouri Alliance has focused on a redirection of residential beds into other services. Through its provider network, it has developed crisis beds, respite beds, and residential placements that from the outset are designed to be very short-term. These services are intended to promote the stability of children as quickly as possible so that they can return to their communities and receive services through community-based providers. Crisis beds are used when children's placements disrupt, providing short-term care for the purpose of assessment and return to the community as soon as needed services can be put into place. Respite beds are used in a planned way to alleviate stress and prevent placement disruption. Short-term residential placements are focused on stabilizing the child rather than affecting significant behavioral changes. The Missouri Alliance plans to further expand this component, as it views redirection of residential beds as a key to the full implementation of a wraparound philosophy.

Exit from Services

Children exit from the initiative in one of two ways: disenrollment or discharge. Disenrollment occurs when the family support team determines that a child has successfully completed the program, as demonstrated by his or her sustained placement in the community for at least three months. The contract provides examples of indicators of the requisite stability and permanency to support a child's disenrollment from the initiative (see Table 31). Although the Missouri Alliance assesses children's status using these indicators, its principal focus with regard to disenrollment is the child's stability in a least restrictive setting for at least three months.

Alternatively, a child may leave the program through discharge, either for administrative reasons or voluntarily. Discharge refers to a child's exit from the program for a reason other than a successful outcome. An administrative discharge occurs when, after the interagency team refers a child to the initiative, IMT determines that the referral is not appropriate, it advises the interagency team of its determination, and the interagency team agrees. A voluntary discharge occurs when all decisionmakers (the interagency team, the family support team, and the state agency staff) agree that the initiative cannot successfully serve the child. Examples of situations leading to a voluntary discharge are: the child is a runaway for more than 14 days; the referring agency will agree only to long-term residential care and will not accept a plan to move the child to a community-based setting; all parties agree, after services have been provided for a period of time, that the child can only benefit from long-term residential care and that community-based services are not appropriate; and the child's parents, when they retain custody, refuse to allow the child to return to the community.

Of the 262 children who were no longer active clients as of December 1, 2001, a total of 143 children (55%) had been successfully disenrolled from the initiative. One-third (32%) were voluntarily discharged, and 12% were discharged for administrative or other reasons (see Table 32).

Length of Time Services Are Provided to Children

The Missouri Alliance has collected and analyzed data on the length of time that children served through the initiative receive services. In a report dated February 7, 2002, the initiative analyzed the length of time that 605 children received services. It analyzed length of stay for children in three categories: children who were active clients on February 7, 2000 (239 children); children who had been disenrolled as of that date (163 children); and children who had been discharged as of that date (164 children). It is not possible, as of this writing, to compare these data to length of stay data for children prior to the implementation of the initiative

Table 31

Disenrollment Guidelines for the Missouri Alliance

- The child demonstrates improved functioning on a standardized instrument designated by the interdepartmental policy authority.
- A child who attends school or a general equivalency diploma program has had no more than 18 hours of suspensions in the past three months.
- The child has had no referrals to the court or to law enforcement agencies within the past three months.
- The child has had a physical and dental examination within the past 12 months.
- The child has not had an acute inpatient psychiatric hospitalization within the past three months.
- The birthfamily has not had any incidences of substantiated abuse or neglect within the past three months.

Table 32

Children Exiting by Reason

Reason for Exit	Percentage
Disenrollment (Successful Outcome Achieved)	55
Voluntary Discharge: Major Reasons	
Parent or youth voluntarily withdrew	11
Family support team recommended long-term residential care	8
State agency discharged against family support team recommendation	7
Runaway	6
Administrative Discharge: Major Reasons	
Moved out of region	4
Arrest	4
Withdrawn prior to enrollment	2
Administrative	1
Death	1

because the state has not completed its data analysis in this regard.

Children who were active clients as of February 7, 2002, had been enrolled for a mean of 9.5 months (median of 5 months) and received services over time periods ranging from 1 day to 2.94 years. Slightly less than one-third of the children who were active clients (31%) had been receiving services for one year or more. The Division of Family Services referred all but two of these children; the DYS referred the two exceptions.

Disenrolled children had been served for a mean of 14.7 months (median of one year) and had received services over time periods ranging from 2.3 months to 2.93 years. The Division of Family Services referred 64% of disenrolled children who had received services for one year or more, with Comprehensive Psychiatric Services (22%), the DYS (13%), and the Division of Alcohol and Drug Abuse (1%) referring smaller percentages.

Discharged children had been enrolled for a mean of 11.6 months (median of 7.8 months) and had received services for periods of time ranging from zero to 2.92 years. Slightly more than two-fifths (43%) of the discharged children had been served for one year or more. DYS referred 46% of discharged children who had received services for more than one year, followed by the Division of Family Services (36%), the Division of Comprehensive Psychiatric Services (12%), and the Division of Mental Retardation and Developmental Disabilities (6%).

The data for the three groups of children (active, disenrolled, and discharged) are compared in Table 33.

The Provider Network

As of 2002, the Missouri Alliance was contracting with between 300 and 400 service providers. Providers offered a range of services and included both comprehensive service providers such as Boys and Girls Town (which provides, among other services, residential treatment, foster care, and counseling) and individual service providers who worked with only one child enrolled in the initiative. Often, enrolled children entered the initiative with established relationships with service providers. In these cases, the Missouri Alliance has contracted with such providers to continue their services for these children as a Missouri Alliance provider. As a result, and contrary to the managed care approach typically used in developing provider networks, the network is extremely broad-based. This approach, however, coincides with the intent of the initiative to maximize service flexibility beyond traditional services and delivery mechanisms.

In general, members of the provider network are subject to maximum payment rates established by the Missouri Alliance for each service (see Table 34).

Table 33

Length of Services Data—February 2002

	Active Clients	Disenrolled Children	Discharged Children
Mean length of services	9.5 months	14.7 months	11.6 months
Median length of services	5 months	1 year	7.8 months
Range	1 day–2.94 years	2.3 months–2.93 years	0–2.92 years
Percentage of children receiving services for one year or more	31	50	43

The alliance, however, negotiates with each service provider, and in cases in which the child requires certain services, higher rates can be authorized.

Monitoring the Initiative

As noted earlier, Value Options, as TSO, received the contract to monitor the Missouri Alliance's performance as CMO for the initiative and assess the program's outcomes. The relationship between Value Options and the Missouri Alliance was initially strained and continued in that vein over the life of the business relationship. The tensions related to reporting and monitoring were exacerbated when the Missouri Alliance's management information system (called FamCare) proved incompatible in certain respects with the TSO's management information system. The two entities invested considerable time and effort in attempting to reconcile data. Although data required by the CMO and TSO contracts were produced, considerable tension existed between the two organizations on the issue. The relationship between the Missouri Alliance and Value Options improved somewhat after Mr. Matt assumed leadership of the Missouri Alliance, but monitoring-related tensions continued.

In June 2001, Missouri made significant cuts in the budgets of most state agencies, and it did not continue the contract with Value Options. As of June 30, 2001, the state assumed responsibility for monitoring the contract with the Missouri Alliance and assigned a staff of two individuals to this function. This arrangement represented a significant departure for the state, which previously had no formal quality assurance and contract monitoring unit. The Missouri

Table 34

Array of Services Provided by the Initiative

Service	Maximum	Service	Maximum
Payment Rate (as of 3/1/01)		Kinship/relative care	$14/day
24-Hour Facility Care Services		In-home respite care	$40/day
Inpatient psychiatric evaluation and treatment	$400/day	Treatment and Support Services	
		Initial psychiatric evaluation	$150/evaluation
Intensive residential treatment	$150/day	Medication management/monitoring	$50/one-half hour
Sex offender intensive residential treatment		Assessment/evaluation services	$65/hour
		Psychological consultation	$50/hour
Sex abuse victim intensive residential treatment		Individual therapy	$65/hour (in home)
			$55 hour (in office)
Residential treatment	$100/day	Family therapy	$65/hour (in home)
Sexual abuse victim residential treatment			$55 hour (in office)
		Group therapy	$20/hour
Sexual offender residential treatment		Specialized sex abuse therapy	$70/hour (in home)
			$60/hour (in office)
Adolescent mother and child residential treatment		Alcohol/drug abuse therapy	$55/hour
		Intensive in-home services	Negotiated rate/day
Family-focused residential treatment	$100/day	Day care	Negotiated rate/day
		Day treatment	$65/day
Residential alcohol and drug abuse treatment	$90/day	Crisis response	$50/per intervention
		Family support group	$12/hour
Group home care	$85/day	Adoption services	$20/hour
Independent supported living	$85/day	Educational services	$55/day
Crisis/respite bed	$60/day	Case management	$30/day
Family Home Care		Child and family support services (depending on level)	$20/day or $12/day
Family foster care	$14/day	Transportation	Negotiated rate/trip
Behavioral foster care	$22/day	Emergency transportation	Negotiated rate/trip
Specialized family foster care	$55/day	Family assistance	Actual expenses
Individualized care payment	Negotiated rate/day		

Alliance has viewed the shift in monitoring responsibilities from TSO to the state as highly positive, particularly because Missouri has taken a more focused approach to monitoring, with an emphasis principally on fiscal performance and issues related to interdepartmental coordination, in contrast to the TSO's intensive monitoring on a range of process-related issues. In addition, the state and the alliance have found that their data systems are highly compatible and that the communication of program data has become smoother.

Funding of the Initiative

Pooled general state revenue funds from the Departments of Social Services and Mental Health fund the initiative. The Department of Social Services (DSS) contributes 67% of funds (the Division of Family Services contributes 60% and the DYS contributes 7% of the case rate for each child). The three participating divisions of the Department of Mental Health (DMH) contribute smaller percentages of the case rate: Comprehensive Psychiatric Services contributes 12%; Mental Retardation and Developmental Disabilities 2%, and Alcohol and Drug Abuse 1%. The remaining 18% is contributed by the Medicaid program, which unlike DSS and DMH, does not refer children to the initiative. The interagency teams generally review and manage referrals in ways that reflect the respective contributions of each of the divisions in the overall composition of the children served, but the process is flexible.

The initiative receives between $600,000 and $800,000 monthly. In February 2002, with a caseload of 240 children, initiative income was approximately $850,000. The projected annual income for the initiative is between $10 and $11 million, based on the total number of children enrolled multiplied by the case rate for each month of each child's enrollment, including case management fees for children referred by the Division of Family Services.

Program budgeting for the initiative is done on an aggregate basis, in which the initiative pools all case rate payments and provides services to all children from this aggregate funding. The care and services provided to an individual child are not planned or provided on the basis of the child's individual case rate. The alliance, however, tracks detailed financial information for each child through its management information system. The system generates lists of children with their levels of authorized costs and their actual expenditures (which can be rank ordered for comparative purposes). It also provides each care manager the average authorized costs and actual expenditures for children in their caseloads.

The Missouri Alliance reports (Richard Matt, personal communication, September 30, 2002) that the case rate remains inadequate in light of the needs of children served. The state set the case rate based on 1996 cost data, with significant reductions for the TSO and the risk pool and without taking into account case management costs. As a result, the initial case rate was substantially below 1996 costs. Although the state has made adjustments, they were not based on data reflecting the increase in the cost of services, including Medicaid services. The case rate adjustments reflect an increase in the case rate for children referred by the Department of Family Services of approximately 14% over a six-year period (slightly more than 2% per year) (Richard Matt, personal communication, September 30, 2002).

Criticisms of the initiative case rate parallel the dissatisfaction regarding rate structures expressed generally by child welfare service providers in the state. In an unrelated but relevant development, the Missouri Child Care Association (MCCA), a trade association of residential care agencies in the state, recently filed suit against Missouri, alleging that the state failed to pay the full cost of children's residential care, in violation of Title IV-E of the Social Security Act. The results of this lawsuit, even if in favor of the MCCA, will not affect initiative case rates because the alliance contractually negotiates fees with each service provider. Founding members of the Missouri Alliance, however, are among the members of the MCCA.

Initiative Outcomes

The outcomes for the initiative can be viewed from three different perspectives. First, the contract provided an extensive list of outcome domains and indicators. Second, broad systems outcomes were envisioned by DSS and DMH when they established the initiative. Third, the actual outcomes which the Missouri Alliances tracks and measures are indicators of program achievements.

Contractual Requirements Regarding Outcomes

The contract between the state and the Missouri Alliance established five domains of outcomes—safety, school, community, family, and health/mental health/substance abuse—and detailed indicators for each domain. Although many of the indicators referenced percentages or number reductions or increases, the contract did not specify actual performance targets for any of the indicators. Table 35 provides the contract-designated outcome domains and indicators. Despite the absence of specified targets, neither the TSO nor the state subsequently established performance targets for the indicators.

Missouri acknowledged that the indicators listed in the contract are quite broad and has interest in narrowing the list to more focused outcomes, possibly tied to national outcome standards and the federal Child and Family Service Reviews. The state noted that the initial list of indicators reflected the interests of the two state agencies in serving both children and parents through the initiative (indicators such as reduction of criminal activity and substance abuse by parents). Nonetheless, the reimbursement rate since inception of the program has been tied to the projected costs of serving a child (based on per child historical expenditures), not multiple family members. The state has indicated a willingness to consider a more child-focused outcome approach.

The contract stated that the Missouri Alliance's performance on the indicators was to be measured against performance of a "current system," in the form of "a control group from a comparable population in a geographical area not included in the Initiative" (Missouri Interdepartmental Initiative Contract, 1998, p. 32). TSO was to develop a control group, conduct on-going data collection and analysis, and, on the basis of the collected data, provide the state with information on which it would base a "report card...that provides summary information of [the Missouri Alliance's] performance" on each of the five outcome domains. TSO never developed a control group, however, and it did not implement the study. The initiative, however, has developed its own approaches to outcome assessment and performance measurement (discussed later).

Systemic Outcomes

A second perspective on initiative outcomes is that of the program's designers, who believed that an interdepartmental pooling of funds would result in two key systemic improvements: a decrease in the number of children entering foster care and a decrease in the number of children entering residential care. The initiative has not fully realized these outcomes. With regard to the number of children in foster care, a highly publicized child abuse case in Kansas City in 1999 had increased the number of children entering foster care in the state, a trend that has continued. The initiative has not had (nor could reasonably be expected to have) an effect on this trend.

It also has not achieved the second systems outcome, lowering number of children entering residential care statewide. The residential care population in Missouri increased by 14% between 1998 and 2001. As an indicator of initiative outcomes, however, the total number of children in residential care in the two regions the initiative has served decreased by 11% during that time.

Outcomes as Defined and Measured by the Missouri Alliance

The Missouri Alliance's perspective regarding initiative outcomes is key. The alliance has focused on two outcomes: (1) placement of children in residential care

Table 35

Array of Services Provided by the Initiative

Outcome Domain	Indicator
Safety	Percentage of enrolled children who are repeat victims of abuse and neglect will be reduced.
	Percentage of enrolled family members who are involved in repeat abuse and neglect will be reduced.
	Percentage of enrolled children who attempt suicide will be reduced.
	Percentage of enrolled children who commit crimes against persons will be reduced.
	Percentage of enrolled children who are involved in noncriminal aggression will be reduced.
	Percentage of children on runaway status will be reduced.
	Percentage of enrolled children who are adjudicated will be reduced.
School	Percentage of enrolled children who obtain high school or general equivalency diploma will increase.
	Percentages of enrolled children who drop out of or are suspended or expelled from school will be reduced.
Community	Employment (part-time or full-time) in terms of the percentage of enrolled children older than 16 who are not attending school will increase.
	Percentage of enrolled children who participate in community activities will increase.
	Percentage of enrolled children who live within one hour driving time of their families will increase.
Family	Percentage of enrolled children under court custody will decrease.
	Percentage of children in a permanent family will increase.
	Placement disruptions for enrolled children will decrease.
	Incidence of crime among enrolled parents will decrease.
	Incidence of substance abuse among enrolled parents will decrease.
	Average length of time for children spent in group care will decrease.

Health, mental health, and substance abuse

Incidence of physical and dental exams and treatment for enrolled children will increase.

The number of Healthy Children and Youth exams (Early Periodic Screening Diagnosis and Treatment) exams for enrolled children will increase.

The number of Healthy Children and You EPSDT exams for enrolled children will increase.

Preventable hospitalizations will decrease.

Incidence of sexually transmitted diseases among enrolled children will decrease.

Incidence of pregnancy among enrolled children will decrease.

Functionality on standardized measures will improve for enrolled children.

Use of mechanical or chemical restraints for enrolled children will decrease.

Use of medication for control of aggressive behavior of enrolled children will be reduced.

Incidence of substance abuse among enrolled children will decrease.

Self-reports on quality of life will improve.

or at risk of residential care in community-based settings, and (2) maintenance of children, once in community-based settings, in the least restrictive settings. Data collection and analysis have focused on these two outcomes both during service provision and after children disenroll. As shown in Table 36, data indicate that when a study compared children's placements at the end of 2001 with their placements at time of enrollment, far fewer children were in residential or inpatient settings and larger percentages of children were living at home or in community-based settings.

Similarly, as Table 37 indicates, when a study compared placements of disenrolled children with their placements at time of enrollment, the children were primarily living in community-based settings. A high percentage of disenrolled children were living in their own homes.

Finally, the Missouri Alliance compared data regarding disenrolled children's last known placements based on their referring agencies. These data demonstrate that the majority of disenrolled children were still in their community-based placements at four months postdisenrollment, regardless of referring agency (86% of children referred by DFS, 97% of children referred by DMH, and 96% of children referred by DYS; see Table 38).

In 2002, the Missouri Alliance initiated the use of the Fidelity Wraparound Index developed by the University of Vermont. The index assesses whether wraparound services have been provided to families and, if so, the effectiveness of the services and the satisfaction of consumers (children and birthparents) and customers (the state agencies that refer children to the program). The Missouri Alliance partnered with Gateway, a Missouri agency with a history of providing wraparound services to conduct telephone interviews with families served through initiative. Final results are not expected until late 2003.

The Future of the Initiative

The future of the initiative is currently uncertain because of state budgetary issues that have affected both the participation of the agencies that were initially involved and the contract rebidding process.

The contract for the Interdepartmental Initiative originally was scheduled to terminate in February 2002. In early 2002, the state extended the contract with the Missouri Alliance until June 30, 2002, and indicated its intention to continue the initiative until the contract could be rebid. Missouri also expressed interest in expanding the initiative to other geographical areas of the state, particularly the Kansas City area, where a large number of children are in intensive residential treatment programs and could benefit significantly from initiative servic-

Table 36

Placement at Time of Enrollment and Current Placement of Enrolled Children,
November 27, 2001 (n = 242) (in percentages)

Placement Type	Placement at Time of Enrollment	Current Type Placement
Inpatient psychiatric hospital	9	5
Detention	5	2
Residential treatment	61	40
Foster care	8	17
Independent living	0	6
Home	17	29
Runaway	0	1

Table 37

Placement at Time of Enrollment and Last Known Placement of Disenrolled
Children, November 27, 2001 (n = 143) (in percentages)

Placement Type	Placement at Time of Enrollment	Current Placement
Inpatient psychiatric hospital	11	1
Detention	7	1
Residential treatment	51	9
Foster care	5	10
Independent living	1	9
Home	24	70
Runaway	1	0

es. The Division of Family Services, in particular, became actively involved in assessing strategies for continuing and expanding the program.

These activities, however, have occurred in an environment of mandatory budget cuts in many state departments. In early 2002, DMH was forced to withdraw its participation in funding the initiative. All DMH-referred children were discharged from the initiative on February 15, 2002, and referred to DMH-contracted community-based mental health programs, whenever possible. DMH, however, extended to the initiative a limited number of its inpatient mental health treatment beds in St. Louis with no charge back for the use of these services, as

Table 38

Last Known Placement of Disenrolled Children by Referring Agency, November 27, 2001 (in percentages)

Placement Type	Department of Family Services (*n* = 98)	Department of Mental Health (*n* = 29)	Department of Youth Services (*n* = 25)
Inpatient psychiatric hospital	1	0	0
Detention	1	0	0
Residential treatment	12	3	4
Foster care	14	7	0
Independent living	4	10	24
Home	68	80	72
Runaway	0	0	0

otherwise required under the contract. DYS also elected to cease the participation of its active clients as of February 15, 2002. The initiative discharged all DYS-referred children, with the exception of four young people for whom DYS will continue to participate in the case rate.

In spring 2002, Missouri extended the contract through June 30, 2003. As of June 30, 2002, however, only the Division of Family Services continued to make referrals to the program. Medicaid has continued to contribute to the case rate. The state also announced that it would revise the initiative contract in a number of ways. It announced that the contract would be replaced with an updated, revised version of an existing Division of Family Services contract, known as Family Focused Residential Treatment (FFRT). The FFRT contract has been in place for almost 10 years but, historically, has not been well-used because of limited interest on the part of residential agencies in developing community-based services and deploying staff off-campus.

The state planned to build on what it had learned from the Interdepartmental Initiative and integrate the desirable features from the initiative contract with the FFRT contract. The state expressed interest in designing a new contract to support the central premise of the initiative (community-based services) while allowing contractors financial flexibility. It anticipated that the financial methodology would be neither a per diem, per bed rate nor a monthly case rate and that the actual level of reimbursement would exceed the current rates for the Interdepartmental Initiative. Services would be limited to children in the custody of the Department of Family Services. It was expected that over the next year, referrals to the Interdepartmental Initiative would be phased out and directed to FFRT.

The state's plan raises a number of issues. On the positive side, it may address the fiscal issues that hindered active bidding interest in the past. The case rate and the definition of the target population in the original program posed significant problems for most private agencies. It appears that the state intends to pursue alternatives other than a case rate adjustment with the new contract,[26] which should stimulate broader interest.

On the more problematic side is the direction that the program is taking. Clearly, the "interdepartmental" nature of the Interdepartmental Initiative has been lost, along with the substantial attendant benefits of minimal and unified eligibility criteria for children and pooled funding. It is not clear how the proposed revision of the FFRT contract will create a program that differs in any meaningful way from other contract-based programs with a single public agency division. It is likewise not clear how the positive outcomes achieved by the Missouri Alliance, particularly more extensive use of nonresidential settings and stability of placements in less-restrictive settings, will be sustained. The Missouri Alliance identified three key areas of achievement of the Interdepartmental Initiative: positive outcomes for children who, by and large, were considered lost or beyond help; the initiative's ability to use funds flexibly to achieve the most successful outcomes for children; and the ability to serve children in need of services regardless of the system with which they are involved (the elimination of a categorical approach). It is not clear how the new approach will ensure that these successes can be sustained.

---

[26] Although not relevant to the new contract given the state's decision, it is interesting to note that people suggested a variety of possible approaches if the state had decided to retain the case rate approach. One was development of a two-tier case rate, with different case rates set for children with moderate and severe needs. A second approach was retention of a single case rate, but with a program design that resulted in a more balanced mix of referred children. A third suggestion was retention of the current case rate, with disenrollment permitted only after a child has demonstrated stability for a six-month, as opposed to three-month, period. If used, this approach might have provided a stronger foundation on which to base assessment of positive outcomes and might have provided the Missouri Alliance (or another care management organization) with the benefit of an ongoing case rate for children whose care has shifted to less expensive, community-based services. To illustrate this point, data indicate that with regard to the 143 children disenrolled from the initiative, total expenditures for their first month of enrollment was $555,000, compared with total expenditures of $221,000 for services during the one month prior to their disenrollment.

Lessons Learned

With regard to recommendations for other communities, the Missouri Alliance and the state advance the following:

■ It is key to involve an independent entity, such as the Missouri Alliance, as the coordinator of services for children referred by multiple public agencies. Public agencies generally are invested in the specific services they provide and the populations they serve, and they find it difficult to develop systems to serve children and families with complex service needs that extend beyond the traditional reach of the agency.

■ The creation of a new entity to assume responsibility for this type of initiative carries with it a number of advantages and challenges for the founders themselves. When a new entity is created by existing entities, each founding entity faces a limited level of financial risk. In addition, a new entity can serve as a middle ground, in which like-minded agencies may come together and commit themselves to developing and implementing innovative service delivery approaches. At the same time, however, founding agencies may find themselves competing with the entity they have created. This relationship may be complex, and founding agencies, as members of the new entity's board, may struggle with their dual roles.

■ Although the Missouri Alliance was incorporated as a for-profit entity, there is no evidence that for-profit status has provided the organization with benefits that would not have been realized if nonprofit status had been sought.

■ It is important to take the long view in developing and implementing an initiative of this nature. The start-up phase is inevitably fitful. The first two years of a new effort, which usually involve the negotiation of the contract and early implementation, are likely to be quite difficult. Initial expenditures are likely to prove to be unrealistic, the fiscal issues may pose particular challenges, and the relationships between the state and provider may be strained. Even when a long history of public-private relationships exists, as is the case in Missouri, an initiative that shifts roles and responsibilities will cause confusion and competition. The participants must give attention to building trust and good interpersonal relationships, and all parties must make adjustments.

- Communities considering a similar initiative should be aware of the slow pace at which service philosophy and orientation change. Even under optimal circumstances, in which service providers embrace new wraparound and family-focused services, they must overcome long histories of providing services in traditional ways.

- Start-up funding is essential to ensure that resources exist to build an appropriate infrastructure. Particularly when the model involves a wraparound approach, it is important to recognize that initial costs will be high.

- It is essential to pay careful attention to the case rate. Ideally, the case rate should be set higher than ultimately may be necessary and then adjusted downward, as appropriate. If possible, the case rate should be set on a daily, not on a monthly basis. A daily rate provides the lead agency with a stronger foundation for budgeting and planning.

- Connected with the case rate is how the initiative defines the target population. If eligibility is limited to only those children with extremely high needs, it is not reasonable to expect either marked success or changes in relatively short periods of time, such as three to six months. If the population is children with severe needs, the initiative must commit significant funding to the program. Alternatively, if the target population is broader-based, so that children with less extreme needs receive services at an earlier point in time, service costs are likely to be lower and the probability of success higher.

- The participants must define the roles of all parties involved in a new program from the start. Specifically, the roles of the state (the contractor) and the lead agency (the contractee) should be clearly delineated in the contract negotiation process. At the policy and program development levels, clarity is needed regarding the roles to be played by state agency staff and lead agency staff (particularly caseworkers) in decisionmaking and assumption of ultimate responsibility for the child and outcomes. Ideally, the lead agency should assume much of the responsibility for decisions related to outcomes for the child, and the state should have strong monitoring and oversight roles in ensuring quality agency performance. In this regard, the contract should focus on outcomes, not on processes.

■ The importance of open and honest communication among all parties cannot be overestimated. Joint orientations of public agency staff and contractor's staff after the contract is awarded but before implementation begins can be extremely helpful. Regular communication among all participating state agencies, the CMO or its equivalent, the TSO or its equivalent, and other relevant parties should be developed at the outset and carefully maintained.

■ Clear communication should also be a goal with regard to contract requirements, even if they appear clear cut. One issue of controversy in the initiative contract was the no eject, no reject clause. Although the Missouri Alliance and the state appeared to have reached a mutual understanding of this requirement, problems arose as children were enrolled and the intense service needs of each child became apparent. At that point, the alliance questioned the scope of the no eject, no reject clause, whereas the state viewed the policy as an inherent component of program design. Because providers may not fully appreciate the effect of this type of mandate, they should fully explore it in the bidding process.

■ A structure involving one or more lead agencies and a TSO that "belongs" to the state, as opposed to the providers, inevitably creates tensions and poses barriers to program development, implementation, and evaluation.

■ When developing RFPs and contracts for these types of initiatives, the state needs to clearly define outcomes and take a realistic view of what can and cannot actually be accomplished.

■ The extent to which a multidepartment collaboration can be sustained over time is an issue that warrants consideration. Although envisioned and initially implemented as an interdepartmental initiative, all departments other than the Division of Family Services decided to withdraw from the initiative. This raises questions about the forces that may work against long-term commitment to such an initiative, particularly when there are significant budget restrictions and when the individuals who initiated the effort are no longer in key leadership positions.

Hamilton County, Ohio: Creative Connections

Hamilton County, Ohio, has two initiatives that fall within the rubric of privatization: True Care Partnership, a behavioral health plan to meet children's and families' needs for basic mental health and substance abuse treatment services, for which Magellan Health Services is the managed care organization; and Creative Connections, an initiative to serve children with high needs from multiple systems (McCullough & Schmitt, 2002).

This case study focuses on Creative Connections, because that initiative is specifically designed to meet the needs of children in the child welfare system.[27] It traces the interagency effort that preceded Creative Connections, then describes the program as it has been implemented over the past five years. The case study also examines the issues that the participants considered during contract renegotiations between Hamilton County and Beech Acres, the lead agency for Creative Connections. Ultimately, the groups did not resolve these issues in ways that allowed Beech Acres to continue serving as lead agency for the program.[28] Nonetheless, these negotiations indentified critical issues that affected the program as originally designed and illustrate redesign features that, potentially, held promise in strengthening the program. Finally, the case study examines some of the programmatic and fiscal issues that arose as the groups implemented Creative Connections and discusses the lessons that the state has learned.

---

[27] In October 2002, the state awarded thenew contract to an Indiana-based behavioral health organization. It will make significant changes in program design.

[28] The written materials utilized in the preparation of this case study are cited. Much of the case study, however, was developed based on a series of interviews with James Mason, Chief Executive Officer, Beech Acres and information that he generously supplied.

The Initial Interagency Effort

Historically, Hamilton County used a cluster approach to service delivery for children in need of assistance from multiple systems. The cluster approach involves a multiagency assessment and planning process. Although this approach has a number of strengths, in the mid-1990s, the public child- and family-serving agencies of Hamilton County concluded that it was not an effective response to the needs of many children. They identified a number of problems, particularly in the areas of efficiency, quality of care, service costs, and designation of roles and responsibilities. In 1994, five Hamilton County public agencies—the Department of Human Services (now known as the Department of Job and Family Services), the juvenile court, the mental health board, the alcohol and drug addiction services board, and the mental retardation/developmental disabilities board—decided to pool funding and develop a managed care approach to serving children with multisystem needs. The county agencies had two major goals: to improve the quality of care for children, and to reduce the rising costs associated with serving children and youth with complex needs (Auditor of the State of Ohio, 2001).

In 1995, the agencies contracted with Family and Children First Management (FCF Management) to implement the managed care program that they had decided to fund. The board of directors included a juvenile court judge, lawyers, physicians, managed care representatives, and a provider representative (Jim Mason, CEO, Beech Acres). FCF Management hired a director with a background in managed health care to implement the program. Under the terms of a relatively simple contract executed between the five Hamilton County agencies and FCF Management, the program began providing services in July 1995. Each of the five agencies determined its own eligibility criteria for children to be enrolled in the program. For example, the Department of Human Services required that a child have had two or more foster care placements prior to referral to the program, and the juvenile court limited admission to children younger than 12 who had committed a felony. The contract between the agencies and FCF Management limited the total number of children served to 286. Each of the five agencies agreed that its referrals would be limited to a pre-established number of children. They allowed Department of Human Services almost one-half of the 130 referrals and allocated fewer slots to the remaining agencies.

To implement the program, FCF Management contracted with 22 direct service agencies (Seibel, 1998). It also contracted separately with three agencies (Beech Acres, The Lighthouse, and St. Joseph's) to serve as "care management agencies" charged with overseeing and coordinating the activities of the direct service providers. This arrangement immediately presented problems. The three care management agencies had no role in selecting the direct service providers and no authority to take action regarding the overall quality of services and care provided. Also, the three care management agencies were quite diverse in their service philosophy and views of program development. The lack of uniformity in these areas presented significant programmatic and reporting challenges, with particular difficulties in the development of an integrated management information system.

By mid-1997, it had become apparent that the program was experiencing severe budget deficits, with a projected loss in the range of $1.5 million in 1998 (Auditor of the State of Ohio, 2001). The five county agencies, which had anticipated cost savings as a result of the new approach, held FCF Management responsible for the failure to control costs and establish a level of financial predictability (Auditor of the State of Ohio, 2001). Stresses developed, and the relationship began to take on the character of a contractor-vendor relationship, instead of a public-private partnership.

In January 1998, the Department of Human Services, in behalf of the five Hamilton County agencies, approached the board of directors of Cincinnati-based Beech Acres and proposed that Beech Acres create a new program to serve the children for whom FCF Management had responsibility. In light of the fiscal issues that had arisen as FCM Management implemented the program, the county agencies concluded that a higher level of financial resources would be needed to successfully implement the program. Given the level of needed resources and limitations on the county agencies' budgets, they sought to place the program with a private agency that could invest significant, independent financial resources into the program. The Department of Human Services viewed Beech Acres as having the necessary organizational and programmatic strengths, financial acumen, and financial resources to build and implement the type of program that the public agencies envisioned. Beech Acres had an endowment that was valued at approximately $60 million. Ultimately, the board of directors of Beech Acres, based on its commitment to community service and its belief that a well-implemented program could both improve the quality of care and reduce costs, approved a set-aside of $6 million to implement a four-year contract with the Hamilton County agencies. The amount of the set-aside was based on a calculation that, had FCF Management continued the program, it likely would have incurred losses in the range of $6 million.

The New Initiative: Creative Connections

Once Beech Acres indicated its willingness to assume responsibility for implementing the new program, the Hamilton County agencies entered into an agreement with the FCF Council to serve as the intermediary for the program. Under the agreement, the five county agencies (known as "the Council agencies" in the contract) agreed to fund the program, and the FCF Council agreed to manage the contract with Beech Acres and report to the council agencies on contract compliance.

The Contract with Beech Acres

In November 1998, Beech Acres executed a four-year contract with the council to serve as lead agency for a program that it would develop. The contract required Beech Acres to purchase, administer, monitor, and evaluate certain delineated services for the clients that the council agencies referred to Beech Acres. The contract (as later amended in March 2001) required Beech Acres, as lead agency, to assume a number of responsibilities, including the following:

Provision of Services

- Develop and manage a group of service providers in sufficient number and in appropriate locations to meet the needs of enrolled children.

- Ensure provision of services at the appropriate level of care required by each enrolled child.

- Maintain a no reject, no eject policy, which prohibited Beech Acres from refusing to accept a referred child unless admission would result in more than 286 children enrolled in the program.

- Agree, in addition to providing services, to make court appearances in behalf of enrolled children and, if found in contempt of court, to satisfy on its own any sanction that a court imposed.

Utilization Review and Quality Assurance

- Establish, coordinate, and maintain a utilization review program, a continuous quality management program, and a financial monitoring plan.

- Modify the Beech Acres quality improvement program to achieve goals and measure performance standards outlined in the contract.

- Maintain a grievance procedure for enrolled children, families, custodians, and guardians.

Information Management

- Develop, implement, and maintain information management systems that meet a range of technical and substantive requirements.

- Ensure that Beech Acres and its subcontractors adhere to professional standards and/or licensing requirements.

- Produce a number of client tracking and financial reports.

- Participate in fiscal audits as required by the council.

Insurance Coverage

- Obtain and maintain professional liability and commercial general liability insurance in limits of not less than $1 million per claim and $3 million in the annual aggregate to cover losses and any liability assessed against Beech Acres.

Contract Termination

- If Beech Acres intended to terminate the contract without cause, to give 120 days written advance notice, with termination fees stipulated based on the quarter and contract year in which the contract is terminated. The council also is accorded the right to terminate the contract without cause with the same notice. If Beech Acres intended to terminate the contract with cause, to give 90 days advance notice and provide the council with the opportunity to cure the breach within 30 days of receiving notice.

The contract further contained extensive requirements with regard to each service provider with which Beech Acres contracted, including mandates related to participation in supervisory conferences, participation in the Beech Acres utilization review and continuous quality management programs, maintenance of professional liability insurance, and preparation of specified financial reports.

The Initiation of the New Program

To implement the contract, Beech Acres created a new intensive service program, Creative Connections. Consistent with the contractual requirements, Beech Acres established five primary goals for the program:

- improve client outcomes;

- predict, control, and limit costs;

- more appropriately match each child's level of need with the level of care he or she received;

- improve access of enrolled children and their families to services; and

- reduce the number of caseworkers who manage services for children served through multiple systems (McCullough & Schmitt, 2002).

Beech Acres is a multifaceted child and family service agency, and Creative Connections is one of the agency's 14 programs. Since its creation, Creative Connections has been housed separately on the Beech Acres campus. It has maintained its own staff, although certain management and administrative functions have been performed by Beech Acres, such as quality assurance, evaluation, financial management, and information technology services (Auditor of the State of Ohio, 2001).

From the outset, the 55- to 60-member staff of Creative Connections was composed of many individuals who worked with FCF Management, including the assistant director, who was hired to be the director of Creative Connections; the financial director; and the individual responsible for developing the network of service providers. Creative Connections also included staff from The Lighthouse, one of the care management agencies that contracted with FCF Management, and Beech Acres staff.

Creative Connections: An Evolving Program

Beech Acres implemented Creative Connections, as initially designed, over a four-year period. As the contract neared expiration in July 2002, negotiations began to examine the structure and operational nature of the program and make any needed changes. Participants identified a number of areas requiring redesign. In the course of these negotiations, the Hamilton County agencies decided to abolish the intermediary role of the council. In the next phase of the program, they decided that the lead agency would contract directly with the five county agencies, to be referred to collectively as the "Multi-County Systems Agencies" (MCSA). They anticipated that the new arrangement would save the county the $70,000 per year associated with the council's management of the contract and would establish a direct reporting and monitoring relationship between the lead agency and the county agencies. The negotiations anticipated that participants would execute a two-year contract.

The following discussion describes Creative Connections as Beech Acres implemented it over the initial period and discusses the programmatic and fiscal directions that the groups considered in the contract renegotiations between Beech Acres and the Hamilton County agencies. Of particular importance in this regard are issues related to the eligibility requirements for children's participation in Creative Connections, the financing structure, the process by which children would be referred to the program, the nature of service provision, and the composition and use of the provider network.

Children Served Through Creative Connections

From inception in 1995, the program has required all referrals of children to come from one of the five Hamilton County agencies. The program does not permit public enrollment of children. Under the initial four-year contract with Beech Acres, Creative Connections (as was the case with the earlier version of the program) was limited to serving 286 children at any point in time. Creative Connections served approximately 330 children each year, with 50 to 60 children leaving the program annually and the same number entering the program.

One of the issues that surfaced early in the implementation of Creative Connections was the eligibility criteria for children's participation in the program. Under the initial contract with the county agencies, Creative Connections served children with highly intensive needs who either required the services of multiple systems or who had an extremely high level of special needs (children described by the Auditor of the State of Ohio [2001] as "the County's most troubled youth" [p. 1–1]). These children primarily were dependent children in state custody (whether placed in-county or out-of-county); children and youth involved with the juvenile justice system and children/youth with serious emotional disturbances (McCullough & Schmitt, 2002). At first, each of the county agencies used specific enrollment criteria, but over time, eligibility for Creative Connections devolved to a single criterion—that the child or youth was in need of residential care. For example, although the juvenile court initially limited referrals to children younger than 12 who had committed a felony, it soon began to refer older youth with serious conduct disorders whose problems could be addressed only through long-term residential treatment. Eventually, all agencies referred only children and youth needing residential care to Creative Connections.

As the five agencies came to rely on Creative Connections for residential services, the program faced significant financial issues and difficulties in demonstrating effectiveness. To a great extent, Creative Connections administrators associated the fiscal and evaluation challenges with the fact that referrals were only of children in need of residential treatment, a problem compounded by the absence of clear disenrollment criteria. As a result of the expectations of both the referring agencies and children's families, Creative Connections found that it was limited in developing and implementing community-based care arrangements as alternatives to residential care. Creative Connections had anticipated that it would serve a mixed caseload of children in terms of level of care and would have control over assessment of, planning for, and placement of children along a continuum of services that ranged from residential treatment to community-based services. Neither of these aspects of the program, however, could be realized as a result of referrals only for residential treatment.

The issues regarding the criteria for children's enrollment in Creative Connections received considerable focus in the contract negotiations in 2002. In the initial round of negotiations, the county agencies and Beech Acres agreed to two major changes in the overall design of Creative Connections: The cap of 286 children was reduced to 250 children because of budgetary considerations, and the allocation of a specified number of referrals from each county agency was abandoned. Each of the five agencies agreed to continue contributing its allocated share of funding for the Creative Connections program but without an assurance of a designated number of treatment slots.

Also, in place of enrollment criteria associated with residential care, three new general criteria were developed for children's enrollment in the Creative Connections program: (1) the child must have a *Diagnostic and Statistical Manual of Mental Disorders* (4th ed.) diagnosis, (2) the child must have a condition or identified risk that crosses two or more service systems, and (3) the living arrangement the child requires must balance with the living arrangements required by the current mix of children enrolled in Creative Connections to maintain a financial risk balance (that is, to permit Creative Connections to manage costs). Perhaps most important, in contrast to the earlier unitary program approach, the parties proposed creating two different service tracks for children: individualized wraparound services, referred to as Track 1, and specialized intensive service needs, referred to as Track 2. In various documents developed in the negotiations, the two service tracks were defined as follows:

> **Individualized Wraparound Services.** "A process that strives to improve the lives of children and families who have complex needs. The process is implemented by a Child and Family Team (individuals who know the child and family best) to identify strengths and needs important to them in achieving outcomes in life domains (social, cultural, educational, etc.). Overall, the process strives to incorporate the strengths, values, norms, and preferences of particular children, families, and communities. Services may include non-

Table 39

Referral Preference Criteria for Creative Connections

Track 1: Individualized Wraparound Services

■ An active case in any Multi-County Systems Agency (MCSA) service system for less than 12 months.

■ Presence of child and family strengths to support a community-based wraparound plan.

■ Presence of a dedicated adult in the child's life.

■ Child is younger.

Track 2: Specialized Intensive Service Needs

■ Two or more failed out-of-home placements.

■ More than 12 to 18 months in any MCSA service system.

■ Extreme risk behaviors (i.e., sexual offending, suicidal behavior, violent behavior).

■ Court-ordered, long-term institutional stay.

■ Medically fragile or specialized intensive service need.

---

traditional, categorical, or other community based resources/services to assist families/children."

Specialized Intensive Service Needs. "Intensive service needs that are restrictive (such as locked acute settings or 24-7 monitoring of medically fragile conditions), costly, and correlated with children who have identified risk factors and poor outcomes."

In addition to establishing the three general criteria for participation in Creative Connections, the proposal also set forth specific enrollment criteria for each track. The contract delineated certain "referral preference criteria" and provided that children who met the most criteria would be considered most appropriate for Creative Connections services. The referral preference criteria for each service track are set out in Table 39.

Under the new design, children appropriately served through Track 1 could be maintained in a community-based, noninstitutional setting, or if placed in an institutional setting, could make progress toward a community-based setting.

Children appropriately served through Track 2 would be children with severe needs, who required highly specialized and intensive services, and who could not benefit immediately from individualized wraparound services and planning for a community-based placement. Beech Acres anticipated that it would assign new children to Track 2 only when children currently enrolled in Creative Connections disenrolled. It also anticipated that the number of children served through Track 2 would decrease over time, although some number of children would at all times be enrolled in Track 2. Under the program redesign, the number of children served through Track 1 would not exceed 180 children, and the number of children served through Track 2 would not exceed 70 children. Creative Connections expected to build local capacity to provide care to children enrolled in Track 2 and that the use of out-of-county placements would decline substantially.

Finally, the new design anticipated a third group of youth to be served—children who were enrolled in Creative Connections before July 1, 2002, and who would need discharge and transitional planning. It was expected that some of these youth would be referred to the adult service system.

Ultimately, the participants abandoned these redesigned features of the program, and they decided to limit participation to only those children whose needs could be met with less expensive treatment services.

Referral to Creative Connections

Under the original model of service provision, one of the five council agencies referred a child to Creative Connections, and Beech Acres, as lead agency, assigned a care manager to the child. The care manager began the planning process for the child by assessing the child's level of risk using the Child and Adolescent Functioning Assessment Scale (CAFAS) and other assessment tools. A child and family team (composed of the care manager, family members, any service providers involved with the child and family, a county case worker if applicable, and others who were resources in the child's life) developed a plan of care for the child within 30 days of enrollment. The child and family team met at least every 90 days to reassess the child using the CAFAS, review the case plan, and make decisions about next steps. In some cases, depending on the child's status and needs, the child and family team met every 30 days. Under this approach, the care manager coordinated the services for children as provided by service providers in the network. The care manager also served as a facilitator, identifying nontraditional, community-based services, that is, services provided by agencies with which Creative Connections did not hold contracts but which could provide long-term supports for the child and the family after the child disenrolled from

Creative Connections.

As part of the internal structure, the initial design organized care managers into teams of five to six care managers and a supervisor. The teams included staff members with utilization management responsibilities and expertise in the development of wraparound resources.

In the proposed redesign of the program, the assessment and service delivery approach involved different service delivery strategies for children enrolled in Tracks 1 and 2. An MCSA oversight committee was to be established to determine whether a child was an appropriate referral to Creative Connections and, if so, in which service track the child should be enrolled. The committee was to be composed of representatives from each of the five county agencies and a representative from Beech Acres. As in the past, referrals were to originate from the county agencies. The parties proposed that the oversight committee use the following process to decide whether a child should be enrolled in Creative Connections:

- Prior to any review of referrals, the MCSA oversight committee receives two types of information: (1) summary aggregate financial information about the budgeted and actual year-to-date costs associated with the care of all children currently enrolled in Tracks 1 and 2; and (2) an estimate of the number of cases that the oversight committee can assign to each track without causing a major deficit in the budget.

- The referral agent (from the appropriate agency) provides the committee with a full referral packet on the child.

- The committee members receive information regarding the estimated costs for the child's care for the balance of the fiscal year if the child is assigned to Creative Connections.

- The oversight committee discusses each case. Each committee member completes a one-page ranking form, in which the member ranks all referred children from "highest" to "lowest" based on the child's potential to benefit from Creative Connections, rather than on the child's need.

- Committee staff sum the rankings for each child and rank the children from highest to lowest priority.

- The staff use rankings to make final decisions regarding acceptance by Creative Connections.

The parties ultimately abandoned this innovative approach to eligibility determination, however, when they discarded the two-track approach.

Service Provision

Under the original model of service delivery, all children enrolled in Creative Connections and their families had individualized plans to meet their specific needs. To develop an individualized plan of care, Creative Connections staff assessed a number of domains, as listed in Table 40.

The worker developed an individual service plan for the child and family. Then, formal service providers, such as foster care or residential treatment providers, or nontraditional providers, which, depending on the nature of the child's needs, might include the YMCA or a local karate school, provided services.

The original contract for Creative Connections required Beech Acres to ensure that certain services were available to children enrolled in Creative Connections and their families, either by directly providing those services or assuring their provision by a member of the network of service providers (see Table 41).

The proposed new model for service provision varied from the original service provision design. The new model had five goals: to improve the functioning of enrolled children and families in targeted life domains; increase the capability of enrolled families to meet the needs of their children; increase access to informal and formal community supports as needed; increase the capacity and capability of communities to support their children and families; and use informal and formal resources optimally. For children and families served through both Tracks 1 and 2, the program specified a community-based wraparound approach as the foundation of service delivery. That approach focuses on connecting children with their families in community settings, thereby reducing dependence on out-of-town providers, engaging families in treatment, and reducing children's lengths of stay.

In the course of the initial negotiations, the county agencies and Beech Acres agreed on certain key services that Creative Connections would provide to children and families enrolled in Tracks 1 and 2. These services, which were organized in the three categories of individualized wraparound services, direct services, and case management, are described in Table 42.

As Table 42 indicates, under the new design, Beech Acres would offer three levels of case management for children enrolled in Track 2: Level 1, administrative monitoring; Level 2, case management—low intensity; and Level 3, case management—high intensity. The MCSA oversight committee, once it determined that a child met the referral preference criteria for Track 2, would assign the child to the appropriate level of case management, based on the following guidelines.

Level 1 (Administrative Monitoring). The case manager would not make face-to-face visits. The case manager, instead, would provide administrative services oversight, such as reviewing service plans and progress, levels of care, financial arrangements, and length of stay, and would collaborate with providers and funding agencies to ensure that appropriate services were provided. Level 1 generally would be used only when one of the county agencies provided primary case management services or the child was placed out of region with no immediate step-down plan.

Level 2 (Case Management—Low Intensity). The Creative Connections case manager would provide all Level 1 services and would make regular face-to-face, goal-directed visits with the child and/or the family as specified in the child's service plan.

Level 3 (Case Management—High Intensity). The case manager would provide all Level 1 services; make face-to-face, goal-directed visits to the child and/or the family every two weeks; and provide specific, targeted, time-limited interventions (typically no more than three months). As envisioned, these interventions might include placement stabilization, transition services, and stepping up or down the child's level of care. Level 3 would be used only when the MCSA oversight committee specified a time-limited goal expectation. If the case manager did not achieve the expected outcome within the specified period of time, the relevant county agency representative and Creative Connections staff would assess the need to continue Level 3 case management.

Under the new program design, an individualized wraparound care coordinator became the key Creative Connections staff person. As proposed in various documents developed in the negotiations, staff in these positions were to be

> a Bachelor and Master level clinician skilled at identifying, facilitating, and engaging family members, system representatives, and community stakeholders (Child and Family Teams) in an individualized wraparound service planning process focusing on child needs and family strengths. An individual who performs outcome-focused, needs-based activities (face-to-face and collateral contacts) which assist families and children by locating, developing, coordinating, and monitoring care and community based services. An individual who ensures that families and children have a voice in identifying their needs, is skilled at accessing/developing community based services/resources, and engages Child and Family Teams

Table 40

Assessment Domains for Children Referred to Creative Connections

Assessment Domain	Areas Explored Within Each Domain
Residence	Do the current living arrangements meet the needs of the child and the family?
Family	Who is the family (as defined by the family)? Do all family members have appropriate access to one another? What is needed for all family members to remain in touch or to stay together? Does any family member have serious unmet needs?
Social	Do family members have friends? Do family members socialize with one another? Do they have fun? Do they have ways to relax?
Emotional/psychological	Does the referred child have any unmet needs? Do any family members have unmet needs? Are there unresolved issues that impede normal interactions within the family or in the community?
Educational/vocational	What is needed to ensure a viable education for the children in the family, particularly the client? Do older children have access to employment? How are the children prepared for the future?
Safety	Are all family members safe? Does any family member face danger? Is any member a danger to himself or herself, or the community?
Legal	Is any family member involved in the judicial system (on probation or on parole)? If so, is he or she represented by legal counsel? Are there any issues regarding child custody?
Medical	Are the health needs of each family member met? Does the family have access to needed medical specialists?
Other potential domains	Crisis intervention, spiritual, cultural, financial, behavioral

Table 41
Services Provided Through Creative Connections

Type of Service	Services Provided
Community support services	Therapeutic community support, support counseling, case aide, housing
Crisis services	Crisis counseling and planning, crisis home, crisis beds, crisis respite
Diagnostic and evaluative services	Inpatient and outpatient assessments, evaluation services, psychiatric reviews/medication checks
Foster care services	Foster care treatment, foster day care, foster home care
Group care services	Therapeutic group care
Home-based intervention services	In-home treatment, day treatment
Independent-living services	Supported independent living and work environments
Psychotherapy	Individual, family, and group therapy; individual, family, and group alcohol and other drug therapy; special therapy
Medical/somatic services	Inpatient assessments and medication trial, outpatient medication trial
Outpatient partial hospitalization services	Camp, reintegration treatment services, consultation with other professionals, partial hospitalization, behavior management services
Residential care services	Residential treatment/child care institutional placement, psychiatric hospitalization, foster day care, shelter care, foster or group home care
Respite services	Temporary babysitting; supervised care; services designed to assist child, parent, family member or foster parent adjust to placement

Table 42

Creative Connections: The New Framework of Services

Service Area	Description of Service
Individualized Wraparound Services	
Individualized wraparound care coordination	Engaging the child and family in identifying their aspirations, strengths, resources, and barriers
	Identifying, engaging, and collaborating with stakeholders to implement child and family teams
	Generating and involving neighborhood and community resources
	Documenting plans, progress, and activities
	Managing costs
	Monitoring service outcomes
	For Track 1 children: Focusing on facilitating sustainable self-sufficiency within their natural support structure
	For Track 2 children: Focusing on monitoring placements and implementing aftercare services
Child and family teams	Developing individual service plans
	Monitoring plan implementation
	Identifying barriers to progress
	Developing resources to enhance progress
	Developing plans to teach dedicated adults how to respond in crisis situations to avoid risk behaviors or out-of-home placements
Individualized wraparound service planning	Use of assessment tools to ensure that the child's and family's strengths and needs guide the planning and delivery of service

Direct Services

Neighborhood/community-based services
(to be used before traditional direct service
providers)

Web-weaving and capability services (such as parent support groups, advo-
cacy training, and peer mentoring)
Faith-based services
Tutors
Community recreational resources
Voluntary community res ources
Volunteers to mentor families

Traditional therapeutic services

Foster care services
Residential care services (including creative approaches, such as dedicated
adults in co treatment opportunities)
Crisis stabilization services
Acute mental health services
Traditional extended care
Brief extended care

Case Management (for Track 2 Children)

Level 1
Level 2
Level 3

Administrative service monitoring
Low-intensity case management
High-intensity case management

in a process of implementing individualized wraparound service plans to help children/families achieve permanency, safety,
and well being outcomes.

As proposed in the new design of the program, a child would be referred to
Creative Connections for individualized wraparound services (Track 1), a care
coordinator would meet with the family and assess the child's needs (using standardized instruments such as the CAFAS), and the care coordinator would put
together a child and family team. The child and family team would develop a care
plan for the child that emphasized natural and community-based supports. The
coordinator would assign team members specific roles and responsibilities and
oversee all efforts. Although Track 1 services were open-ended, the program anticipated that for most children and families, individualized wraparound services
would be provided for 12 to 18 months. The parties did not finalize specific discharge criteria before the negotiations with Beech Acres ended and the county
agencies abandoned the two-track approach.

Similar to the team model in the original program design, Creative
Connections also planned to use care coordination teams. Each team was to consist of a supervisor; six care coordinators, one of whom would focus on the development of informal resources and one of whom would focus on quality assurance
and utilization management; and a parent with strong community relationships
to assist the team in identifying informal services and supports.

The care coordination team also would manage the costs of all services for the
children served by the care coordinators on the team. The program would calculate the monthly budget for the team (the case rate times the number of children),
and the team would make decisions regarding expenditures for children while
remaining within budget. Based on the projected case rate being negotiated (discussed later) and a projected caseload of 10 children per care coordinator (a total
of 60 children per team), the program expected that each team would have a
monthly budget of approximately $200,000. Beech Acres anticipated that there
would be three clinical teams for children enrolled in Track 1 (individualized
wraparound services) and that these teams would be assigned to specific geographic areas. Beech Acres also anticipated that there would be one care coordination team for children enrolled in Track 2 (specialized intensive service needs
program).

A new aspect of the redesigned program was a focus on parent advocacy, in
recognition of the fact that a dedicated adult's active participation in a child's plan
of care is critical to the successful treatment of the child. Among the approaches
that Beech Acres considered in relation to the new parent advocacy component of

Creative Connections were parent support groups, parent peer mentoring, parent advocacy training and coaching, and a parent advisory committee. Beech Acres also considered development of a parent advocate (a paid parent and/or a parent of a child who formerly was enrolled in Creative Connections) to ensure parent inclusion in the care coordination teams and to coach care coordinators in their efforts to empower families to serve as active members of the child and family teams. The elements, unfortunately, were eliminated once negotiations between the county agencies and Beech Acres ended.

The Provider Network

As lead agency, Beech Acres has provided or overseen the provision of services to children enrolled in Creative Connections. During the implementation of the original program, Beech Acres provided a limited level of direct services to children, primarily residential care and therapeutic treatment programs representing less than 10% of Beech Acres' total operating budget. A network of service providers in Hamilton County and, to some extent, residential care providers outside Hamilton County provided the majority of Creative Connections' services.

When Beech Acres first established Creative Connections, it did not use an RFP process to select service providers. Instead, Beech Acres enlisted service providers who had served children through the program administered by FCF Management. As providers were needed for additional services, Beech Acres requested proposals from providers competent in the needed service area and selected the providers with the strongest proposals. This process involved a formal contracting procedure that determined the scope of services, the contracted rate, and credentialing requirements. In 2000, Creative Connections used 95 service providers, who primarily offered counseling, foster care, partial hospitalization, residential treatment, and mentoring services. As Table 43 indicates, the largest portions of the Creative Connections budget for 2000 were for residential and group services, allocations that would be expected given the client population served.

Prior to the proposed new program model in 2002, Creative Connections began to critically examine each service that it provided and determine whether the service was actually needed and whether the agencies providing services met expected outcome achievement and cost standards. Anthony Broskowski, in his actuarial analysis of Creative Connections in 2001, identified a number of concerns in these areas, including:

- issues related to the development and management of the provider network (with particular concerns about the concentration of funding in the hands of a small number of service

Table 43

Calendar Year 2000: Services and Percentage of Total Budget

Service	Percentage
Residential treatment (multiple levels)	39
Group home	10
Client support services	5
Therapeutic foster care	7
Partial hospitalization	3
Mentoring	3

providers);

■ the fact that in some instances, fees had been separately negotiated for providers offering similar services;

■ considerable variation in the monthly minimum and maximum fees for each service type; and

■ the absence of an explicit and uniformly applied set of clinical
protocols for decisions regarding service utilization (with decisions made, instead, on provider considerations).

Based on its own assessment and Broskowski's analysis, Creative Connections
began to implement strategies to reduce the number of service providers and
ensure that all providers shared a similar service philosophy and approach, the
goal being to institute a more effective provider network management system.

Under the program redesign, Beech Acres anticipated that the program's
provider network for children enrolled in Track 1 would expand to more fully
incorporate nontraditional, community-based services and support providers. It
did not expect the provider network to change significantly for children enrolled
in Track 2, although it did expect major changes in relation to the development
of a fuller range of community-based residential programs.

Consistent with Beech Acres' focus on community-based care, which predat-
ed the contract renegotiations, was the development of a partnership between
Creative Connections and Children's Hospital to expand the availability of local,
multilevel, out-of-home care services. Beech Acres' partnership with Children's
Hospital was to expand local capacity to treat children enrolled in Creative
Connections but placed in out-of-county residential care—providing those children with needed services in Hamilton County. Creative Connections was to provide a range of services—including emergency care, longer term acute care, tradi-

tional extended care, and brief extended care—through the partnership with Children's Hospital.[29]

The proposed new agreement between Beech Acres and the county agencies would have created a more formal relationship between the parties in the development of the Creative Connections provider network. The county agencies would have designated a provider contract manager to coordinate, manage, and communicate provider rate structures, provider agreement administration, and credentialing of all in-region, traditional providers. Creative Connections would do the same for all community-based traditional and nontraditional service delivery providers and all out-of-region traditional providers. The parties believed the provider contract manager for the county and Creative Connections would develop a standardized process to be used in all provider contracting and network management activities. The process would include a standard rate structure; defined criteria and procedures for contracting outside the standard rate structure; credentialing requirements; provider selection criteria; expectations of providers regarding utilization review, participation in child and family teams, and discharge planning; outcomes management; and provider service issues and conflict resolution practices. These provisions had not been fully detailed at the time the negotiations ended.

Creative Connections Outcomes

Outcomes have been a key focus of Creative Connections since its inception. Four perspectives on outcomes exist: performance indicators under the Creative Connections contracts, contractually established fiscal penalties for inadequate performance, data regarding outcomes for children in Creative Connections, and the program's evaluation processes.

Performance Indicators. The original contract for Creative Connections con-

---

[29] Beech Acres tried to build local capacity for the residential treatment of children placed out of county from the inception of Creative Connections. From the outset, it was clear that Hamilton County lacked residential treatment resources. From a fiscal perspective, it was clear that a small number of children with very costly needs dramatically skewed the funding structure of Creative Connections. In 2000, for example, services for the 27 children placed out of county cost $121,000 per month (total of $3.2 million that year). The children had chronic, serious needs for which few options were available other than extremely costly residential treatment. Although it might have been possible to develop a community-based program of wraparound services closer to home, fiscal analyses suggested that such services were likely to cost even more than the residential care the child was receiving.

tained a range of indicators, measures, benchmarks, and data reporting requirements that appeared throughout 11 separate contract exhibits. These outcome-related elements were not closely correlated and, as a result, proved extremely difficult to implement. In March 2001, the participants amended the contract, and made the performance measures considerably more streamlined and outcome-focused. Seven indicators were developed for the Creative Connections program, with benchmarks established for each indicator. The seven indicators in place from 2001 through the termination of the contract in 2002 were:

1. Enrollees receive residential treatment only when it is essential to decrease impairment; aggregate lengths of stay decrease for enrollees in institutional placements.

2. Appropriate services are available within the region and the county.

3. Beech Acres performs functions designated by the council agencies.

4. Placement services are stable and meet the child's treatment needs.

5. Individual plans of care and quarterly individual progress reports are responsive to the needs of enrollees and agencies.

6. Services for enrollees are high quality, responsive, and appropriate in meeting desired outcomes.

7. Beech Acres monitors and tracks financial status, quality improvement, and aggregate reporting of contract requirements.

Table 44 provides examples of benchmarks for each of the seven indicators that went into effect in the third year of the Creative Connections original contract.

With the redesign of Creative Connections to a two-track service delivery program, separate indicators were to be developed for Tracks 1 and 2. Before termination of the negotiations between Beech Acres and the county agencies, indicators, measures, and benchmarks had been proposed for Track 1 services (see Table 45). Three instruments had been proposed to support the assessment of the indicators and measures for individualized wraparound services: the Ohio Youth Problems Scales, Functioning, and Satisfaction (Ohio Scales), CAFAS, and the Child and Adolescent Level of Care Utilization System (CALOCUS). Creative

Connections was to use CAFAS, CALOCUS, and the Ohio Scales to assist child and family teams in appraisals of child and family strengths and risk factors. Teams were to complete CAFAS and CALOCUS at intake, at 6 months of service, at 12 months of service, and annually thereafter. Teams were to complete the Ohio Scales at intake and update them quarterly.

Fiscal Penalties for Inadequate Performance

The original Creative Connections contract with Beech Acres linked performance to financial penalties. The contract identified certain benchmarks as "reimbursable performance indicators." The contract provided that in a given contract year, a certain level of administrative and care management costs could be withheld as a performance penalty if the council determined that Beech Acres had failed to meet the designated indicators. Beech Acres had to provide quarterly reports on these indicators, and on the basis of these reports, the contract authorized the council to determine whether Beech Acres had failed to meet the indicators. In such a case, the council was allowed to deduct funds up to the maximum level set by the contract from Beech Acres' next quarterly payment. If the failures occurred in the final year of the contract, the contract required Beech Acres to reimburse the council an amount equivalent to the penalty. The contract set both maximum total aggregate penalties in each contract year and maximum penalties for failure to achieve specific reimbursable performance indicators. The total maximum performance indicator penalties were set at $100,500 for Contract Year 1, $150,000 for Contract Year 2, $225,000 for Contract Year 3, and $225,000 for Contract Year 4. Table 46 provides the maximum penalties for failure to achieve the individual indicators in the third year of the Creative Connections original contract.

As part of the renegotiations, the groups proposed a more simplified performance indicator penalty, which would be imposed if Creative Connections failed to meet or adequately demonstrate achievement of the performance indicators. The county agencies would have been permitted to withhold a certain level of administrative cost reimbursement only, in contrast to the provision under the original contract that permitted withholding of administrative and care management costs reimbursement.

Outcome Data

Although challenges associated with the information management systems limited the ability of Creative Connections to aggregate outcome data, the program was able to analyze outcomes for children served through the program based on CAFAS scores. These analyses indicated that enrolled children had lower CAFAS

Table 44
Creative Connections: Indicators and Benchmarks

Indicator	Benchmark
Enrollees receive residential treatment only when essential to decrease impairment; aggregate length of stay (LOS) decreases for enrollees in institutional placements	Average hospital LOS will be 220 days
	Average LOS for residential care will be 330 days
	At least 50% of enrollees will be in community-based settings
	Less than 20% of enrollees who are in out-of-home placement will experience an inpatient hospitalization during any one-year period.
	Of outlier costs, 15% will shift to community-based services
Appropriate services are available within the region and the county	The number of enrollees who are placed outside of Hamilton County as compared to the prior contract year will decrease by 10%
Beech Acres will perform designated council agencies functions	All enrollees will have face-to-face contact with their care managers (CMs) within five days of enrollment
	At least 90% of enrollees will have face-to-face contact with a CM at least twice a month
Placement services are stable and meet the child's treatment needs	75% of placement moves will be planned by the CM, and no enrollee will experience more than two unplanned moves while in out-of-home care in any 12-month period
	Less than 10% of planned moves will be to the same or to more restrictive settings
	Less than 15% of unplanned moves will be the same or more restrictive settings

Individual plans of care and quarterly individual enrollee progress reports are responsive to the needs of enrollees and council agencies

90% of all plans of care (POCs) have documented progress notes that specify the input of treatment teams in the planning

90% of all POCs, amendments, and quarterly progress reports are completed within 30 days

90% of planned Medicaid services are realized

There is no increase in the total cost per enrollee over the previous contract year

Services for enrollees are high quality, responsive, and appropriate in meeting outcomes

90% of all enrollees meet level of care criteria

Rates of reported suicide attempts are less than 5%

90% of enrollees and families maintain or improve school functioning

At least 50% of all enrollees, families, CMs, and custodians indicate a positive satisfaction rating of services provided under the contract

70% of council agency representatives are satisfied with services

70% of providers are satisfied with contractor's performance

Beech Acres monitors and tracks financial status, quality improvements, and aggregate reporting of contract requirements

100% of all reports are submitted in a timely manner and are adequate to keep the council informed of contract performance status

Table 45

Proposed Indicators, Measures and Benchmarks for Track 1: Individualized Wraparound Services

Indicator/Measure	Benchmark
1. Comprehensive wraparound planning facilitates improved child functioning	
1a. Enrollees demonstrate improved overall functioning.	1a. Ohio Scales/Child and Adolescent Functioning Assessment Scale (CAFAS) scores reflect significant improvements in overall functioning.
1b. Enrollees demonstrate improved school functioning.	
1c. Enrollees commit fewer juvenile offenses.	1b. Significant decreases in suspensions and detentions are reported.
1d. Enrollees increase prosocial behaviors.	
1e. Enrollees have a decreased number of self-harmful behaviors and/or suicide attempts.	1b. Significant increases in days attending school are reported.
1f. Enrollees are maintained in the planned living environment.	1b. CAFAS scores demonstrate significant improvements in school functioning.
	1c. Ohio Scales/CAFAS scores indicate statistically fewer arrests and delinquent behaviors.
	1d. Ohio Scales Functioning subscale indicates statistically significant improvements in prosocial behaviors/strengths.
	1e. Rates of reported suicide attempts are less than 5%.
	1f. 95% of children will not be absent without permission.
	1f. CAFAS scores indicate statistically significant improvements in home functioning.
2. Comprehensive wraparound planning improves family functioning.	
2a. Parents/dedicated adults report increased family empowerment.	2a. Of families in focus groups, 80% report increased capability access resources for their child.
2b. Parents/dedicated adults report satisfaction with services.	2b. Of families in focus groups, 90% report satisfaction with Creative Connections.
2c. Families have fewer incidences of abuse and neglect.	2c. There is a consistent reduction of substantiated reports of abuse and neglect.

3. Clinically appropriate services are provided in the least restrictive environment possible.

3a. Enrollees are placed in clinically appropriate settings as identified by quality assurance/utilization review policies and procedures.

3b. Changes in placement are to the same or less restrictive settings.

3c. Clinically appropriate services exist within the region.

3d. Contractor has a competent network that meets the treatment needs of the enrollees.

3e. Providers demonstrate positive enrollee outcomes.

3a-b. Child and Adolescent Level of Care Utilization System scores are congruent with current level of care for 100% of enrollees.

3b. Less than 11% of enrollees have placement changes to the same or more restrictive settings.

3c. Of enrollees, 80% receive service within the region.

3d. All providers maintain licensure.

3d. All traditional providers are credentialed annually.

3e. A system to profile providers by outcomes achieved is developed in Contract Year 1.

4. Community-based supports are available and used.

4a. Individual service plans use formal and informal community supports to meet enrollee needs.

4b. Network of community-based informal supports is available.

4a. Percentage of planned informal supports increases relative to baseline. Baseline determined by percentage of informal supports identified July 1, 2002.

4b. Of enrollees, 75% use available community-based informal supports.

5. Children have permanency and stability in their living situations.

5a. Changes in placement are directly related to helping the enrollee achieve treatment plan goals.

5b. Services provided directly address risks identified on assessment tools.

5a. Of placement moves, 75% are directly related to treatment plan goals.

5a. All enrollees experience two or fewer unnecessary moves in any 12-month period.

5b. Of services provided, 90% directly address risk areas.

5b. Enrollees and families demonstrated decreased risk behaviors from enrollment to 6, 12, and 24 months in care.

6. Of sampled providers and consortium members, 90% are satisfied with Creative Connections.

7. Creative Connections services are cost effective.

7a. The plan of care indicates a service mix with the appropriate balance between family support and Medicaid-eligible services.

7b. Percentage of care coordination time is Medicaid billed bursed.

7c. Monthly spending does not exceed case rates.

7a. Of planned Medicaid services, 90% are realized.

7b. A percentage of care coordination time for Medicaid-eligible children is billed to Medicaid. and reimbursed.

7c. No spending exceeds case rates.

Table 46

Reimbursable Performance Indicators and Maximum Penalties in Contract Year 3

Indicator	Measure	Maximum Penalty
Enrollees receive residential treatment only when essential to decrease impairment; decreased aggregate length of stay for enrollees in institutional placements.	Residential total aggregate length of stay decreases by 30 days for the contract year.	$5,000
	The number of enrollees in community-based settings increases by 15%.	10,000
	Costs for outlier enrollees are shifted from hospital and residential treatment to community-based treatment.	5,000
Appropriate services are available within the region and the county.	All enrollees placed out-of-county and out-of-region are in clinically appropriate settings as identified by quality assurance/utilization review (QA/UR) policies and procedures.	20,000
	90% of services authorized and billed aresubstantiated by QA/UR protocols.	5,000
Contractor performs designated council agencies functions.	The care manager sees each enrollee face-to-face within five days of enrollment.	5,000
	90% of enrollees have-face-to-face contact with the care manager at least twicea month unless otherwise approved by the enrollee's plan of care.	25,000
Placement services are stable and meet the child's needs.	A UR review of 100% of all planned moves to the same restrictiveness level takes place.	5,000
	A UR review of 100% of all unplanned moves takes place.	5,000
Individual plans of care, individual service plans, and quarterly individual enrollee progress reports are responsive to the needs of enrollees and council agencies.	Each plan of care indicates the service mix, including the appropriate balance between family support and Medicaid-eligible services.	5,000
	Of planned Medicaid services, 90% are realized.	5,000
	There is no increase in the total cost per enrollee.	30,000

Services for enrollees are high quality, responsive, and appropriate in meeting outcomes.	Enrollees receive treatment in the least restrictive, most appropriate environment.	5,000
	Caregiver demonstrates that enrollee's basic needs are continually being met.	5,000
	Enrollees overall significantly demonstrate statistical improvement based on a standardized measure.	10,000
	All individual outliers undergo UR every quarter.	15,000
	Contractor provides quarterly QA reports in a manner as described in indicators 1 through 6.	10,000
Contractor adequately tracks financial status, quality improvement, and aggregate reporting of contract requirements.	Contractor provides quarterly fiscal reports that track monthly, quarterly, and year-to-date financial activity as well as available actual cost date for services authorized and rendered.	20,000
	All reports are submitted in a timely manner and are adequate to keep the council informed of contract performance status.	10,000
	Contractor provides comparison of actual administrative costs, care management costs, and direct service costs to authorized and projected costs.	13,000
	Contract reports actual aggregate deficit (compared with projected).	10,000
	Contractor provides quarter-end planned outlier costs for estimated expenditures for community-based services as costs shift from hospital to residential care.	10,000

scores over time—findings that indicate improved stability in children's level of care. Average CAFAS scores, for example, from July 2000 to September 2001 fell from 90 to 80 (Beech Acres, 2001). Data also indicated that the greatest changes occurred for children between the time of their enrollment and 3 months of services and then again at 12 months of services (Beech Acres, 2001). In addition, CAFAS scores demonstrated that children were able to maintain positive changes through 24 months of services (Beech Acres, 2001). Specifically, analyses of CAFAS scores (Beech Acres, 2001) showed that children enrolled in Creative Connections demonstrated:

- statistically significant functional improvements in overall role performance from enrollment to three months and enrollment to six months;

- significantly improved community functioning, such as fewer delinquent behaviors, during the first six months of enrollment;

- significantly improved functioning at home during the first six months of enrollment;

- moderate improvements in school functioning (not statistically significant); and

- statistically significant improved interactions with others following six months in the program.

Creative Connections did not analyze CAFAS scores in connection with outcomes associated with the placement of children at less restrictive levels of care as children stepped down from residential care to group care, to family foster care, and, finally, to home with community-based services. Other data, however, indicated that on an aggregate basis, children enrolled in Creative Connections were served in less restrictive environments. Using a rating scale in which Level 6 was hospital care, Level 5 was residential care, Level 4 was group home care, Level 3 was foster care, Level 2 was independent living, and Level 1 was community-based services, the average level of care for enrolled children declined over time. In July 2000, the average level of care for enrolled children was 3.05, between foster care and group care. By September 2001, the average level of care for enrolled children was 2.75, between independent living and foster care, with the average level of care scores steadily declining in October 2000 (Beech Acres, 2001).

The Creative Connections Evaluation Processes

Under the original contract, the council, as intermediary, was to conduct an annual evaluation of Creative Connections, including an assessment of the extent to which indicators and benchmarks had been achieved. Creative Connections was required to submit documents, data, and aggregate reports. If the council deemed any data to be inadequate, Creative Connections was required to "make every reasonable effort to obtain additional data so that information relating toperformance indicators, standards, and enrollees is accurate and reliable." (Hamilton County Creative Connections, 2001, p. 23) .The contract also required the council to provide Creative Connections with a copy of the its annual evaluation within 30 days of completion. The first evaluation was to be completed 30 days prior to the close of the first year of the original contract, and each subsequent evaluation was to be completed by February 28th of the applicable year (2000, 2001, and 2002), but these were not completed. The original contract also required Beech Acres to coordinate an independent evaluation of its provision of direct services through the Pacific Institute for Research and Evaluation programs and to cooperate "with any independent evaluation of services and costs that may become available through the Council". (Hamiliton County Creative Connections, 2001, p. 23).

The new program design emphasized a utilization management process with required reviews and analyses of qualitative and quantitative outcome data on a monthly basis and at the time of each new admission and discharge. The program was to analyze children's lengths of stay in Tracks 1 and 2, the extent to which child and family goal attainment was achieved, and the resources that were being expended. These analyses were to be used to evaluate the cost-effectiveness of each of the services and to strengthen the ability of the care coordination teams to provide the most appropriate services to meet each child's and family's needs. The new design introduced the role of a utilization management manager, who would serve as a resource to the care coordination teams and ensure a disciplined application of data regarding child outcomes, community outcomes, provider performance, lengths of stay, and service costs.

In the newly designed program, utilization management would have had three components: prospective review, concurrent review, and retrospective review. **Prospective Review.** The prospective review was to take place at two levels: an individual level prospective review and an aggregate prospective review.

> ■ **The Individual Level Prospective Review** (ILPR). ILPR involved the care coordinator, the child and family team, and the utilization review care manager for the child's care coordi-

nation team. ILPR was to occur annually, beginning with the initial child and family team meeting. CALOCUS was to determine the child's current needs, with quarterly placement and service plans developed over the course of the year following the child's initial enrollment in Creative Connections. These plans were to be developed for each year that the child continued to be enrolled in the program.

- **The Aggregate Prospective Review (APR).** APR was to synthesize utilization review data gathered by the care coordinator and the child and family team, project the level-of-care needs for all children, and assess the fiscal ramifications of these projections. The analysis was to be done for all enrollees in Creative Connections, for enrollees by care coordination team, and for the enrollees assigned to each care coordinator. APR also was to use plan-of-care information monthly to determine the average length of care for enrollees.

The program designed prospective reviews to provide data for fiscal analyses. These data were to be used to determine the total fiscal liability for Creative Connections, offset by funding under its contract with the five Hamilton County agencies; the extent to which Medicaid-funded services were being maximized in children's plans of care; and the fiscal implications for placement of new enrollees into Track 2.

Concurrent Review. The concurrent review was to involve each care coordinator's monthly review of the placement plans for each child assigned to him or her. The care coordinator would identify the children who could not be maintained in their current placements and specify why the child's placement must be changed. Information related to variance from the child's planned placement was to be entered into the utilization review database and aggregated for purposes of determining the factors associated with placement change. The aggregate data were expected to identify trends to enhance the ability of Creative Connections to predict placement success.

Retrospective Review. The retrospective review was to take place at two levels: an individual level retrospective review and an aggregate retrospective review.

- **Individual Level Retrospective Review (ILRR).** ILRR was to involve the care coordinator, the child and family team, and the utilization review care manager for the child's care coordination team. ILRR was to occur quarterly, beginning with the child and family team meeting that took place four months after the individual level prospective review plan was initially prepared. The child and family team was to review the child's placement, the projected costs associated with the child's plan of care, and the actual costs. The information would identify the strengths that supported the child's projected plan of care or barriers that precluded realization of the plan.

■ **Aggregate Retrospective Review (ARR).** ARR was to involve an analysis of the utilization review data to determine the variances between the actual costs of services provided and the projected costs. The analysis was to be done for all children enrolled in Creative Connections, for enrollees by care coordination team, and for the enrollees assigned to each care coordinator. ARR also was to use service information monthly to determine the average length of care.

As was the case with the prospective reviews, retrospective reviews were to provide data for fiscal analyses.

Financial Aspects of Creative Connections

Two financial issues were key in both the original program and in the negotiations to redesign the Creative Connections: fiscal methodology and stop-loss.

Fiscal Methodology

Medicaid funding and pooled funding from the five Hamilton County agencies financed Creative Connections. The Department of Job and Family Services (the child welfare agency) contributed the majority of the funding (72.89%), with the mental health board (14.4%), the mental retardation/developmental disabilities board (7.79%), the juvenile court (4.36%), and the substance abuse treatment board (0.49%) contributing smaller proportions of the funding (McCullough & Schmitt, 2002). Creative Connections funding represented approximately 8% of Hamilton County's total child welfare spending (McCullough & Schmitt, 2002).

In the original program, the financial methodology was a case rate that applied to all children served by Creative Connections. During the first year of the original contract, the case rate was $3,130.29 per enrolled child. Administrators calculated the case rate for subsequent years based on a formula established by the contract: the lesser of (1) the annualized actual project cost for the immediate preceding year increased by an amount corresponding with the consumer price index and decreased by projected funds from other sources (cluster payments, interest, Medicaid, individual outlier reimbursements, and first and third party payments); or (2) the annualized county contribution for the immediate preceding contract year increased by an amount corresponding with the consumer price index.

By way of illustration, the basic contract rate for the third year of the original contract (June 1, 2000, to June 30, 2001) was $3,296.75, reflecting a 3.7% increase in the county contribution, based on the March 2000 consumer price index. A monthly Medicaid rate of $284.26 enhanced the basic case rate. With additions to the case rate from annual cluster payments, interest, and individual outlier reimbursements, the final case rate for the third year of the original contract was $3,977.13. This rate, however, fell short of the full-service monthly case rate of $4,433.11, which took into account the total direct service costs, care management costs, and administrative costs.

In each year of the original contract, the preset case rate, which applied regardless of the status of the individual enrollee, proved to be adequate for some children but wholly inadequate for other children, depending on their client category. Table 47 provides data on average monthly costs by client category, based on aggregate data from Creative Connections clients active as of November 1, 2001, and calculated over the time period July 2000 through September 2001.

The aggregate effect of actual costs for Creative Connections as originally designed is illustrated by the overall budget for the program. Table 48 provides the revenue and expenses details for the third year of the original contract. It shows the shortfall between projected income and projected costs. After adjustments to the aggregate deficit, the budget for the third year of the original contract projected a net deficit of $854,542.20.

Over the life of its original contract with the Hamilton County agencies, Beech Acres absorbed the bulk of the program's deficit—80% of the deficit in third year of the contract, with the county agencies absorbing the remaining 20%. As Beech Acres anticipated when it entered into the original contract for Creative Connections, it consistently drew on the board-approved set-aside from the endowment. As of June 2002, Beech Acres had invested $5 to $6 million of its own funds in the program.

With the proposed redesign of Creative Connections, two financial methodologies were proposed: a case rate for children enrolled in Track 1 and fee-for-service for children enrolled in Track 2.

Track 1: Individualized Wraparound Services. As redesigned, Creative Connections would have used two county case rates for children enrolled in individualized wraparound services: one case rate for "placement children," that is, children in out-of-home care settings, and one case rate for "in-home children,"

Table 47

Average Monthly Planned Costs by Client Category

Client Category	Average Monthly Planned Costs
Physical disability	$2,905.28
Serious emotional disturbance	
Low	4,427.42
Mid	5,705.28
High	8,374.54
Conduct disorde r/delinquency	4,865.41
Autism	5,893.98
Sex Offender	
With mental retardation	5,989.78
Without mental retardation	7,298.61
Mental retardation/mental illness	7,040.91

children served while they remain with their birthfamilies. Beech Acres proposed the two case rates for children in Track 1 based on an assumption of a balance of children in Track 1 with the following living arrangements: 43% in therapeutic foster care, 27% in group homes or independent living settings, and 30% in residential institutions. As noted earlier, the MCSA oversight committee would have assessed the overall mix of children referred to Track 1 and maintained a balance of children that mirrored these percentages. Because of the fiscal effect of the original model, the new design attempted to put into place procedures that would avert "adverse referral patterns" to Track 1 (that is, referrals of a disproportionate number of children with extreme risk factors, long histories of residential placement, or the absence of any protective factors).

The proposed county case rate would have been $120.75 per day for Track 1 placement children. This rate assumed that Creative Connections would generate an additional $5.06 per day, per child in the form of Medicaid revenue to offset the total direct care service costs for enrolled children. Based on this assumption, the total case rate was calculated at $125.80 per day. For Track 1 in-home children, the county case rate would have been $33.09 per day. This assumed that Creative Connections could generate an additional sum per day, per child in the form of Medicaid revenue to offset the total direct care service cost for enrolled children. When negotiations between the county agencies and Beech Acres ended, they had not yet determined the projected Medicaid revenue rate or set the final case rate for this group.[30]

Track 2: Specialized Intensive Service Need Program. Under the redesign, the payment methodology for Track 2 children would have been fee for service. The MCSA oversight committee would be charged with ensuring that the costs associated with serving children through Track 2 services were managed within a limited budget. Under the redesign of the program, the county agencies would have reimbursed Creative Connections for the actual costs of services for children enrolled in the specialized intensive services need program, excluding Medicaid reimbursement.

Administrative Costs. In addition to the case rates for Track 1 children and fee-for-service reimbursement for Track 2 children, the new design would have reimbursed Creative Connections' administrative service costs for the whole program. The permissible level of administrative service costs was to be approximately $1 million per year.

These new fiscal methodology approaches were not finalized, however, and were abandoned when negotiations between Beech Acres and the county agencies ended. The new contractor agreed to the use of a case rate only approach.

Stop-Loss Provisions

Both the original contract for Creative Connections and the negotiations regarding the redesign of the program addressed stop-loss, although in different ways.

The original Creative Connections contract contained highly detailed provisions regarding stop-loss at the individual care level and at the aggregate level.

Individual Stop-Loss. Under the original contract, the individual stop-loss provision was triggered if, at any time, the actual costs of providing services to an individual enrolled child (known as an "outlier") exceeded $7,000 per month for three consecutive calendar months. If, in any calendar month following that three-month period, the direct service costs for the child was between $7,001 and $15,000 per month, Creative Connections and the council would share those costs equally. If, after the three-month period, the direct service costs exceeded

---

[30] The case rate proposal would have been applied to a significant number of children already enrolled in Creative Connections who required residential treatment. Under the new design, these children would have been moved into Track 1. Beech Acres calculated that as a result of these children's actual expenses, it would have sustained a loss of more than $100,000 in the first month of the new contract alone. Beech Acres proposed methodologies other than the use of a case rate under such circumstances. The county, however, only would agree to end the participation of certain children in the program, not to reexamine the use of a case rate. Ultimately, Beech Acres determined that although it could accept financial risk under a performance-based contract, it could not accept the level of financial risk that a case rate under these circumstances would present.

Table 48

Revenues and Expenses for Creative Connections: Year 3 of Original Contract

	Rate	Units	Unit Description	Total
Revenue Source				
County case rate	3,296.75	3,432	Monthly	$11,314,437.21
Individual outlier reimbursement through contract	360,000.00	1	Annual	$360,000.00
Individual outlier reimbursement through Beech Acres	360,000.00	1	Annual	$360,000.00
Medicaid	284.26	3,432	Monthly	$975,580.32
Cluster	500,000.00	1	Annual	$500,000.00
Interest	9,375.47	12	Monthly	$112,505.64
First- and third-party payments	27,000	1	Annual	$27,000.00
Total project revenue				$13,649,523.17
Total project revenue per case, per month		3,432		$3,977.13
Expense				
Direct service costs	3,184.35	3,432	Monthly	$10,928,674.57
Care management	537.08	3,432	Monthly	$1,843,255.95
Administrative	711.68	3,432	Monthly	$2,442,498.45
Total project costs				$15,214,428.97
Total project costs at full service case rate				$4,433.11

$15,000 per month, neither Creative Connections nor the council was to be responsible. In these cases, Creative Connections was authorized to negotiate with the referring county agency (child welfare, the juvenile court, mental health, alcohol and drug addiction services, or mental retardation/developmental disability) to pay the direct service costs. If Creative Connections was not able to obtain the referring county agency's agreement to assume costs for the child at that level, it was permitted to disenroll the child from Creative Connections without violating the contractual no eject, no reject mandate.

Aggregate Stop-Loss. To limit the potential total risk and annual profits for Beech Acres, the contract also required that Beech Acres submit quarterly financial reports. If the annual Creative Connections program revenue exceeded program costs, the difference (called the annual aggregate financial surplus) was apportioned based on the level of revenue excess. If the annual aggregate financial surplus was $333,333 or less in the first year or $500,000 or less in Years 2, 3, or 4 of the original contract, Beech Acres would retain the entire annual aggregate financial surplus. If the annual aggregate financial surplus was more than $333,333 in the first year or more than $500,000 in Years 2, 3, or 4 of the original contract, Beech Acres and the council would share equally any amount in excess of those limits. The same formula applied to losses, with Beech Acres absorbing all losses less than $333,333 in the first year or $500,000 in Years 2, 3, or 4 of the original contract and sharing any losses that exceeded those amounts with the council (McCullough & Schmitt, 2002). Beech Acres sustained losses in each year of the program and absorbed most them.

Taking a different approach to stop-loss, the parties to the new contract negotiations proposed a three-month financial risk period for children enrolled in individualized wraparound services. If a child receiving Track 1 services moved from an out-of-home placement to an in-home placement, Creative Connections would continue to receive the $120.75 per day rate for three months, as long as the child's placement did not change. If a child receiving individualized wraparound services moved from an in-home placement to an out-of-home placement, Creative Connections would continue to receive the case rate ($32.87 per day) for three months. If a child in individualized wraparound services had to be stepped-up to residential treatment, Creative Connections would be at risk for a three-month period (that is, the program would continue to receive the predetermined case rate for that child). Should the child continue to require residential treatment for more than three months, the county agency responsible for the child would assume full financial responsibility for the child's care. Finally, if on authorization from the MCSA oversight committee, a child moved from Track 1 to Track 2, Creative Connections would receive the authorized case rate for the child at the time of the placement move for an additional three months, in addition to being reimbursed for service costs on a fee-for-service basis.

In addition to these fiscal risk provisions, the parties proposed that the MCSA oversight committee and Creative Connections review the individualized wraparound services case rates both for placement and in-home services three months after implementation of the new contract to compare revenues and actual direct service costs. The contract permitted an upward adjustment of the case rates if actual direct service costs exceeded the established case rates for reasons unrelated to the performance of Beech Acres in implementing Creative Connections, such as actions taken by the county agencies. The contract would not permit adjustments if actual direct service costs exceeded case rates due to Beech Acres' failure to control service frequency, service volume, or unit costs. These proposals, however, were not finalized.

Assessment of Creative Connections

Researchers have favorable evaluated Creative Connections on a number of fronts. In August 2001, the Auditor for the State of Ohio (2001) conducted a performance audit of Creative Connections and the behavioral health initiative implemented by Magellan Health Services and concluded that both initiatives had been successful in providing improved services for children. Beech Acres has identified major successes in four programmatic areas: improved coordination of care, improved quality of care, extension of services to many children and families who previously would not have been eligible for services, and development of new local services.

From the outset of Creative Connections, however, a number of program and fiscal challenges were evident. The auditor's report noted that certain fiscal aspects needed improvement, including the extent to which there was use of self-referrals by Beech Acres, more thorough documentation of Beech Acres' expenditures, and the need to integrate Beech Acres' care management and financial reporting computer systems so that the council could more accurately assess client care and financial performance (Auditor of the State of Ohio, 2001). Beech Acres itself identified a number of programmatic issues that posed challenges in the implementation of Creative Connections. Beech Acres highlighted difficulties in establishing adequate information system technology, hiring and retaining adequately trained leadership and staff, using the programmatic structure as established under contract and handling its fiscal implications, and blending the functions and philosophy of community service with the varying providers' approaches (McCullough & Schmitt, 2002).

The issue of leadership for Creative Connections quickly emerged as a key challenge for the program. Within five months of the program's creation, it became apparent that the newly appointed director, formerly of FCF Management, could not build the program as needed. She was replaced in early 1999 with a second director, recruited from Beech Acres. This individual resigned after 11 months. The executive director of Beech Acres then became acting director while overseeing a national search for a permanent director for Creative Connections. After a six-month search and interviews with many candidates, in late summer 2000, Creative Connections hired a new director with a managed care and mental health background.

The executive director of Beech Acres, drawing on his management of Creative Connections, identified several areas on which the new director should focus: development of the information technology system, further development of the network of service providers, and refinement of performance indicators, which required contract renegotiation with the Hamilton County agencies. A focus on these areas proved to be extremely challenging for the new director, and she resigned in June 2001. At that point, the executive director named two Beech Acres staff members—one with administrative and network provider development expertise and one with clinical expertise—to codirect the program. This arrangement continued through the summer of 2002. At that time, had negotiations been successful, the new contract's changes would have taken effect. Based on expectations of a successful resolution of the contract negotiations, the codirector with clinical expertise assumed director status, and Creative Connections phased out the administrative director position and created a new leadership position involving oversight of all Creative Connections' business processes.

Beech Acres (Jim Mason, personal communication, August 14, 2002) points to frequent director turnover, resulting in six different leaders in 3.5 years, as a key internal challenge. It further notes that the instability of leadership accentuated other internal challenges related to development of the information management system and other programmatic issues.

Staffing challenges also affected Creative Connections. Jim Mason, Beech Acres CEO, described the initial Creative Connections program design as "not a program for sissies" (personal communication, August 14, 2002), pointing to the extremely high level of needs of all children served, the clinical complexity of these children's problems, and the constant casework and case management demands associated with their care. The care managers primarily were young people with bachelor's degrees who each carried a small caseload of 9 to 10 children. When Creative Connections was initially established, it decided to hire a large number of staff, each of whom would carry a small caseload. Under the original program design, each care manager had a general caseload (that is, a single caseload may have been composed of children who were mentally retarded, were sexual offenders, had serious emotional disturbances, and were drug-addicted). The intense needs of all enrolled children had serious implications with regard to staff turnover. Crisis situations involving one or more children became part of each day's routine, and, as Jim Mason described the situation, staff were required to develop a "firefighter mentality" (personal communication, August 14, 2002).

The proposed new program approach would have addressed some of these issues. Beech Acres planned to develop a staffing pattern in which care coordinators would have different levels of skills and proficiency in wraparound planning and implementation. Each level—associate, practitioner, master, and mentor— would represent a higher level of expertise. Through orientation programs, training, and supervision, care coordinators would become proficient in wraparound philosophy and service delivery, including engaging children and families; assessing child, family, community, and personal strengths, risks, and barriers; facilitating child and family teams; enrolling community resources; using resources well; and using data to evaluate outcomes and processes to improve personal and system performance. Under the new approach, each care coordinator's caseload would be 8 to 10 children. The only exception would have been for care coordinators who solely provided monitoring when children were placed in hospital or residential settings and had no plan for stepping-down to community-based settings.

An important new aspect of Creative Connections that was proposed in the contract re-negotiations with Beech Acres, but that will not be implemented by the new contractor, was community outreach regarding wraparound services. Both Beech Acres and the Hamilton County agencies recognized that a wraparound system of care was likely to succeed only if the leadership and line staff of each subsystem serving children and families understood wraparound services and were committed to them. During the contract negotiations, Beech Acres proposed the development of a stakeholder enrollment program for all relevant community participants. This program would have developed a shared knowledge base and understanding of wraparound services, facilitated and enhanced commitment to the wraparound system, and created a community team that would work effectively in behalf of children and families. It would have included educational opportunities for key decisionmakers in each system, including administrators and direct line staff from each of the county agencies and from agencies in the provider network; parents, dedicated adults, families, and community supports; judges; guardians ad litem; and school representatives. The activities that Beech Acres proposed to engage stakeholders were an orientation to wraparound principles and tools; programs on the implementation, maintenance, and evaluation of the wraparound system and the strategic role of decisionmakers in successful wraparound systems; training on all aspects of child and family teams; and quarterly practice and learning sessions.

It appears that these new aspects of the program design, had they been implemented, would have resolved some of the more significant challenges associated with the original program. It became apparent that the initial decision to develop Creative Connections as a managed care program serving only children and youth with very high service needs undermined any meaningful possibility of financial stability. As Anthony Broskowski's (2001) analysis concluded, fiscal success was unlikely, given the carve out service population of children and youth who required very expensive care, the use of a fixed case rate for care, and the placement of Beech Acres, as lead agency, at full financial risk. Broskowski's assessment concluded that the original structure was "fatally flawed" from a fiscal perspective because Creative Connection only received the most expensive cases, and the case rate was not actuarially tied to the long-term expenditure pattern for this group of children. Referred children were "already locked into a pattern of service delivery based on very early and possibly ineffective clinical decisions" (Broskowski, 2001, p. 6), that is, the decision already had been made that children needed residential treatment at the time they were referred. Creative Connections was not able to use "one of the most potent tools of managed care, namely the ability to decide where the case begins to receive services" (Broskowski, 2001, p. 6), and the structure gave Creative Connections no incentive to reduce costs associated with an individual case, because a child successfully placed in a less restrictive, less expensive setting and then discharged was simply replaced with the case of another child who was likely to be more difficult and require more expensive services. As a result, Creative Connections, as originally designed, was at financial risk but had no opportunity to realize or retain savings. The new, proposed programmatic and fiscal approach, in which a mix of children with varying levels of service needs would be enrolled in Creative Connections and the fiscal methodology would involve both a case rate and fee-for-service, may have addressed many of these issues.

Broskowski (2001) also identified issues regarding the benchmarks used to evaluate the original program. He emphasized the need to develop benchmarks based on the experiences of other communities, with a particular focus on: (a) other communities' rates of residential placement based on all children in the community and on children currently being served, (b) average lengths of stay in residential settings, (c) other communities' success in preventing out-of-home placement, (d) lengths of service provision, and (d) other communities' practices regarding transferring children from unsuccessful treatment providers to providers with better track records. Although the proposed approach did not specifically reference cross-community analysis and comparison, it may have provided the basis for a stronger, more appropriate program evaluation by delineating different benchmarks for children enrolled in the two service tracks.

Lessons Learned

With regard to the recommendations that might flow from the experience of Beech Acres in developing and implementing Creative Connections, the agency advances the following:

- The development and implementation of programs such as Creative Connections are not for the faint of heart. Changing complex service delivery systems, particularly when multiple systems are involved, is a major undertaking. In general, systems are averse to change and resist major redesign. Efforts to change a traditional child welfare, mental health, or juvenile justice model of service delivery to a community-based wraparound system represent major redesigns. A new program must overcome institutional resistance, and it must be able to provide traditional services while simultaneously developing new types of services that will ultimately take the place of traditional services.

- The commitment of top leadership in both the public and private sectors is critical for this type of initiative, both in initiating the effort and sustaining it. It is noteworthy that in 2002, when the contract for Creative Connections was being renegotiated, none of the five Hamilton County agencies were directed by the individuals who headed them in 1998, when Creative Connections was created.

- In any new privatized initiative, the public agencies contracting for services and the private lead agency should have a shared vision of the program. The public and private sectors should agree on the principles that will guide the program and the ways communication will take place. They should have face-to-face dialogue about what will be done, how the program will operate, and the roles and responsibilities of each party.

- At the outset, it is extremely difficult to accurately predict what it will cost to provide services through a new service delivery model. In most instances, public agencies do not have cost data that permit reliable estimates of actual costs. As a result, any financial data that is generated in the course of planning and/or implementing a new initiative should be used as a guide and not as factual. Like many other aspects of new service systems, the fiscal component should be treated as a hypothesis to be tested.

- It is essential that initiative clearly define the target population, both in relation to which children will be initially enrolled and which children will continue to be admitted. Particularly with risk-based contracts, it is financially and programmatically imperative to clearly understand the exact nature of the needs of the children to be served. At the same time, it is not recommended that a program serve only children with severe needs. Without a mix of children with a variety of needs, it is difficult from a managed care perspective to appropriately design and fiscally manage a program. At the same time, as Creative Connections learned, children with severe needs referred by multiple agencies are extremely diverse and require program staff to become expert in many practice areas. Staff must be competent to work successfully with children who are diagnosed as mentally retarded, are autistic, have serious emotional disturbance, or have conduct disorders. The program must define its population in such a way that staff can identify and develop a core set of professional competencies.

■ In developing Creative Connections, Beech Acres quickly became aware of the service gaps that existed in the community—a situation likely to be found in many other communities. Many of the proposed services could not be offered by existing providers. At the same time, Beech Acres encountered challenges in building a provider network that would offer services in a different way. Beech Acres found that many service providers were unwilling and, in some cases, unable to develop new service structures and technologies consistent with the philosophy and goals of Creative Connections. This experience is, in all likelihood, one that other communities may encounter.

■ In connection with the issue of provider network development, the experience of Beech Acres suggests that parties need to give attention to the relationship between no reject, no eject requirements that bind the lead agency, and the ability of the program's provider network to meet the needs of enrolled children. When a lead agency agrees to a no reject, no eject provision, it must have access to a provider network that offers a range of services that can appropriately meet the needs of each enrolled child. In the case of Creative Connections, the Hamilton County service system had a limited capacity to provide residential treatment services. As a result, Creative Connections found itself using expensive, geographically distant, out-of-county service providers for children it could not reject but for whom no local service was appropriate. The expenses associated with providing this care limited the program's ability to use its resources to build local residential treatment capacity.

- Any new initiative needs a high level of competence in process engineering. Expertise in designing and implementing new processes, including examining and revamping the paperwork processes, is critical.

- Finally, in light of its ultimate decision not to continue as lead agency for Creative Connections because of the county's fiscal mandates, Beech Acres (Jim Mason, personal communication, August 14, 2002) emphasizes that private agencies must recognize that fiscal considerations inevitably drive government decisionmaking. It is critical that private agencies acknowledge and assess the political and fiscal realities of undertaking significant systematic change in partnership with the public sector.

Wayne County, Michigan: The Foster Care Permanency Initiative

Michigan's child welfare department, the Family Independence Agency (FIA), began the Foster Care Permanency Initiative as a pilot project in 1997. The initiative had two goals: to reduce the amount of time to achieve permanency for children in foster care and to increase the percentage of children who achieve permanency. The initiative is based in Wayne County, Michigan, which includes Detroit and a few surrounding suburbs. The majority of children in foster care in Wayne County are from Detroit, the nation's 10th-largest city with a population of 961,000 in 2000, and are African American.

This case study examines the development of the initiative, its implementation over a five-year period, its strengths, and the challenges it experienced.[31] In October 2002, the initiative will assume the status of a permanent program, with 17 Wayne County agencies participating. Michigan plans to expand the initiative to additional areas of the state, including other urban settings and a group of rural counties. It is expected that variations of the initiative will eventually be implemented statewide.

The Changing Climate in Michigan

The public's desire to contain taxes, coupled with an increasingly conservative view of the role of social programs, led to change in government leadership in

---

[31] The sources for this case study are reports issued by the Michigan Family Independence Agency (FIA), the Child Welfare League of America Managed Care and Privatization Child Welfare Tracking Project (1998 and 2000), and interviews with Knud Hansen, Acting Director, Office of Audit Services, Michigan FIA; Lynn Nee, Departmental Manager of Program Development Unit, Michigan FIA; and Jim Gale, Vice President, Research and Development, Orchards Children's Services, Wayne County, Michigan.

Michigan in the 1990s. Michigan took a particularly active role in welfare reform compared with other states. The name of the DSS was changed to the Michigan FIA to convey to clients the agency's expectations of responsibility and independence. Responding to the taxpayers, the legislature demanded that all government-funded services, including foster care, comply with the increasingly repeated refrain, "do it faster, better, and cheaper." Michigan's legislature directed FIA to propose a new foster care system that based payment on performance outcomes. FIA had to complete this no later than December 1996 or January 1997. The legislature made clear that managed care principles, including capitated rates, would be desirable features of any proposal.

At the time of this mandate, FIA already had a successful history of performance-based payment in adoption services. FIA had instituted a graduated payment system for adoption services designed to produce desired outcomes within specific time frames—a system that, in effect, averaged the cost of service. According to FIA data, the performance-based adoption program increased the annual number of adoptions and decreased the number of children in foster care awaiting adoption. USDHHS (2002) found that the markedly higher rate of adoption of children in foster care in Michigan was associated with higher rates of adoption for children in older age ranges and higher rates of adoption for African American children.

After receiving the directive to create a foster care payment system tied to performance outcomes, FIA turned to the private sector, as it had with its performance-based adoption program. Reactions from the private sector varied considerably. Some individuals and agencies, as well as some FIA staff, were uncomfortable with changes in the foster care system and opposed the integration of managed care concepts and the foster care program. Others felt that change was inevitable and actively participated in efforts to develop a new approach. Long, intense discussions ensued with several agencies, but FIA and the private agencies were unable to reach an agreement regarding a redesign of the foster care system in a way that complied with legislative mandates.

The Creation of the Foster Care Permanency Initiative

Given the impasse on a broader redesign of the foster care system, one of the private foster care agencies in Wayne County, Orchards Children's Services, independently developed a proposal to provide foster care services.[32] Under the lead-

---

[32] Orchards Children's Services is the largest private provider of foster care services in Wayne County, serving approximately 20% of the foster care population. It was an active participant in the initial discussions regarding a redesign of foster care.

ership of its assistant executive director, Deborah Dinco (now the agency's executive director), it proposed a pay for performance contract. Gerald Miller, head of FIA, and representatives from the Department of Management and Budget were interested in the proposal and asked Orchards Children's Services to work with the Wayne County FIA, Office of Child and Family Services, to identify potential partners for a pilot project. Three private agencies, Catholic Social Services of Wayne County, Homes for Black Children, and Spectrum Human Services, joined Orchards Children's Services. As a result, a partnership of four private agencies (the "initiative agencies") and one public agency (Wayne County FIA) initiated the foster care pilot project. Wayne County FIA participated in the initiative in the role of payor and government overseer.[33]

Prior to the implementation of the Foster Care Permanency Initiative, Michigan had changed the status of private sector foster care agencies from subcontractors to vendors—a status change that had important implications for the development and implementation of the initiative. As vendors of foster care services, agencies in Michigan are expected to deliver an end product in exchange for fees paid, as would be expected of vendors that construct roads or deliver office supplies. In foster care services, the end product is outcomes that achieve permanency for children within a certain time frame. Implicit in this arrangement is the assumption that the vendor has the resources to deliver the agreed-on outcomes. Unlike services such as road building, however, foster care services are affected by a range of variables not within the control of the vendor: Agencies must defer to court decisions, which have final authority regarding outcomes for children in foster care; foster care agencies serve involuntary clients (birthparents), whose level of cooperation in achieving outcomes may be limited; and foster care agencies must rely on a limited number of foster families, whose skills and commitment levels may vary but who are an integral component of the system. Because so many factors were seen as outside the control of foster care agencies, the partnership of private agencies and the public agency rejected the use of capitated payments, a model common to managed care in the health care arena, as the fiscal methodology for the initiative. Instead, they agreed on a methodology that combined performance-based payments on achieving specified outcomes and a reduced per diem rate (the payment structure is described more fully later). The initial planning process did not include birthparents, foster parents, or representatives of the judicial system. The initiative later found failure to involve these stakeholders to be an error, particularly given the crucial role that the courts play

---

[33] The Family Independence Agency provides direct foster care services for 20% of the children in care in Wayne County, but did not participate in the pilot project in that role.

in determining how quickly children move through the foster care system. In future planning efforts, the initiative included a wider audience.

Unrelated to the initial development of the initiative but occurring simultaneously were major changes in FIA itself. A new FIA director was appointed, and FIA offered early retirement options to all state employees. These developments affected FIA because many seasoned employees left the department. This significantly affected the initiative because it was developed in an environment filled with stress and uncertainty.

The initiative has had three distinct phases since May 1997. Phase I began in May 1997 and involved the Wayne County FIA and the four private foster care agencies. Phase II, which began in April 2000, saw the addition of two private agencies and a shortening of the time frames for meeting permanency goals for children. A third phase began in October 2002. In Phase III, the FIA plans to implement the initiative countywide, and as of this writing is in the process of doing so.

Phase I

The Foster Care Permanency Initiative began operating on May 12, 1997, with two primary goals: (1) to shorten the time to permanency,[34] and (2) to increase the percentage of children and youth who achieve permanency. The pilot was built on several principles: All children who enter foster care have been traumatized to some extent, or they never would have required removal from their families, agencies must assess the individual needs of children and families and respond appropriately, and the provision of new and additional services to families early promotes engagement with parents and successful outcomes. The design of the pilot made clear that private agencies were to focus on outcomes rather than on the volume of children and families served.

In Phase I, the four private participating agencies entered into three-year contracts (renewed in April 2000 in Phase II for another three years). Under the contracts, FIA retained primary responsibility for all management functions. The private agencies assumed responsibility for the provision of all foster care services, which were to be individually tailored to meet the needs of children and families, and which were required to meet the goal of child-centered, family-focused permanency planning. Phase I proved challenging in many respects, including the development of payment systems, overcoming resistance to the initiative, staff turnover, and staff training.

---

[34] When the initiative began, the average length of foster care stay in Wayne County was 36 months.

Program Eligibility

From the inception of the initiative, children have been referred in three ways, depending on their ages and other demographic factors:

■ Youth ages 12 or younger are referred the Initiative through the Family Assignment System;

■ Youth ages 12 or younger who do not live in Wayne County may be referred to the initiative by the court; and

■ Youth ages 13 years and older who are siblings of youth who were referred to the initiative through the Family Assignment System.

In addition, under certain circumstances, such as when a shelter determines that a child could benefit from foster care services, youth older than 13 who are not siblings of youth assigned through the Family Assignment System may be served by the initiative. Regardless of the basis for the referral, agencies must accept all referred children and youth, that is, they have a no reject, no eject policy.[35]

As the eligibility criteria suggest, the referral of children and families is primarily through the Family Assignment System. That system has been in place in Wayne County since April 1, 1985. The Family Assignment System operates to assign all children (ages 0 to 19) who enter foster care in the county to private child-placing agencies. FIA developed the Family Assignment System to eliminate the need for interim placements of children in shelters and ensure appropriate allocations of referrals to all private agencies that hold foster care contracts with FIA (a total of 17 agencies in Wayne County). The Family Assignment System assigns families to participating agencies on a rotation basis, based on a calculation of the total number of available foster families who provide a general level of care among all participating agencies and the percentage each agency holds of the total available families. The following types of families are referred through the Family Assignment System:

■ Families whose children are 12 or younger and who are entering foster care for the first time. When families have children 13 or older, FIA assists with shelter arrangements for up to 30 days for the purpose of assessment.

---

[35] As has always been the policy with the family assessment system, initiative and noninitiative agencies have the right to refer children who require exceptional services (the most intensive level of services for children with the most severe emotional and physical needs) to four noninitiative agencies that provide specialized foster care services.

■ Families of children placed in residential shelters for assessment purposes when the facility has recommended general foster care.

In addition, if a child already in foster care requires a specialized foster care placement, the agency next on rotation may agree to place the child and receive credit for making a Family Assignment System placement. When siblings of children already in care come into care or families are referred who either had previous contact with an agency or are receiving other services from an agency, these cases generally are excluded from assignment on rotation and, instead, are referred to the agency that has the current or previously active case.

In the first year of the initiative, the private agencies served approximately 650 children—roughly 40% of the children in foster care in Wayne County that year. The percentage has remained consistent throughout the initiative. Following the first year of the initiative, it has served approximately 850 children in foster care annually.

Fiscal Methodology

The initiative is funded entirely with child welfare dollars, and the designers intended it to be cost neutral. The planners created the funding structure, however, to provide foster care agencies with flexibility to ensure that they provide appropriate and effective services. The principal aspect of this design was a reduction in the per-diem rate typically paid to foster care agencies and a reallocation of the resulting savings into lump sum incentive payments tied to performance goals.

The financial arrangements consist of a per-diem rate and three lump-sum payments—an initial referral payment, a performance standard payment, and a sustainment payment—that are paid at designated milestones in each case. In determining the initiative per diem, FIA first blended the rates paid to the four initiative agencies for specialized and general foster care prior to the new program, taking into account children's average length of stay in care and the average time frame for achieving specific goals, such as a return to birthfamily or termination of parental rights. It then increased that rate by 12% to help insure the financial solvency of each participating foster care agency and ease agencies' concerns about the financial effect of the new approach. FIA then allocated the funds into two components: a reduced per diem and a pool from which it would draw incentive payments. It set the initial per diem rate at $14.94, compared with a per diem of $16.96 for noninitiative agencies. The per diem applies for all children served by the initiative agencies. This approach represents a departure from previous practice, in which children received one of two rates based on an assessment of the level of need (general or specialized care) and received services based on the category to which they were assigned. Although the per diem is the same for all children, initiative agencies have maintained three levels of foster parent stipends—general, special, and exceptional—for room and board and clothing allowances, based on the assessed needs of children.

FIA created three types of incentive payments. The initial lump-sum payment, made at the time of referral and paid to the agency for each referral it receives, was $1,770. The second lump sum payment, the performance standard payment, was $1,500. FIA makes that incentive payment if one of the following occurs:

- A successful placement, defined as a return to the child's parent, placement with a relative or legal guardian, or independent living, is made within 315 days for a placement in Wayne County or 265 days if the case was from outside Wayne County, from the date the child's case was accepted (that is, the date the court accepted jurisdiction over the child's case by issuing its preliminary court order); or

- A court terminates parental rights within 600 days for Wayne County cases or 420 days for outside-county cases, from the date the child's case was accepted.

The plan used geographically based differences in time frames for the performance standard payment because it initially was assumed that better socioeconomic conditions outside Wayne County, among other factors, would permit permanency to be accomplished more quickly. The program eliminated the out-of-county distinction in Phase II, however, because few children fell into this category and the distinction created confusion in the processing of payments. The third lump sum incentive payment, called the sustainment payment, was $730. It is made when a child sustains a successful placement for at least six months or is placed for adoption within six months of the termination of parental rights. Under the payment methodology, if a child returns to foster care within one year of a "successful placement," the initiative agency is permitted to receive a second initial referral payment, a second performance standard payment, and the reduced per diem rate. The agency is not allowed, however, to receive a second sustainment payment for these children.

The Michigan legislature, in response to private foster care agencies' calls for higher levels of reimbursement, has periodically increased foster care rates for all initiative and noninitiative agencies, typically by 3%. For example, in November 1997, the initiative per diem rate was increased to $15.25. The legislature also

Table 49

Perdiem and Lump Sum Payment Structure for Phases I and II

	Noninitiative Per Diem	Initiative Per Diem	Referral Lump Sum	Performance Payment	Sustainment Payment
Phase I					
5/97	$16.96	$14.94	$1,770	$1,500 (315/600 days)	$730 (6 months)
11/97	$17.47	$15.25	$1,900	$1,585	$795
4/99			$1,990	$1,700	$930
1/00			$2,045	$1,745	$955
Phase II					
5/00		$13.20/ increased to $13.60 in 10/00	$2,150	$1,850 (290/515 days)	$1,250 (6 months; $1,550 (12 months)
2/01			$2,210	$1,900	$1,290/$1,600

periodically has increased the initiative incentive payments. The legislature increased payments five times between November 1997 and February 2001. Table 49 documents all payment rates and their chronologies (changes in Phase II are discussed more fully later).

Initiative agencies have faced challenges in connection with the new payment methodology, particularly in adapting their internal payment systems. Prior to the initiative, the agencies' sole funding was a per child, per diem rate, which simply required a determination of the number of children under the agency's responsibility each day. Under the new payment methodology, the agencies can process the per diem payments through their established payment procedures, but they are required also to submit specific payment requests for each incentive payment for each child. The new system requires an agency to report both the number of children in care each day and the status of each child in the permanency planning process.

The Service Delivery Model

The changes in fiscal methodology paralleled significant changes in the service delivery model. As indicated above, the initiative did not tie services to the category to which a child was assigned (general or specialized care). Initiative agencies had flexibility regarding the types of services that children received and the length of time that services could be provided. They were no longer subject to service requirements that applied outside the initiative, such as the requirement that all children in specialized foster care receive 50 minutes of weekly therapy.

The initiative contracts stipulated that agencies must provide certain services: case management, permanency planning with families, kinship care, family foster care, treatment foster care, family reunification, supported visitation, and foster parent mentoring. Other services were not mandatory but were to be provided, as appropriate. Services to parents could include, but were not limited to, home-maker services, budgeting, parenting skills, safe child behavior management tech-niques, substance abuse services, problem-solving skills development, anger management, job preparation, lifeskills development, counseling, and domestic violence. Services to children could include, but were not limited to, problem solving, lifeskills development, academic tutoring, self-protection techniques, and counseling.

The initiative also included postreunification services. Initiative contracts required private agencies to provide services following the return of children to their birthparents or following placement in the home of relatives. These services were directed toward reintegration of the child into the family and assurance of the child's safety in the home. In cases in which initiative agencies referred families to postreunification services, the contract required the agency to maintain case management responsibility to ensure that it delivered the services and coordinated them with other services. The FIA family reunification contract administrator had to approve the provision of post–family reunification services beyond a six-month period.

The service delivery model recognized that there would be cases in which a child could not be reunited with birthparents or relatives, and it would be determined that termination of parental rights was not contrary to the best interests of the child. In such cases, Initiative agencies had to assist FIA in petitioning the court for termination of parental rights and continue to provide needed services to the child and the family until the child was adopted.

The service delivery model also required that involvement of families in service planning, delivery, and evaluation. Families were to be involved in service delivery planning for their children, and case management activities were to focus on family members in addition to the identified child. The service delivery model also required frequent contact between case managers and families and parent-child visits at least every seven days.

The flexible funding approach has made it possible for initiative agencies to address some of the more significant barriers to reunification, including housing. For example, because many families, particularly those who receive Temporary Assistance to Needy Families benefits, lose income when their children enter care, they also lose their housing arrangements. Initiative agencies have been able to assign case aids to help parents locate housing and may use flexible funds to purchase furniture and major appliances or for rental assistance. Initiative agencies, such as Orchards Children's Services, also have developed programs to involve extended family members in the short-term care of children and have provided kin with needed resources, such as extra beds, so they can assume temporary responsibility for the care of their relative children. The flexible funding approach also has made it possible for initiative agencies to offer intensive postreunification services in the form of weekly visits that gradually decrease as the families become well connected with the community.

The new service delivery model has led to significant staffing changes at initiative agencies. Orchards Children's Services, for example, has reduced the number of clinical staff at the agency and has begun to use the services of community mental health agencies when children require mental health services. It also has increased the number of case managers and case aides to do the legwork, such as exploring housing opportunities for families, thereby freeing case managers to focus on case management services.

Performance Standards

The initiative contract for Phase I only specified performance standards related to events that establish agencies' eligibility for the performance standard payment (a successful placement or termination of parental rights within the specified time periods) and the sustainment payment (sustaining a successful placement for at least six months or placement for adoption within six months of termination of parental rights). The contract stipulated that these performance standards would be achieved for 80% of the children and families accepted for services and, therefore, for whom the agency would earn incentive payments. Although the initiative agencies made strides in implementing the program during Phase I, some of the smaller agencies struggled with tracking program outcomes, an issue that FIA and the agencies attempted to address more fully in Phase II.

Phase II

Phase II began on April 1, 2000, when the contracts with the original initiative agencies were renewed for three years (until March 31, 2003) and two additional agencies (Lutheran Child and Family Services and Judson Center) were selected for participation, bringing the total initiative agencies to six. The RFP process elicited proposals from five agencies, in which they described how they would modify their services to conform to the initiative model.

In Phase II, based on the agencies' experiences during Phase I, the contract modified the performance standards on which the payment structure was based. The time frame from initial placement to termination of parental rights was reduced from 600 days to 515 days (approximately 17 months) for all referred children. The standard for achieving a successful placement was reduced from 315 days to 290 days. In both instances, the experiences of agencies during Phase I indicated that the "best guess" time periods that were used initially could be reduced. The standard for the time frame from termination of parental rights to adoption was increased from six to seven months to make the standard consistent with the performance payment system used in the state's adoption program.

The payment structure was modified in May 2000. The structure reduced the per diem rate to $13.20 ($2.05 less per day) and increased the incentive payments again. The new structure increased the initial referral payment to $2,150 and the performance standard payment to $1,850. In addition, it redesigned the final sustainment payment to be paid at two intervals. Under the redesign, $1,250 was paid at the original 6-month follow-up period and a second installment of $1,550 was paid at 12 months. The redesign reflected a desire to sweeten the financial rewards for achieving the shortened time frames established at the beginning of Phase II and offer further support for a focus on children's stability. In October 2000, the new structure raised initiative per diem from $13.20 to $13.60. In February 2001, it increased the incentive payments yet again. As of this writing, the initial referral payment is $2,210, the performance standard payment is $1,900, the 6-month sustainment payment is $1,290, and the 12-month sustainment payment is $1,600.

In addition, Phase II offered agencies an incentive payment of $40 per child if a child remained in the same school that he or she attended immediately preceding placement until the end of the school year or case closure, whichever occurred later. Agencies could qualify for the incentive payment, however, if the "same school" goal could not be achieved because of the child's progression due to age and class advancement, redistricting of the school area, school closure, or a school's decision to move the child to another location to address the child's special needs. Agencies rarely have sought the educational incentive payment, because in most cases, children are placed with foster families who live in different communities than the children's birthfamilies, and the Family Assessment System does not take home address into account in assigning families to agencies on a rotating basis. FIA has indicated that it may develop a more substantial incentive payment of $500 to promote agencies' efforts to maintain children in their original schools. The effectiveness of a larger incentive payment, however, is questionable, given the current system of assigning families to agencies.

Phase II increased the age limit for referral to the initiative from 12 years (unless an exception applied) to 18 years of age. Under the original program design, the system referred children ages 12 and younger to initiative agencies and placed them immediately with foster families, and generally placed children 13 and older in a shelter for assessment, with the goal of placing them with foster families at a later time as appropriate. It was determined, however, that the system was not placing many youth ages 13 and older with foster families, and they were remaining in congregate care. Phase II changes in the initiative assigned children ages 13 to 18 differently. They are referred through the Family Assignment System both to a shelter for assessment and to an initiative agency for placement with a foster family. Under the new process, agencies are required to place a teen with a foster family, a parent, a relative, or a legal guardian within 30 days of the child's acceptance.

Agencies that achieve the 30-day placement goal for youth ages 13 and older are eligible for an incentive payment of $1,000. Agencies may provide the foster parents of these youth with a portion of or the entire incentive payment. The program pays a second incentive payment of $1,000 if the youth remains in a family-based setting (a nonresidential care placement) for six months. The initiative agencies, however, have struggled to recruit and retain foster families for youth. One approach being explored is an additional higher level of payment for foster families (beyond the current "exceptional" level of care) who accept teenagers or children with multiple problems. To date, FIA has not supported this approach.

Phase II saw two new programmatic features incorporated into the initiative: a focus on building a strong team effort between FIA and the initiative agencies, and the expansion of supportive services as part of the array of provided services. As Phase II of the initiative was developed, the initial initiative agencies expressed considerable anxiety about the planned changes in the time frames for achieving the specified goals. FIA and the agencies began to meet on a regular basis to address these concerns. At the same time, the agencies expressed a need for a formal process through which the they could exchange information about their approaches to developing components that the initiative required, such as appropriate staffing levels, billing systems, and information management technology. Although Phase I planning had included regular meetings, they had not consistently taken place.

In Phase II, FIA and the six initiative agencies began to hold monthly administrative meetings. The meetings have rotated from agency to agency, and the groups invite providers of supportive services. Generally, 30 to 40 individuals attend each meeting. The format is that of an open forum with a pre-established agenda, which often includes issues related to payment and service provision. If the agenda includes significant policy issues, the group invites Jim Beougher, director of Child and Family Administration at FIA, to attend. In addition to the monthly administrative meetings, participants also arrange regular monthly meetings to address issues associated with the Family Assignment System. Most recently, these meetings have focused on the implementation of Phase III of the initiative.

The second key feature of Phase II was a broader inclusion of supportive services to more effectively meet the needs of children and their families, an effort funded with state and federal child welfare dollars. In Phase II, FIA entered into contracts with service providers to provide three categories of services: supported visitation, assisted care, and intensive family reunification services. In supported visitation, trained social workers attend visits between birthparents and their children, often in the homes of birthparents, and assist birthparents in structuring and maximizing the benefits of visits with their children. FIA entered into a contract with PACT (Parents and Children Together) at Wayne State University to provide supportive visitation for families served by initiative agencies. Phase II also incorporated assisted care services for all difficulty-of-care levels. A trained professional provides assisted care to a foster family for up to 20 hours per week. Assisted care consists of respite care or mentoring services for foster parents who are struggling to maintain the child's placement. Finally, FIA entered into separate contracts with the Judson Center and Orchards Children's Services to provide intensive home-based services for families successfully reunified with their children. These services are provided for four to six months by a master's level professional social worker and two case associates, who together carry a caseload of 12 families. Supportive visitation, assisted care, and intensive home-based services have greatly enriched the resources available to initiative agencies that are striving to provide quality services and meet performance goals. These services, however, add substantially to the overall cost of the initiative, raising the question of whether the effort can continue to be viewed as cost neutral, as originally intended.

Outcomes and Quality Requirements

In the contracts for the Foster Care Permanency Initiative, FIA specified quality requirements and outcome performance measurements in a number of areas, including:

- system performance indicators related to program effectiveness,

- performance indicators related to cost,

- criteria related to access and availability of services and utilization patterns,

- criteria related to appropriateness of services,

- outcomes related to child functioning,

- outcomes related to achievement of permanency planning goals, and

- requirements that initiative agencies adhere to professional standards and licensing requirements.

As an example of specific criteria related to access and availability of services, initiative contracts require that parental visits with children by parents or legal guardians occur within seven days of the children's assignment to the agency. As an example of specific criteria regarding appropriate services, initiative contracts required that supported visitation occur twice a week when children are younger than 5. To promote child functioning, the contracts for the initiative direct agencies to work to maintain children in the same school. Finally, as an example of both service appropriateness and access and availability criteria, the contracts require agencies to remain responsible for one year following a child's discharge from foster care and to resume services for the child if he or she returns to foster care during that time period.

Data indicate that the initiative agencies successfully achieved performance outcomes related to timely achievement of permanency. In Phase I, the average number of days from case acceptance to placement for the four initiative agencies was 133 days, substantially below the outside time limits of 315 days for Wayne County and 265 days for out-of-county children. During the first part of Phase II, April 2000 through December 2001, they reduced the average even further, to 74 days. They also reduced the average number of days from case acceptance to termination of parental rights from 272 days in Phase I (again substantially below the outside time limits of 600 days for Wayne County and 420 days for out-of-county children) to 211 days in the first part of Phase II.

Between April 1997 and March 2001, the initiative served 2,589 children. Of those children, 1,283 children were reunified, either with a parent (43%) or a relative (57%). The agencies reunified great majority of these children (83%) within the required time frames. In addition, the agencies freed 656 children for adoption, 81% within required time frames. Agencies placed three children in independent living, two of whom achieved this goal within required time frames. As of March 2001, for the remaining 647 children, the permanency outcome was pending, and 83% were still within the allotted time frames.

The initiative has not affected the percentages of children who historically have been reunified, placed with relatives, or adopted, but it has expedited the achievement of these goals. Although the significant addition of services for birth-families in Phase II may increase the percentage of children who return home, the percentage of children who reunify (50%) has remained relatively constant over time and is comparable to Wayne County data prior to the initiative.

A critical aspect of outcome achievement is each agency's ability to track children's cases individually, report on the status of each child, and qualify for each incentive payment, thereby remaining financially solvent. In July 2002, Orchards Children's Services, for example, tracked the status of 440 children. To ensure the careful monitoring of the progress of each child, the agency implemented a procedure in which agency staff meet weekly to review progress and resolve problems that prevent children from moving from foster care to permanency at an appropriate pace. Experienced administrators work directly with less experienced junior caseworkers, melding the overall administrative vision with individual casework. Not only has this procedure proved extremely useful in tracking children and ensuring progress in line with requirements for incentive payments, it has given administrators the opportunity to learn directly about the barriers to reunification and other permanency options and evaluate the need for administrative changes to address key barriers.[36]

Third-Party Evaluation

In June 2001, FIA commissioned William Meezan, of the University of Michigan School of Social Work, to conduct a third-party evaluation of the initiative. Under the study design, he will study the performance of the six initiative agencies and compare them with three noninitiative agencies. The study, to be completed in June 2003, will sample children from each agency and examine child and family demographics, services, and outcomes. The agencies are fully participating in development of the study, and they meet twice a month to discuss evaluation issues. Among the questions that the evaluation will attempt to answer are:

- How does the shift to an incentive-based, managed care approach affect how services are provided to children and families?

- What organizational accommodations have the initiative agencies made to shift to a new service delivery and payment system?

---

[36] Interestingly, the tracking systems that initiative agencies have implemented also have affected casework. For example, Orchards Children's Services closely monitors the services and goods provided to each family. If a family receives a refrigerator, for instance, the agency documents receipt. If the family returns to the agency for services and no longer has the refrigerator, the agency uses that information in assessing the stability of the family.

- What is the effect of a shift to an incentive-based, managed care system on the internal functioning of the initiative agencies and the ways they provide services?

- Do children served by initiative agencies have better outputs (defined as the number of children who achieve specified outcomes) than children served by other foster care agencies in Wayne County?

- What factors are associated with better outputs for children served by initiative agencies?

- What factors are associated with better outputs for children served by noninitiative agencies?

- Do children and families served by the pilot nonprofit agencies have better outcomes than children and families served either by other nonprofit child welfare agencies in Wayne County?

- What factors are associated with better outcomes for children and families served by initiative agencies?

- What factors are associated with better outcomes for children and families served by noninitiative agencies?

Phase III

Administrators planned extensively to implement the initiative county-wide effective October 2002.[37] With county-wide implementation in Phase III, the number of initiative agencies will increase from 6 to 17. Program enhancements will occur in four key areas: (1) more comprehensive, ongoing training involving private agencies at all levels, from boards of directors to front-line staff; (2) more extensive training for other stakeholders, such as FIA staff and family court judges, to ensure their understanding of all aspects of the initiative; (3) more effective and efficient data collection; and (4) more efficient processing of incentive payments, which is currently manual. As in the past, FIA will not participate in the initiative as a service provider, given its role of payor. Some advocates, however, have chal-

---

[37] The Family Independence Agency also is involved in a planning process to develop a pilot project to expand the initiative to other geographical areas of the state, including rural counties and other urban settings. The long-term plan is to implement variations of the initiative statewide.

lenged FIA to meet the same outcomes it requires initiative agencies to meet for the children and families that FIA serves directly.

Of relevance to the county-wide implementation of the initiative is Wayne County's interest in developing a foster care assignment system based on geographic catchment areas. The development of such a system, which would allow foster care agencies to provide neighborhood-based foster care, would have important implications for the initiative. As the following discussion suggests, however, this type of change is not easily implemented.

Since 1999, a planning process has been in place to develop and implement a foster care geographic assignment process in Wayne County. FIA and the private agencies that receive referrals through the Family Assignment System have had numerous discussions regarding such an approach. During fall 2000 and winter 2001, data availability problems and the restructuring of the Wayne County FIA stymied discussions. In September 2001, however, the planning group developed a geographic assessment model that both FIA and Wayne County private foster care agencies subsequently approved. Despite the ostensible agreement, however, the implementation of the system has been postponed. This situation appears to be the result of ongoing concerns on the part of the private foster care agencies that families' housing instability and frequent moves make a geographic assignment system impractical.

As of this writing, some people are interested in supporting a gradual move toward geographic assignment in line with an initiative that has been implemented in Detroit. The Family to Family Initiative, developed by the Annie E. Casey Foundation, supports communities in providing neighborhood-based foster care to increase the number and quality of foster families, reducing reliance on institutional or congregate care, and improving resources in the communities from which children in foster care come. It is anticipated that over time, the Family Assignment System will be modified to assign families to private foster care agencies based on geographic location. When this new system is implemented, it will have a significant effect on the initiative as it becomes a countywide permanent program in Phase III.

Overall Assessment of the Initiative

Assessments of the Foster Care Permanency Initiative suggest that the extent to which success has been achieved is related to several factors:

- a data system that produces accurate and consistent data for evaluation;

- sufficient monitoring and technical assistance to quickly resolve problems;

- clearly defined, effective services delivered at strategic points so that agencies are able to reach specified outcomes within required time frames; and

- investment of significant time on the part of the public and private agencies to develop solid working relationships and effective communication.

It is evident that the Foster Care Permanency Initiative is the product of significant planning and careful crafting of fiscal methodology. The goals of the initiative are clear, outcomes are meaningful, performance targets are specific and based on data and program experience, and the payment methodology has allowed agencies to achieve significant changes while remaining financially solvent.

Among the key features of the initiative that have promoted its success are the use of a pilot project to test the cost and service assumptions, with a gradual expansion of the program over an extended time; the public agency's willingness to revise programmatic elements and payment levels based on data and program experience; regular meetings between FIA and the agencies to resolve programmatic and fiscal issues; and a focus on fiscal incentives, rather than fiscal penalties, that are expressly tied to outcome achievement.

Two areas where FIA and initiative agencies continue to strive for greater success are keeping children geographically closer to their birthfamilies when they enter foster care and placing teens with foster families rather than congregate care settings. A number of solutions have been considered, such as increasing the incentive payment from the current ineffectual $40 to a more substantial $500 when children stay in the same school they attended while living with their birthparents. These two issues continue to need attention in Phase III.

As indicated earlier, the Foster Care Permanency Initiative is an incentive-based model in which penalties are not assessed against agencies that do not perform well—a feature that may be viewed a strong element in its success. Poor performance in this model, nonetheless, has significant financial consequences for initiative agencies. Because they have agreed to accept a significantly reduced per diem rate, the agencies must have systems in place to ensure that they qualify for all incentive payments. The payment system also requires that agencies set aside funds to serve the inevitable number of families whose children will reenter foster care and for whom agencies will not be able to qualify for certain incentive payments.

Although no initiative agency has filed for bankruptcy, the payment system has caused fiscal problems for some agencies, particularly smaller agencies that are working to establish effective tracking and payment processing systems, both of which are essential to effective agency performance. Agencies such as Orchards Children's Services, however, have developed successful approaches in these areas. Orchards Children's Services created a trigger system that sounds an alert after a child has been in foster care for a certain number of days. The alert signals that any barriers to permanency must be addressed immediately so that the child can be reunified or the agency can move to terminate parental rights within the required time frames.

As the initiative becomes a countywide, permanent program in Phase III, FIA and the private agencies anticipate new challenges. They expect the strengths of the initiative, as developed through the pilot phase, however, to provide a solid foundation for the program.

Maine: The Community Intervention Program

In 1998, Maine developed the Community Intervention Program (CIP) to provide assessment and intervention services to families at low to moderate risk for child abuse and neglect. The Maine Department of Human Services contracted with seven private agencies across the state to provide front-end child welfare services to families reported for child maltreatment, a function ordinarily performed by government agencies. This case study examines the development and implementation of CIP and the issues that the program currently faces.[38]

CIP generally has met its goal of making in-person contacts with families at low to moderate risk of child abuse and neglect and offering services to these families. After four years of operation, however, CIP's intent and focus are changing, as administrators make plans for state child protective service workers to resume responsibility for safety assessments on all reported families, including the families at low to moderate risk who have been served through CIP. Under this plan, the function of CIP agencies would shift from safety assessment to casework services for referred families.

The Creation of CIP

As an initial step in the implementation of the federal Family Preservation and Family Support Program, created legislatively in 1993 and implemented in Maine beginning in August 1994, the Maine Bureau of Children and Family Services, a

---

[38] The sources for this case study are reports issued by Maine and Families United and interviews with Chris Beerits, Deputy Director, Bureau of Child and Family Services; Lee Hodgin, Assistant Deputy Director, Bureau of Child and Family Services; Michael Norton, Director of Public and Legislative Affairs, Bureau of Child and Family Services; and Kim Day, Program Director, Families United.

233

division of the Maine Department of Human Services (DHS) convened an advisory board to make recommendations to DHS regarding community-based services for families and children. The Family Preservation and Family Support Services Advisory Board was composed of a broad representation of federal, state, and community stakeholders.[39] The advisory group's mission statement was relevant to later efforts to develop CIP:

> To promote community-based efforts to enhance the ability
> of all families to create stable, safe, and nurturing environ-
> ments that promote healthy child development and family
> self-sufficiency through services developed in partnership with
> families and built on family strengths. (Maine Department of
> Human Services, 1998, p. 4)

During the same period that the advisory group met, the Bureau of Children and Family Services conducted a needs assessment as part of its development of the state's FY 1995-1996 plan for child welfare services. The assessment focused, in part, on families who were appropriately referred to child protective services but who were not assessed and served. In 1994, approximately 38% of referrals that met the criteria for child protective services assessment were not assigned for assessment because of limited staff resources. The state plan identified this population as the target for the Family Preservation and Family Support initiative. In 1996, three agencies, Community Concepts, Waldo County Preschool & Family Services, and Youth and Family Services, received contracts to provide services to families in three counties who were at risk for child abuse and neglect. It was anticipated that the government would offer similar services across the state over the next five years.

Legislators and high-level administrators of DHS again noted the large number of unassigned child protective services intake reports in early 1998. At that time, there were more than 3,700 reports of child abuse and neglect that had not been assigned because of the limited number of state child protective services staff

---

[39] The participants included representatives of key state agencies and departments, the Council of Churches, the Maine Foster Parent Association, the Child Welfare Training Institute, consumers and parents, Family Crisis Services, the Native American community, legislators, Head Start, community action programs, the courts, the Juvenile Justice Advisory Committee, the Maine Children's Alliance, providers of services to children and families, group homes, the Maine State Housing Authority, child care and homemaker service providers, the Maine Association of Mental Health Services, Cooperative Extension, the Coalition for the Homeless, Child Abuse and Neglect Councils, the United Way, and the Administration for Children and Families.

focused on cases that presented a high risk of harm to children. It was clear that the public child welfare agency lacked sufficient staff to investigate and assess all reports of child abuse and neglect, but DHS decided not to expand the government provision of these services through hiring additional staff. It opted, instead, to contract out these services with private agencies, the first such decision by DHS to partner with community-based agencies. The contracts with Community Concepts, Waldo County Preschool & Family Services, and Youth and Family Services provided some precedent for this approach. The service design as envisioned by DHS, however, differed from the earlier program because it included initial safety assessment services.[40]

Originally called the Community Integration Program, planners created what became known as CIP very quickly. In less than one year, the project moved from conceptualization to implementation. The planning process involved the Commissioner of DHS and senior staff of the Bureau of Child and Family Services. DHS requested proposals to provide CIP services from agencies in the 13 counties of the state, with the intent of selecting a service provider for each of the eight local service regions into which the counties were organized. In the spring and summer of 1998, DHS published a notice of the services sought, held a bidders' conference, and solicited letters of intent from bidders. Bidders submitted 32 proposals, and the department awarded contracts to seven agencies. In six of the eight regions, CIP began operating in November 1998 under contracts held by Community Concepts, Families United, Home Counselors, Waldo County Preschool & Family Services, Youth Alternatives of Cumberland County, and Youth & Family Services. In the remaining two regions, CIP began operating in January 1999 under contracts held by Youth Alternatives of York County and Home Counselors. None of the selected agencies had experience in providing child protective services prior to the award of the CIP contracts.

CIP Operation

CIP has operated through one-year contracts with seven private agencies since its inception. It provides assessment services for families at low to moderate risk of child abuse and neglect and provides ongoing services to families for a period of six months if families agree to receive services.

---

[40] Community Concepts, Waldo County Preschool & Family Services, and Youth and Family Services eventually provided safety assessments when they were incorporated into the Community Intervention Program in 1998.

Eligible Families

Three groups of families are eligible for CIP services, although the focus has been primarily on the first group:

1. Families for whom child protection reports have been made and for whom DHS has determined there is a low to moderate risk of child maltreatment. In these cases, a regional supervisor for DHS, the agency that receives all reports of suspected child abuse and neglect, assesses whether the risk of harm to a child in the family is low, moderate, or high, based on information obtained in the telephone intake call and any past contact with the family. DHS refers cases assessed to be of low to moderate risk to the CIP agencies without making in-person contact. DHS investigates and assesses all other reports of child maltreatment.

2. Families who have an open child protective services case, who have a DHS case plan in effect, for whom risk to children in the household has been substantially reduced, and who are cooperating with DHS in completing the case plan.

3. Families who have been the subject of a child maltreatment report, for whom a safety assessment has been completed, and who request follow-up services.

For the first group of families, CIP agencies conduct assessments and provide short-term case management for up to six months.

Cases referred to CIP agencies are opened on the first day following the agency's home visit with a family that agrees to work with the agency. Referred families' cases are closed if: (a) the family is determined to have a high likelihood of repeated abuse or neglect and in consultation with DHS staff, the severity of potential abuse or neglect is determined to be high (in which case, DHS assumes responsibility for the case); (b) during or after the initial assessment, it is determined that there are no child safety concerns that warrant intervention; (c) the client terminates the relationship; (d) the agency terminates the relationship because the family does not wish to receive services or is unwilling to address child safety concerns; (e) services have been successfully completed; or (f) the family relocates to another agency's service area within the state.

Coordination Between DHS and CIP Agencies Regarding High-Risk Cases

When the CIP agency determines that a family referred to the program as presenting low to moderate risk actually presents a higher level of risk, it refers the case to DHS. As mandated reporters, CIP agencies report to DHS any information that could be reasonably interpreted as indicative of an increase in the risk of harm to the children in the home, such as a new injury, disclosure by children of additional types of maltreatment not previously known, and new or escalated behaviors by parents that pose additional risk. Agencies first discuss all reports with the designated DHS district child protective services supervisor. The DHS district administrator is charged with ensuring a response to CIP agency reports at all times and with developing a dispute resolution process to resolve disagreements between the CIP agency and DHS regarding the level of harm presented in any case.

The CIP agencies and DHS have developed specific protocols regarding agency reports. First, if the DHS child protective services supervisor determines that the information provided by the agency does not elevate the risk level to high, the report is noted and no further action is taken. If the CIP agency disagrees with this decision, it may use the district's dispute resolution process. Second, if the reported situation meets the criteria for a new incident,[41] the DHS child protective services supervisor instructs the CIP staff to call central intake and make a report. Third, if the reported information does not meet the criteria for a new incident, but in the opinion of the DHS child protective services supervisor, the family should be assigned for assessment, the new information is noted in the narrative log of the existing report (at that point considered a closed report) and the report may be reopened by DHS.

The CIP Service Model

The services provided by CIP agencies respond to the two goals listed as performance criteria in the CIP contracts: (1) Children at risk of abuse and/or neglect and their families will receive needed services appropriate to their level of risk; and (2) communities in Maine will provide collaborative, coordinated service delivery systems that meet the needs of families.

---

[41] The criteria for a new incident are that the incident involves a different type of abuse or neglect than the maltreatment in the current case, new allegations of physical or sexual abuse of any child exist, new allegations of any type of abuse or neglect by an abuser other than the abuser named in the current case exist, or new allegations of neglect exist that fall in the moderate to severe range.

CIP agencies do not provide the range of casework services associated with traditional child protective services. They are not authorized to substantiate reports of child abuse or neglect or initiate court action in behalf of a child determined to be maltreated. They do not have statutory authority to obtain the type of information that DHS may obtain in the course of its investigations or to access information from the mental health system. The agencies cannot issue investigatory subpoenas or obtain criminal history information, and they cannot interview a child without prior parental notification and consent. Should it be determined that the case requires such investigatory mechanisms, a DHS caseworker handles the case.

Under the CIP contracts, agencies must have telephone contact with families within 48 hours of referral (a requirement that was subsequently modified, as discussed later). They must make face-to-face contact with families within seven days of the DHS referral, assess each family's strengths and vulnerabilities using an assessment instrument developed by the Maine DHS/Bureau of Child and Family Services, and develop a case plan jointly with the family. The time frames for contact reflect the program's emphasis on expeditious contact with families. With regard to case plan development, the early CIP contracts did not specify the time frame. Initially, however, the expectation was that the case plan would be developed within 15 days of case opening, an expectation that proved unrealistic. In 2000, the Bureau of Child and Family Services revised the contracts to include a time frame within which case plans are to be developed with families, with a time period of 30 days from case opening specified. In addition, the contract requires CIP agencies to hold review meetings with each family and with all service providers every 90 days to mobilize community support and develop collaborative efforts in behalf of families.

The agencies provide direct services to families and coordinate services through other resources for families who voluntarily opt to work with the agency. It is estimated that CIP agencies typically spend 25% of their service delivery time providing direct services and 75% of their service delivery time coordinating services with other providers. None of the CIP contracts state the specific services that CIP agencies are to provide or that families may expect on accepting services. Nonetheless, typical services in families' case plans include counseling, parent education, and substance abuse treatment. As the contracts make explicit, the focus of all services—including assessment, case planning, and case management—must be directly related to addressing child abuse and neglect and its underlying causes. Although some ancillary issues may be addressed in a limited manner to engage the family, evidence must exist that the primary thrust of the work relates to child safety and prevention of maltreatment. CIP caseloads are to be 18 to 20 cases per caseworker.[42]

One express requirement of the CIP service delivery model is that cases are to be closed within six months. All ongoing services are provided by other community resources. Although not expressly stated in the contracts, CIP agencies are not permitted to place families on waiting lists for CIP services. The limitation of six months for service provision to families is based on a desire to ensure that all families who are referred can receive services and that no families are required to wait for services because CIP staff are providing longer term services for current clients.

The DHS–CIP Agency Working Relationship

CIP agencies must report routine information regarding cases to the DHS district office every two weeks. They provide information on new cases; cases that are closed, including the reasons for closure;[43] and service provision on all open cases. CIP agencies must also complete a standardized family assessment worksheet on each family, document all services that are provided, and report this information to DHS.

Each DHS district has a liaison (usually the program administrator) who identifies CIP implementation issues and other problems that routinely arise in connection with the program. The liaison works with the agency to resolve these issues. As an example, over the course of CIP implementation, DHS district office administrative support for the program was a critical need. One area in which effective communication between DHS and the CIP agencies proved vital was in locating and maintaining contact with referred families.[44] CIP agencies often face considerable challenges in obtaining information on families because of confi-

---

[42] The Child Welfare League of America's *Standards of Excellence for Services to Strengthen and Support Families with Children* (1989) set the maximum caseload at 15 families.

[43] Community Intervention Program (CIP) agencies must send closing notices to the Department of Human Services on the day the case is closed. Within a week of case closure, they must send closing summaries that describe the issues related to child abuse and neglect that the CIP agency addressed.

[44] Locating and maintaining contact with families is a particular challenge for the Community Intervention Program (CIP) because the population of families that the program serves tends to move frequently. The mobility of referred families affects the quality of services that can be provided and causes administrative stresses as cases are opened and closed and then reopened as families relocate to other regions. The challenges are particularly great for CIP agencies that hold contracts for smaller geographic areas.

dentiality issues and the fact that the agencies themselves do not all use the same information management system. In response to information needs, each DHS district office has a clerk to provide the CIP agencies with needed information on families, obtain information that the agencies require from other states regarding families they are serving, and assist CIP agencies in locating families through other government records. Some districts and CIP agencies have developed better working relationships than others in this regard, reflecting the effect of interpersonal relationships on the implementation of new public-private initiatives.

Every four to six weeks, meetings take place between the staff of CIP agencies and DHS, including a high-level representative from the Bureau of Child and Family Services, who attends as a liaison, and representatives from the DHS Quality Assurance and Finance divisions, as needed. Although the meetings began at the inception of CIP, it was only over time that CIP and DHS representatives became a cohesive group who viewed their efforts as collaborative.

Recent Changes in CIP

CIP has been subject to criticism, particularly in the form of negative press reports. The principal complaint has been that the agencies do not make face-to-face contacts with referred families to assess the safety risks to children. In 2001, DHS instituted a number of changes in an attempt to respond to this concern. Effective October 2001, DHS changed CIP contracts so that agencies are no longer required to attempt a telephone or written contact before making the initial home visit. In addition, DHS required agencies to document all in-person contacts with referred families, send letters to families who refuse an initial CIP visit to encourage them to accept services, and attempt a home visit again after these letters are sent.

Effective October 2001, DHS program administrators at the district level began to hold monthly meetings, in addition to the larger group meetings described earlier, with the individual CIP agencies to identify and resolve any barriers to in-person contact with referred families. These meetings have proven highly useful to the CIP agencies and DHS. Although initially the meetings focused more on work processes, they have become a mechanism for reviewing cases and new information about families, improving practice, and resolving CIP agencies' concerns about specific program issues. Importantly, the meetings have provided the basis for building strong working relationships between DHS and CIP staff at the district level.

Key Challenges

Administrative coordination, access to other community-based services, staffing, and staff training have posed significant challenges for CIP. Coordination and service problems have arisen principally in relation to the referral and reporting processes. As these problems have been identified, however, DHS and CIP agencies have worked together to develop solutions. Initially, for example, DHS simply transferred the cases of families whom DHS had directly served (and for whom the safety risks had been reduced substantially) to CIP through written referrals. Families expressed discomfort with this referral method, and in its place, a process was developed in which a DHS caseworker facilitates the initial introductory meeting between the CIP agency staff and the family. In an administrative area, it became apparent that DHS was faxing new referrals to the CIP agency and that no system was in place to verify the CIP agency's actual receipt of the referrals. The program resolved this issue through a process by which DHS generates a monthly list of all referred cases that the CIP agency can review against its own list of newly referred cases.

CIP agencies also have faced difficulty obtaining services for their clients on a priority basis. CIP families frequently require transportation, housing services, homemaker assistance, and home-based counseling services, but unlike DHS clients, they do not have priority on waiting lists for these services as they are not considered to be at risk of losing their children. In some instances, CIP agencies have been able to obtain services such as housing when they are underutilized by DHS. In many instances, however, CIP clients are wait-listed, a problem accentuated by the six-month limitation on CIP services. This issue has not been readily resolved because many needed resources continue to be quite limited.

Caseworker turnover presents particular challenges for many CIP agencies. Some CIP agencies have resorted to nationwide searches for experienced staff and still have staffing shortages that make it extremely difficult to ensure that all referred families are contacted within seven days. Staffing problems have been accentuated by the growing number of DHS requests that CIP agencies, in consultation with DHS, assess families determined to present moderate to high risk of child maltreatment. The CIP payment rates that apply for low- to moderate-risk families apply for the assessment of and provision of services to this higher risk group of families, despite the fact that highly experienced staff are needed to serve families with more complex problems.

The issue of referral of high-risk families to CIP agencies raises a number of questions regarding the scope of CIP services and the adequacy of the current resources (staffing and financial) to effectively serve referred families. The issue has been difficult to fully assess because it is not clear to what extent DHS refers high-risk families to CIP. In 2001, CIP agencies investigated slightly more than half of the total referrals for child abuse and neglect for the state (CIP agencies investigated 4,901 reports, and DHS investigated 4,795 reports). It is believed by many CIP agencies that low- to moderate-risk families comprise approximately 40% of the total reports for abuse and neglect, suggesting that a large number of high-risk families are being referred to CIP agencies.

Finally, significant challenges exist related to staff training, particularly in relation to the responsibilities of CIP agency staff in conducting safety assessments. CIP agencies have requested more extensive training from DHS on quality assurance issues, case documentation, confidentiality issues, and child and family assessment processes. Because DHS has placed priority on more thorough training for DHS child protective services caseworkers, however, it is not clear to what extent resources can and will be made available for CIP agency staff training.

CIP Funding and Fiscal Methodology

CIP agencies receive funding under their contracts with DHS and are reimbursed through Medicaid for Targeted Case Management. State dollars provide the funds for CIP. As a result, agencies can use funding flexibly to pay for services and items not traditionally allowed under child welfare funding, such as to purchase clothing or pay for home or car repairs, as long as the expenditures are relevant to reducing child abuse and neglect. CIP agencies also strive to qualify all eligible families for Medicaid. Because CIP agencies are only allowed to serve families for six months, Medicaid eligibility is crucial to many families' ongoing access to services. At the same time, Medicaid reimbursement for targeted case management provides key funding for CIP.

With regard to DHS funding, it was not clear initially at what level CIP should be funded to cover program costs. In FY 1999, DHS funded CIP at $2,965,000, and in each subsequent year, the legislature appropriated higher levels of funding: in FY 2000, $3,828,000; in FY 2001, $3,907,000; and in FY 2002, $4,140,000. To date, funding of CIP appears to have strong political support, motivated, at least in part, by fears of negative media coverage should a child be seriously harmed after a report of child abuse or neglect was received but not assessed.

It also has not been entirely clear how the available funds should be allocated among the participating agencies. Payment is based on per family, per month rates, but the CIP contracts set a fixed total payment for each CIP agency. Fiscal data for October 2001 through June 2002 indicate that four of the eight regions had a budget surplus and four required additional funds to provide services for the remainder of the contract year. DHS reallocated funds among the agencies on an as-needed basis to ensure that all CIP agencies could continue to provide services.

With regard to CIP's fiscal methodology, the original approach was that of cost reimbursement to each agency based on actual expenditures. In January 2001, DHS used program data to establish a statewide reimbursement rate in the form of a per month, per family rate of $305.29. In July 2001, DHS reviewed the rate based on actual expenditures for the prior six months in each region. At that time, DHS developed per month, per family rates for each of the eight regions individually, based on the cost of living in each region, with costs being higher in southern Maine. The rates varied from a low of $305.29 to a high of $385.28. The current per month, per family rate ranges from $311.63 to $393.62.

For families who are Medicaid eligible, CIP agencies bill Medicaid for targeted case management services. Medicaid reimburses the agencies at rates that currently range from $205.67 to $259.78 per month. DHS pays the agencies the difference between the Medicaid reimbursement rate for targeted case management and the established CIP rate. For families who are not Medicaid eligible, the agency receives the full CIP reimbursement rate per month from DHS.

CIP Outcomes

CIP has defined outcomes in three areas: safety, family stability, and community involvement. As of the FY 2002 contracts, the CIP outcomes were:

Safety

- The worker will make no new reports of abuse and neglect in 80% of the families after the first agency visit.

- All service plans will clearly address the family-specific safety and risk factors.

- No children will have serious injuries or accidents that require medical attention as a result of child abuse or neglect in any families served by the agency.

Family Stability

- Children's basic needs for food, clothing, and shelter will be met in 90% of cases.

- Of the families served, 80% will not require referral back to DHS.

- Of the school-aged children, 90% will regularly attend school.

- Of the families, 90% will meet the physical and mental health needs of children.

- Agencies will close 80% of all open cases within six months with a closure reason of "no apparent child abuse/neglect concerns" or "services substantially complete."

- Agencies will close 80% of all open cases with an adequate level of care and protection for children in the home.

Community Involvement

- Workers will document service collaboration in 80% of families receiving services after two months.

- Services will be directly related to safety and risk in 85% of families after two months.

- Within four months from the beginning of service delivery, 90% of families will receive services in their communities, allowing CIP to terminate services within the next two months.

CIP contracts provide that DHS may take corrective action if an agency fails to meet the specified outcomes. If an agency fails to successfully take corrective action and continues to fail to attain achievable goals, DHS may terminate the contract with the agency and rebid the contract. Thus far, no agency has been subject to a corrective action plan. In fact, the CIP contractors have remained the same since the inception of the program.

CIP has struggled to develop and define meaningful outcomes to measure program success. As the above outcomes indicate, considerable ambiguity exists in the outcome measures and the definitions of key concepts. For example, the safety outcome related to clearly addressing "family-specific safety and risk factors" requires a subjective judgment. Worker can interpret the "basic needs for food, clothing, and shelter" referenced in the first family stability outcome in a variety of ways, and different evaluators may define regularly attending school, as in the third family stability goal, differently. As examples of inadequate definitions, it is not clear what services may be considered directly related to safety and risk, the second community involvement goal, nor is it clear what constitutes an "adequate level of care and protection for children in the home," the sixth goal under family stability. An additional problem is that the time frames for measurement are not always clear, making it difficult to determine whether the outcome has been achieved and to compare outcomes across CIP agencies. Finally, it is not clear how CIP assigned the performance targets or whether they were based on actual program data or experience.

Nonetheless, it is clear that CIP has achieved a level of program success. CIP has substantially increased the number of families appropriately referred for child protective services who are assessed for safety risks to their children. In 1998, as noted earlier, 3,700 child protective services reports were not assigned for assessment. In 2001, CIP reduced that number to 200 reports. Families are accepting CIP services in high numbers. Statewide, 77% of the families contacted by CIP agencies agreed to receive services. One unexpected consequence of the CIP assessment process is an increase in the number of reports of suspected child maltreatment to DHS. Reports increased from approximately 7,800 reports in 1998 to approximately 9,700 in 2001. CIP caseworkers made many of these reports themselves, based on information that they observed personally or on information that their clients shared regarding concerns about the safety of children in other families who live in their neighborhoods.

A Snapshot of the Program: The Families United CIP

The implementation of CIP can be best illustrated through the experiences of one program. Families United holds the CIP contract to serve Penobscot, Piscataquis, Hancock, and Washington counties, a geographic area that includes one of Maine's largest cities and a large rural area. It began providing CIP services in December 1998 with no prior child protective services experience, its focus previously being mental health services and home-based family preservation services, although its executive and clinical directors were child protective workers earlier in their careers. Families United hired a former DHS caseworker with child protective services experience as its CIP director.

Child protection and safety assessment were entirely new concepts for the agency and required significant philosophical changes in the agency's approach to families. Because Families United had traditionally provided mental health services like most CIP agencies, it was accustomed to a strength-based approach, in which staff served as advocates for clients in the context of therapeutic relationships. CIP required the agency to adopt a risk-based model, in which assessments of families and service provision involve close evaluations of families' problems as well as strengths. Vague contract requirements regarding services (leaving agencies, in some sense, to find their own way) and a rapid program implementation process made the transition to a new service delivery model more difficult. The agency also discovered that the CIP contract was one-way in design: It specified the CIP agencies' responsibilities but did not obligate DHS to provide training or technical assistance.

Families United, like the other CIP agencies, developed its own approach to assessment and service delivery. Families United makes unannounced first visits to referred families, instead of an initial telephone call or written contact, reasoning that telephone calls may create anxiety in anticipation of scheduled visits. Although it is not required to do so, Families United uses the DHS method of interviewing. The staff is trained in forensic interviewing and uses it to interview children first with the parent's permission and then discuss the allegations with parents.

The agency also developed an extensive assessment process based on the work of CWLA using an assessment form that is more extensive than that required by the state. The caseworker speaks with all members of the referred family and interviews at least three collateral contacts, such as teachers or doctors. The caseworker visits the family at least once a week until he or she completes the assessment. The workers records all information on the DHS assessment forms for reporting purposes and uses it to develop case plans with families.

Families United has extremely high family engagement rates: An average of 80% of all families referred to the agency accept services, which is somewhat higher than the statewide initial service acceptance rate of 77%. Its caseworkers remain responsible for families' cases from the point of initial assessment to case closure. Caseworkers carry 26 to 28 cases per month, including open cases, cases to be closed, and families who currently are refusing services. Although the caseloads tend to be higher than the 18 to 20 cases that represent the maximum for the program, families are not wait-listed. Data suggest that many of the families served by Families United are referred more than once for services. Since December 1998, Families United has received 3,551 referrals. These referrals, however, represent only 2,855 families, indicating that approximately 20% of referrals involve families who have been referred to the CIP at least once in the past.

Families United reports that CIP has allowed them to become not only a trusted source of support for families, largely because they are not viewed as "the government" and they connect families with community resources, but a bridge between DHS and the community (Kim Day, personal communication, September 4, 2002). Families United, for example, has invited the police department to participate in forensic training and members of the community to serve on its agency board. Families United staff members are actively involved in community activities, such as a fundraising walks, in which they identify themselves by wearing Families United t-shirts.

Assessment of the Initiative

In general, CIP is viewed positively as an additional aspect of the child protection infrastructure for the state, although it is still in development. Data indicate that it has ensured that more families at risk of child abuse and neglect receive assessments and services. The long-term funding of CIP, however, is of concern, as Maine is facing increasing budget constraints. It is not clear how continuation of the program will occur if resources become limited, particularly because the program was not designed to decrease the foster care population and its attendant costs by investing in front-end services.

Although using private agencies to assess reports of child abuse and neglect is innovative, the program design, when compared with other initiatives, lacks many of the features common to those efforts (financial risk sharing, performance-based contracting, and greater accountability on the part of private agencies under government oversight). Nonetheless, this initiative has many strengths: the focus on front-end services, use of an approach that is consistent with many child welfare initiatives across the country that emphasize community-based child protection, emphasis on developing close working relationships between DHS and private agencies, the responsiveness of DHS to programmatic challenges experienced by the private agencies, and efforts to ensure the financial stability of the private agencies through reimbursement rate revisions (although the exact mechanisms for setting reimbursement rates—particularly the data that support adjustments—were not well defined).

On the other hand, CIP has a number of aspects in which greater clarity would enhance the overall program design and outcomes. The CIP contracts, unfortunately, are vague in terms of the services that the CIP agencies are to provide and how the agencies' performance will be measured. Because CIP agencies have considerable latitude with regard to service provision, two less-than-positive approaches could conceivably be taken: The agencies could opt to provide less than the optimum service to the families or, alternatively, they could extend themselves so significantly in providing services that they encounter financial difficulties. The absence of clearly defined performance outcomes accentuates the problem. The current system of reporting outcomes and costs does not allow for comparisons across agencies to assess either program success or fiscal accountability. Although Maine has been willing up to this point to increase funding and reallocate funds among agencies as needed, it is not clear how the program will be affected if the state experiences budget shortfalls and can no longer adjust funding for CIP as needed.

The Future of CIP

Maine designed CIP in response to concerns that child services were not contacting and assessing families determined to be at low to moderate risk of child abuse and neglect. The program, at the very least, has effectively addressed that problem. DHS is currently considering a shift in CIP's focus, in which state child protective staff would once again assume responsibility for conducting all initial safety assessments and CIP agencies would provide follow-up casework services and coordinate services for families. This proposal is somewhat surprising in light of recent trends, in which DHS has assigned CIP increasing numbers of moderate-to high-risk referrals. Nevertheless, the assumption underlying the new proposal is that state child protective workers could conduct safety assessments on all referrals if CIP agencies would coordinate all services for families and if legal assistance, particularly in the preparation of court documents, were more available to state child protective workers. Although the legislature has funded additional casework and supervisory positions for DHS, the agency hired only eight new staff members in 2001. The remaining new hires were delayed because of the state's budget shortfall. This development may affect progress in the direction proposed by DHS. As of this writing, a plan to address a reallocation of safety assessment responsibilities had not been developed.

Although realigning the respective responsibilities of the state child protective services and CIP may resolve some of the more challenging issues, the shift may cause some of its more powerful features to be lost. Specifically, CIP has maintained high engagement rates with the families with whom agencies work, largely because the agencies are perceived as community based. It is unclear if Maine could achieve the same engagement rates if it conducted initial assessments and then transferred cases to the CIP agencies.

PART III

Key Themes in the Privatization of Child Welfare Services and Recommendations

The privatization efforts of the six jurisdictions that this study examined provide a foundation on which to base a number of conclusions about current efforts to privatize child welfare services. Although it cannot be said that the six jurisdictions are representative of all child welfare privatization efforts, they demonstrated sufficient similarity to allow researchers to make certain observations. The following discussion synthesizes the major findings from this study, and based on the lessons learned from the studied jurisdictions, makes recommendations for communities that may be considering an initiative with privatized and/or managed care features.

1. Privatization Principally Follows a Lead Agency Model, But Initiatives Vary Substantially

The case studies make clear that a variety of contracting strategies are used in child welfare, none of which expressly uses the terms *privatization* or *managed care*. The dominant model, however, is the lead agency model—the approach that was used by Kansas, Florida, Missouri, and Hamilton County, Ohio. Maine used a modified version of the lead agency approach, contracting with agencies that are permitted to subcontract with other community-based service providers but which do not serve as lead agencies. Michigan, by contrast, took the more traditional approach of contracting with private agencies to directly provide services.

Many features of the privatization initiatives differed. The programs, for example, differed in the populations served—ranging from general child welfare populations (Kansas and Florida), to specific populations of at-risk families (families at low to moderate risk of child maltreatment in Maine), to small populations of children with severe needs (Hamilton County, Ohio, and Missouri), to children in foster care (Wayne County, Michigan). The initiatives also varied in the types of child welfare services that were provided, ranging from front-end services in Maine to highly intensive services in Hamilton County, Ohio, and Missouri. Initiatives also varied from an organizational standpoint. Some initiatives were relatively stable and either fully operating or in the midst of operational expansion (Wayne County, Michigan; Kansas; and Florida), whereas others were in a state of flux as a result of contract renegotiations and program changes (Maine; Hamilton County, Ohio; and Missouri).

Other differences emerged in the role that the public agencies played in relation to the private agency or agencies and in the structure of each initiative. In Kansas, for example, the state's role has been limited to contract management and oversight, with the public agency contracting with a limited number of lead agencies across the state. Each lead agency in Kansas specializes in a specific child welfare service (family preservation, foster care, and adoption) and serves a defined geographic area (regional for family preservation and foster care, statewide for adoption).

Florida also has used a decentralized model, but the lead agencies in that state assumed responsibility for a wide range of child welfare services in the defined geographic area. Maine used a decentralized model, in which the contractors provide front-end services for families at low to moderate risk of child maltreatment, and the state provides the same services for families at moderate to high risk of child abuse and neglect. In Wayne County, Michigan, the state agency used a public/private partnership model, contracting with six agencies and continuing to directly serve some children. Finally, in Hamilton County, Ohio, and Missouri, the public agencies developed more centralized models, closely managing the relationship with a single contractor, although initially crafting an oversight role for an intermediary—a role that was ultimately eliminated in both initiatives.

The entities that assumed responsibility as lead agencies also varied in significant ways. The lead agencies in Kansas', Ohio's, and Michigan's service providers are traditional, nonprofit private agencies with established histories as child welfare service providers. The Missouri Alliance, the lead agency for the Interdepartmental Initiative for Children with Severe. Needs and Their Families, is a newly formed, for-profit entity established by traditional child-serving agencies, most of which are nonprofit residential care agencies. The YMCA in Sarasota County, Florida, the lead agency for Community-Based Care in that county, is a traditional, community-based service agency with no history as a child welfare service provider. By contrast, the lead agency for Broward County, Flordia Community-Based Solutions, is a newly formed nonprofit that was established by a large child care agency. The seven CIP agencies in Maine are community-based nonprofits that historically have provided mental health services.

Finally, financial variations were evident. Four of the six of the jurisdictions used risk-shifting contracts, either through the use of case rates (in Kansas initially; in Hamilton County, Ohio; and in Missouri) or global budgeting (in Florida). Wayne County, Michigan, did not use a risk-shifting approach, but instead used a substantially reduced daily rate for foster care combined with incentive payments tied to timely achievement of permanency outcomes. Agencies that fail to qualify for incentive payments are, essentially, financially penalized because the reduced per diem payment levels are not designed to cover the actual cost of care. Maine uses a more traditional fixed rate contract that does not preclude contractors from petitioning the state for additional funds if they incur cost overruns, as has happened throughout the history of the program.

2. Neither Cost Savings Nor Greater Efficiency Is a Well-Established Outcome of Privatization Efforts

The experiences of the jurisdictions described here suggest that communities embarking on privatization initiatives should not expect to save money, and although they may reasonably anticipate some improvements in efficiency, they generally should not expect dramatic gains.

It Does Not Appear That Money Will Be Saved Through Privatization, Although the Level of Public Dollars Expended May Be Controlled

Although some commentators maintain that "improvements in performance (as a result of privatization) also eventually should lead to lower costs" (Reason Public Policy Institute, 2000, p. 36), neither the data analyzed by CWLA nor this study bear out this expectation. CWLA's 1999 analysis of child welfare managed care and privatization initiatives found that:

> States that had hoped for dramatic cost savings have probably been disappointed. In most instances, the best that could be expected with available funding was cost neutrality but with improved quality and access to services by greater numbers of children and families in need (p. 23).

In the 2000-2001 follow-up report, McCullough and Schmitt (2002) observed that child welfare initiatives "rarely indicated that containing or reducing overall child welfare costs" was a principal initiative goal, although there were cost control expectations underlying many of the initiatives. They also found no direct correlation between assumptions about costs and actual cost performance. Some initiatives that they studied did not intend to save money but actually did so, and other initiatives sought cost neutrality but, in fact, spent more money (McCullough & Schmitt, 2002). Interestingly, they found that although only 7.7% of the initiatives that reported cost information had anticipated that the new program would cost more than the previous system, 25.6% of the initiatives actually did so. Although in another 7.7% of the initiatives uncertainty existed at the outset regarding the cost effect, 28.2% reported, based on actual performance, that they were not certain whether the new initiative cost more, less, or the same as the previous system (McCullough & Schmitt, 2002).

This study found that most jurisdictions expected to control public child welfare costs through their initiatives. Florida, for example, developed a financing strategy in which the budget set for each county's (or group of counties') initiative would approximate—and often be lower than—the appropriation to the relevant public agency district office before the implementation of Community-Based Care. Florida expects lead agencies to access nonstate funding sources to meet the full cost of care. Likewise, the Hamilton County, Ohio, public agencies that funded Creative Connections did not anticipate cost savings in implementing the program but allocated a fixed amount for the program and expected that Beech Acres, as lead agency, would subsidize the cost of services to the eligible population of children using its own dollars. In Wayne County, Michigan, cost neutrality has been the goal, and it has been achieved by reducing the per diem rate and instituting incentive payments at key points in the progression of each case. As Michigan has added additional services with the support of other governmental sources, however, the overall cost of the initiative has increased, raising the question whether cost neutrality has been sustained.

A slightly different expectation existed in Missouri, where the state did not anticipate cost savings in the sense of reducing the child welfare or mental health budgets of the public agencies. Instead, Missouri believed that the number of children entering foster care would be reduced and the number of children needing residential care would decrease, both of which would reduce costs. At the same time, however, the state expected that the resources that formerly were targeted for highly expensive care would be reallocated to community-based services.

Finally, in Maine, no specific focus was put on cost issues. Instead, Maine designed the program to address an issue of concern (clearing a significant backlog of uninvestigated reports of child maltreatment), and the legislature appropriated increasing levels of funds each year.

Regardless of their original cost assumptions, it appeared that most jurisdictions had difficulty reaching conclusions about the effect of privatization on costs. In some cases, a comparison of pre- and postprivatization costs could not be made. Hamilton County, Ohio, for example, tracks initiative costs, but the costs of serving the same population before privatization are not available. Similarly, Kansas could not determine the cost of services before privatization, an issue that had important implications for setting case rates, and, as a result, it is not possible to accurately compare pre- and postprivatization costs, although the legislature concluded that far more money has been spent since privatization.

In Missouri, the state attempted to calculate preprivatization costs for a group of children in residential care as the basis for setting case rates for the Interdepartmental Initiative. Although service providers have raised questions about the completeness of these data, that is, whether they reflected all costs associated with these children's care, this effort and that of Wayne County, Michigan, came as close to determining actual cost of care as was found in any jurisdictions studied.

The 2001 evaluation by USF compared Florida counties with and without Community-Based Care programs regarding their average expenditures per child, per child-day, and per total child population. USF found the expenditures in each of these categories increased for both groups of counties in some fiscal years but not in others. In the most recent fiscal year (2000-2001), some Community-Based Care sites had lower expenditures and some had similar average expenditures as non-Community-Based-Care sites. Cost calculations in non-Community-Based-Care counties could be seen as offering an estimate of preprivatization costs, although the costs in other communities are not necessarily comparable to the Community-Based Care communities. Even if they validly provided such a comparison, the findings were so diverse by fiscal year that a definitive conclusion could not be reached regarding whether Community-Based Care costs more, less, or the same as services before privatization.

It is important to note that costs appear to have been at least one factor in significant redesigns of two programs that were studied. In Missouri and Hamilton County, Ohio, fiscal considerations led to major programmatic changes in both areas and limitations in program eligibility in Hamilton County, Ohio. Neither program will likely continue to reflect the original intent behind each effort and will likely lose the benefits of important lessons learned from their implementation experiences.

Given the promise of fiscal benefits that have been associated with privatization (Hatry & Durman, 1985; Nightingale & Pindus, 1997), it is not entirely clear why money has not been saved or, at minimum, costs well controlled when child welfare services have been privatized. One critical question in this regard is how much child welfare services *should* cost—a question for which there appear to be no ready answers. Few jurisdictions are able to calculate the public sector's historical costs of service provision as a baseline. At the same time, it is not clear what costs should be expected when (a) traditional services are delivered with higher expectations of quality and outcome achievement, which all the initiatives are attempting, and (b) new services and service delivery approaches are integrated into the array of services, as occurred in most jurisdictions. It may be unreasonable to expect that the direct costs attributable to service delivery could be reduced when services are expanded, are made more accessible to a larger number of children and families, and improve in quality.

At the same time, even if cost savings theoretically were possible through privatization, the design of the programs in some jurisdictions appeared to make it virtually impossible for costs to be controlled, much less lowered. In Hamilton County, Ohio, and in Missouri, for example, the only children and youth who the original program designs served had severe needs. These high-cost populations were very small in number and were not balanced with a population of children and youth with more limited needs. At the same time, both lead agencies were subject to a no reject, no eject policy, so they could not balance the service population with a mix of children. As a result, these programs could not reasonably expect to realize cost savings through greater efficiency (Sara Rosenbaum, personal communication, February 12, 2002).

The prospects for saving money or controlling costs also appear undermined to a varying extent, depending on jurisdiction, by the costs incurred in implementing new initiatives. Some analysts point out that regardless of actual service costs or whether they can be reduced, the public sector inevitably incurs additional costs in establishing privatization initiatives. USGAO (1997), for example, noted that:

> Potential savings from privatizing social services can be offset
> by various factors such as the costs associated with contractor
> start-up and government monitoring....State and local agencies
> may incur additional costs for transition, contract manage-
> ment, and the monitoring of their privatization efforts. (p. 6)

Similarly, in its analysis of the costs associated with privatization, the American Federation of State, County, and Municipal Employees (AFSCME, 2000) found that administrative costs typically increase in the public sector. New costs are incurred as public agencies assume responsibility for overseeing the bidding process, administering contracts, and monitoring. The studied jurisdictions had little information about the public sector costs associated with the transition to privatization, contract management, and monitoring (an issue, as discussed later, that posed challenges in most jurisdictions).

It is interesting that in one of the studied jurisdictions, Missouri, the state anticipated that it would incur costs in connection with monitoring, but it attempted to meet those costs by "backing out" a substantial sum from the calculation of the case rate for services. In a similar vein, Florida attempted to keep a certain percentage of its Community-Based Care budget for the public agency's provision of monitoring and other services. The percentage, however, has proved difficult to definitely determine, injecting a level of budgeting uncertainty into the Community-Based Care budgeting process.

Finally, AFSCME (2000) observed a tendency among public agencies to retain contractors, regardless of performance, due to costs associated with creating a relationship with new contractors. This study, however, did not support this observation. In fact, in Hamilton County, Ohio, the county agencies made the decision to go elsewhere when Beech Acres, after investing almost $6 million of its own money, declined to accept further financial risk by accepting the newly proposed, inadequate case rate.

Greater Efficiency Is Undermined by a Range of Organizational and Systemic Factors

A consistent theme in the writings of proponents of privatization is that reliance on the private market will inevitably result in greater efficiency (Blank, 2000; Nightingale & Pindus, 1997). Nightingale and Pindus (1997) wrote that "privatization is a way to bring the advantages of competition and flexibility to the delivery of public services" (p. 13), thereby heightening efficiency and creating greater responsiveness to consumer needs and innovation. Not all commentators, however, are convinced that privatization of child welfare services will automatically bring about greater efficiency. Some observers, for example, have pointed out that if a public child welfare agency retains responsibility for case management and for third-party and judicial reviews, it is unlikely that the private sector could demonstrate greater efficiency in service delivery (AFSCME, 2000). At the same time, if private agencies are required to assume a variety of formerly public functions, such as developing working relationships with the courts, efficiency may be as difficult to achieve under private auspices as under public ones (AFSCME, 2000).

Based on the studied jurisdictions' experiences in privatizing child welfare and, in some cases, introducing managed care principles into their privatization approach, it appears that greater efficiency has been difficult to achieve. Wayne County, Michigan, appears to have produced the strongest results in terms of heightened efficiency through the redesign of its payment system, its public/private partnership model, and its willingness to fund additional services to support timely achievement of key outcomes. Most initiatives, however, struggled to design and implement more efficient systems, although the factors that undermined efficiency varied from one program to another.

In some cases, the respective roles and responsibilities of the public and private sectors were not clear or were duplicative, which undermined the quest for greater efficiency. In Missouri, for example, the complex relationships among the public agencies, the lead agency (the Missouri Alliance), and TSO—particularly the overlapping responsibilities of the Missouri Alliance and TSO—worked against the achievement of greater efficiency. In other cases, such as in Kansas initially, inadequate case rates undercut greater efficiencies. Finally, in some instances, managed care principles were inappropriately introduced given the population served. In Hamilton County, Ohio, for example, Creative Connections initially was designed to serve a group of children with different levels of need, for whom managed care principles might have applied appropriately, but shortly, virtually all children served required expensive residential services and, thus, became a population for whom managed care efficiencies could not be realized.

In some cases, greater efficiency (in the sense of streamlining services to produce better outcomes) may not have been a reasonable expectation because the needs of children and families were such that private agencies had no greater control over problem resolution than public agencies. In Kansas, for example, designers assumed that the public agency was the problem and, once out of the way, system efficiency would automatically improve (Kansas Action for Children, 1998). Although they had consensus that the public agency had a number of problems, it became apparent that service demand and corresponding costs were the result of multiple factors, including of families' social and economic conditions, which privatization could not be expected to resolve no matter how efficiently it was implemented (Kansas Action for Children, 1998).

An interesting question related to privatization's promise of greater efficiency is whether privatization is the ultimate form of service provision or has within itself "the seed of its own demise." Milward (1994), for example, noted the irony of privatization: It is promoted as the solution to government inefficiency and mismanagement but can only work well if government manages the process well. The experiences of the six jurisdictions examined in this study illustrate this point: To the extent that privatization worked, it generally was only where the public agency developed strong management, monitoring, and quality assurance capabilities and appropriately structured the initiative, with Michigan being the strongest example. If government must be highly competent and a "smart buyer," it would appear that privatization may well force a significant enhancement of government capacity, in which case, it would seem, government could resume the functions that it previously discarded (Milward, 1994). Interestingly, government reassumption of responsibilities is being considered in Maine, where the state is proposing to reclaim the responsibility of assessing families reported for child maltreatment who are determined to present low to moderate risk.

3. Privatization Initiatives Struggle to Measure Outcomes and Benchmarks that Allow Assessment of Actual Performance

Proponents of privatization consistently list improved quality, along with cost savings and greater efficiency, as a key benefit of privatization (Hatry & Durman, 1985; Nightingale & Pindus, 1997). Critics of privatization, however, refute this contention, arguing that services provided under such arrangements decline in quality. Whether quality improves through privatization appears to depend on the extent to which outcomes and performance measures are clearly defined and the nature of the monitoring.

The importance of outcome definition and measurement in privatization efforts has been emphasized consistently. The Leadership 18 Group (2000), for example, focused on the critical need to establish and monitor outcomes measures. USGAO's study of social service privatization (1997) found that "most state and local government officials...were satisfied with the quality of privatized services" (p. 2) based on the contractors' general expertise in providing services and their management flexibility. Importantly, however, researchers also found that some public agency officials were not satisfied because the outcomes achieved for children and families were no better than the outcomes achieved by the public agency.

Most commentators agree that outcomes associated with privatization should be clearly defined but that in most cases, they are not developed with the necessary specificity. Nightingale and Pindus (1997, p. 13), for example, pointed to the lack of accountability and performance criteria in privatization contracts. Petr and Johnson (1999), based on their study of Kansas' early privatization efforts, found that Kansas, like many jurisdictions, lacked a data-oriented foundation for the development of outcomes and performance standards.

Although there were clear exceptions, many of the programs studied here struggled to clearly state desired outcomes and develop appropriate, data-based performance targets. This study identified several problems with regard to outcomes, although these problems varied from one jurisdiction to another:

Poorly Defined Outcomes. Poorly defined outcomes were one of the more prevalent problems in the area of outcome definition and measurement. In Missouri, many outcomes had a subjective quality that made it impossible to state the exact nature of the outcome (for example, "The percentage of enrolled children who are involved in non-criminal aggression will be reduced" and "The percentage of children who participate in community activities will increase"). Similar problems were found in the outcomes specified in the Maine CIP, which included such outcomes as "Children's basic needs for food, clothing, and shelter will be met," and "Families will meet the physical and mental health needs of the children."

Too Many Outcomes for Children and/or Their Families than Could Possibly Be Monitored Or Measured. In some contracts for privatization, the number of specified outcomes was staggering. In the contract for Missouri's Interdepartmental Initiative for Children with Severe Needs and their Families, for example, the contract specified 30 outcomes for children and their families. The original Hamilton County, Ohio, contract listed numerous outcomes for the program, many not correlated with one another, that were spread through 11 separate contract exhibits.

Attentuated Family Outcomes Beyond the Scope of the Program. In one case, the privatization contract specified outcomes for parents that extended far beyond the scope of the program and the competencies of the staff. The contract for Missouri's Interdepartmental Initiative, which focused on children with significant mental health problems, included outcomes related to changes in parental behaviors that the initiative itself could not reasonably be expected to affect, such the incidence of parents' substance abuse and criminal activity.

Variability in the Outcomes Used to Assess Performance. This issue was relevant in statewide initiatives where the "same" program was implemented in different geographic areas of the state or by different private agencies. Kansas and Florida reflected very different approaches to outcome development. Kansas developed standardized, statewide outcomes for each of the three child welfare program areas (family preservation, foster care, and adoption). Florida, in contrast, proposed statewide outcomes early in its planning process but did not require counties to use a defined set of core outcomes. Each county, instead, developed its own outcomes and performance targets. As a result, it has not been possible to assess the overall performance of Community-Based Care.

Even when outcomes are well developed in the sense of incorporating clearly defined concepts, issues were found in connection with performance targets. As Broskowski (2001) emphasized, benchmarks must be based on historical data or the experiences of comparable communities. This study noted problems, however, in some of the jurisdictions studied. In several programs, the initiatives failed to specify any performance targets, or they set performance targets that lacked validation with program data. In Missouri, for example, the contract did not specify baselines for the 30 indicators, nor did the program create baselines as it was implemented and workers gained experience in providing services. The contract stated that a baseline would be established through a control group of a comparable population in another geographical area, but this approach was never implemented, nor could it reasonably have been done. In Maine, designers selected performance targets without any indication that these percentages had been validated with historical data or with comparable data from other communities.

Some jurisdictions, however, demonstrated strengths in the development and refinement of outcome measures. Wayne County, Michigan, used well-developed outcomes and benchmarks from the outset of its initiative, that is, a limited number of clearly defined outcomes that specified what was to occur, within what time frame, and with regard to what percentage of children. The Foster Care Permanency Initiative is currently attempting to further refine the outcomes through an external evaluation that examines initiative performance versus the performance of noninitiative agencies. The Sarasota County, Florida, YMCA has clearly defined its performance measures and annual objectives for Sarasota, Manatee, and DeSoto Counties. It has tracked performance measures in the areas of safety and permanency over time, which has permitted assessments of Community-Based Care in those counties. Community-Based Solutions, the agency that is to serve as lead agency in Broward County, Florida, likewise, has proposed clearly defined outcomes and performance targets that would permit such an assessment.

Two jurisdictions have made significant efforts to refine and strengthen their outcome measures. In Kansas, the initial outcomes and performance targets, which were not validated with historical data, were intensely criticized from the outset. When it rebid the privatization contracts in 2000. Kansas took the opportunity to revise its outcomes, operational definitions, and performance targets based on the three child welfare programs' experiences. The outcomes and performance measures currently in place reflect the initiative's four-year experience in service provision through privatization and demonstrate attention to the issues that were most problematic in operationalizing the prior outcomes. This approach is recommended to other systems that may begin with less than fully validated outcomes and performance measures.

In a similar vein, in 2000, Beech Acres and the Hamilton County agencies worked together to amend the Creative Connections contract to designate seven outcomes with highly specific, measurable benchmarks. The contract amendment represented a major improvement in the original contract's approach to outcomes. During the contract negotiations, as designers conceptualized two service tracks, they brought the same specificity to the development of outcome measures and benchmarks for each service track, with the additional feature of more extensive use of standardized assessment tools, such as CAFAS.

4. Personal Commitment and Leadership Are Vital to Ensuring that Privatization Efforts Are Developed and Sustained

One clear theme found in the six jurisdictions was that the overall success of a privatization initiative is associated with certain factors: strong leadership at the top, long-term commitment to the initiative, and strong interpersonal relationships.

Strong High-Level Leadership Is Essential to the Success of Any Privatization Effort

In virtually every jurisdiction, stakeholders emphasized the critical importance of strong high-level leadership in planning and implementation. Commentators on privatization have suggested that leadership translates into "a political champion who can provide the needed energy and leadership" and "withstand withering opposition to reform" (Reason Public Policy Institute, 2000a, p. 1). The commitment of top leadership is essential to mobilizing the will to develop new service approaches and sustaining commitment to endeavors that, inevitably, will need years of development to reach the envisioned goals.

The governor's directive for privatization in Kansas and the privatization mandate of the Florida legislature may be viewed as top leadership prompting privatization in those states. It is important, however, to distinguish the role of leadership from top-down management. In Kansas, many perceived privatization as imposed from the top in ways that did not promote cooperation or collaboration. Kansas Action for Children (1998), for example, criticized the effort as directed from the top without the engagement of foster parents, legislators, judicial stakeholders, or school districts, particularly special education programs. Unlike the approach taken in Kansas, the Florida state legislature's mandate included a requirement for broad-based community planning and participation—a feature seen as one of the strongest aspects of that privatization effort. These experiences suggest that top leadership plays a vital role in precipitating change, but that top leadership also must ensure that the community understands and supports the effort.

The experiences of the jurisdictions also suggest that top leadership is vital in sustaining implementation efforts and in weathering the inevitable setbacks that characterize early efforts. The Missouri Interdepartmental Initiative demonstrates the importance of political champions through the early years of implementation. The leadership of the directors of DMH and DSS made the initiative possible. Both leaders, however, left their positions within a few years of the implementation. Had these leaders remained in place, the subsequent withdrawal of DMH's financial support and the restructuring and downsizing of the effort may not have occurred. Similar issues arose in Hamilton County, where, at the time that the contract for Creative Connections was renegotiated in 2002, the directorships of all five county agencies had changed since the initiative was created in 1998.

A similar notion applies in jurisdictions where legislatures have precipitated privatization efforts—legislators need to remain fully engaged. In Florida, the public child welfare agency has invested considerable time in working with the legislature and ensuring that legislators understand and support the initiative. The result has been legislative support for a longer implementation period, development of community alliances, and development of risk-sharing methodologies. In Maine, pressure came from the legislature to develop CIP, and the legislature has continued to appropriate increased funding for the effort. Nonetheless, a question remains as to whether the goals have been clearly enough articulated or the outcomes sufficiently demonstrated to ensure ongoing legislative support, particularly in an environment of budget reductions.

Participants Must Make a Long-Term Commitment to Privatization

Given the magnitude of changes that privatization requires, it became clear in this study that the development and implementation of privatization initiatives are long-term propositions. Florida's Community-Based Care program emphasizes the importance of taking a long-term view of its effort, recognizing that the level of change being made requires a commitment to planning, transitional efforts, and work over the course of years to establish a new system. Similarly, the executive director of the Missouri Alliance emphasized the necessity of a long-range view, noting that start-up is fraught with challenges, if not significant problems, and that the program development, cultivation of interpersonal and community relationships, and refinement of public-private working processes require time. The executive director of Beech Acres likewise noted that an extensive period of time is needed to overcome institutional resistance to change.

Interpersonal Relationships Are Key

In each of the privatization initiatives, the role of interpersonal relationships in promoting success or, alternatively, undermining progress was evident. In some cases, the relationships between the leaders of different state agencies—as in Missouri, where the directors of DMH and DSS had a strong working relationship—made the initiatives possible. In other cases, the relationship between a visionary local leader and other community leaders—as in Sarasota County, Florida, where the YMCA executive director instilled trust and cooperation among community leaders—helped ensure a level of local success not achieved as readily in other communities in the state. In other situations, interpersonal relationships undermined progress, particularly when key leaders or managers were not willing to work collaboratively with other key stakeholders, did not readily share vital information, or worked against, rather than in support of, the formulation of a shared vision.

Of relevance in this regard was the finding that in those jurisdictions that interposed an intermediary between the public agency and lead agency, the quality of relationships between the public and private sectors suffered. In Missouri, for example, TSO served in an intermediary capacity with regard to contract compliance and monitoring outcome achievement. It appears that TSO aligned itself in an almost adversarial role with the public agencies against the Missouri Alliance, a situation that undermined the development of a sound working relationship between the state and the lead agency. In Hamilton County, Ohio, the contract provided for an intermediary (the council) to monitor Creative Connections. As in Missouri, this arrangement created barriers to communication and collaboration between the lead agency and the five public agencies. The result was a sense that neither side—the public agencies nor Beech Acres—truly understood the other.

5. It Is Essential that the Public and Private Agencies Clearly Define Their Roles and Responsibilities

A theme identified in all jurisdictions was the importance of a clear delineation of roles and responsibilities of the public and private agencies and any other players with key structural roles. Clarification not only supports greater efficiency, but provides a framework for implementing and assessing the effect of the effort. In several jurisdictions, it was apparent that the respective roles were not clear. In some cases, the partners made efforts to clarify roles and responsibilities of the state and the lead agency, but questions still remained. Florida, for example, described in detail the roles and responsibilities of the state and the lead agency in Community-Based Care but, in reality, roles have evolved over time. Questions continue to be raised as to the role the state intends to play in Community-Based Care, including to what extent it wishes to continue the traditional role of the state in child welfare. Florida, to its credit, has attempted to address some of these ambiguities through the statewide Community-Based Care Leadership Forum.

In Maine, a key issue for the private agencies has been the one-way nature of the contracts for CIP. The contract specifies private agencies' roles and responsibilities, but the public agencies' responsibilities—for training private agency staff, providing technical assistance, or coordinating with other government agencies—are not clear. Fundamentally, the ultimate responsibility for the services at the heart of CIP may not be fully resolved. The state initially declined to expand public agency staff to assess low- to moderate-risk families reported for abuse and neglect and turned to the private sector, but it now appears unsure whether the private agency contractors should continue in this role.

In Missouri, the lack of clarity regarding the roles and responsibilities of the participants in the Interdepartmental Initiative has been seen in a variety of ways. First, the contract between the state and Missouri Alliance, as lead agency, did not specify the roles of the state agency. Second, the responsibilities of the Missouri Alliance and the technical assistance organization in their respective contracts reflected considerable duplication, particularly with regard to information gathering and quality assurance. It was unclear which entity had final responsibility for these activities. Third, at a more fundamental level, the role of the Missouri Alliance in ensuring the success of the program became less clear over time. The Interdepartmental Initiative was designed as a multisystem effort to expand the availability and utilization of community-based services. The roll out of the program, however, as described by the participants, suggests that the state began to see the Missouri Alliance as responsible for the effort. As the state implemented the program, it tended to attribute programmatic weaknesses to the Missouri Alliance, rather than to broader systemic factors that required problem solving through a collaborative approach. As the Missouri Alliance took on additional responsibilities for the direct provision of services, it may have been targeted even more pointedly as responsible for problems.

It is important to note that none of the contracts contained clear language regarding the obligations of the public agencies, with the exception of the Michigan contract, which had a paragraph titled "Family Independence Agency [FIA] Responsibilities." Even in Michigan's specification of the public agency's roles and responsibilities, however, the contract made no mention of the public agency's obligation to make timely payment to the private agencies or provide technical assistance in response to their needs.

6. Attention Must Be Given to Building and Funding the Necessary Infrastructure for Any Privatization Effort

Individuals involved in the privatization initiatives repeatedly highlighted the need for a well-developed infrastructure. The major components they emphasized were: (a) a mutually shared vision of the initiative, (b) an adequate management and staffing structure for the new initiative, (c) adequate financial support during the start-up period, and (d) strong connections with the community, including the courts, mental health agencies, education agencies, and community leaders.

A Mutually Shared Vision of the Initiative

The prospects for success of any privatization effort appear related to the extent to which the vision for the effort is shared by the public agency, the private agency, and the community as a whole, including the courts and mental health service system. In some jurisdictions, partners made a considerable effort to develop a vision for the initiative that the community could support. In Sarasota County, Florida, YMCA worked closely with community leaders, advocates, and other representatives to develop program goals and a program design that the community could endorse. Similarly, Michigan worked to ensure that a mutually shared vision shaped the development and implementation of its initiative. At the inception of the program, people made considerable resistance to a redesign of the foster care system, but FIA and the private agencies worked together closely to develop a program that providers could accept and that offered the benefits that children, families, and the community expected. More intensive efforts to work with the community are planned in Phase III of the initiative.

Jurisdictions that have planned significant shifts in child welfare service delivery, such as moving away from traditional approaches to wraparound processes, have emphasized the importance of a mutual vision for these efforts. In Missouri and Hamilton County, Ohio, for example, the program designs represented significant departures from previous service delivery approaches. In both programs, the private agencies emphasized the importance of the public agency's and the community's being on board with these major service delivery shifts. In both cases, however, the private agencies experienced disconnections with the public agencies about the vision for the program, with resulting frustrations and significant barriers to success.

Kansas, as a result of the extremely short time frame for the planning and implementing privatization, faced particular problems in developing and achieving a shared vision for its effort. A critical oversight was the public agency's failure to engage the court system and other key community stakeholders, such as foster parents, in the planning process. Although research has noted improvements in engaging all relevant players and developing a shared view of the initiative, ongoing tensions have complicated efforts to achieve and document success.

An Adequate Management and Staffing Structure for the New Initiative

Management and staffing are critical components of any privatization initiative. Management is an issue for both the public agency that assumes oversight responsibility, often with new functions associated with contract monitoring and quality assurance, and the private agency that assumes new functions in the context of service delivery and fiscal management. With regard to public agency management, Reason Public Policy Institute (2000b, pp. 1–3) promoted two management components as essential to the success of privatization initiatives: a high-level executive to establish, maintain, and cultivate relationships with private entities, and a central unit where a "critical mass of knowledge" regarding privatization can reside and provide a basis for "publicizing and riding herd" over entities that "drag their feet" in the privatization process.

The wisdom of this advice seems questionable, at least in the sense that the public sector can force the implementation of privatization through "riding herd" over private sector partners whose views of the initiative may differ from their own. Nonetheless, a central unit that has organizational status and management capacities in the public agency appears to play an important role in successful efforts. The Missouri initiative, for example, never formed IPA, which was envisioned as a central body to oversee funding, planning, and policy development for the initiative. This absence may have played a role in the problems that the initiative subsequently experienced and in the later decisions of DMH and DYS to terminate participation in the initiative. Had there been such a central policy and oversight entity, the initiative may have had a strong ally to help it weather the many complex issues it faced. Florida created a central unit for Community-Based Care in an effort to oversee and coordinate that initiative. Given the magnitude of the effort, however, some have concerns that the Community-Based Care unit may not be positioned sufficiently high in the bureaucracy to ensure adequate support for the initiative.

The development of new management structures within private agencies also was found to be essential. This need was less evident in Michigan, where the contracting agencies historically had provided child welfare services and were not taking on new roles as lead agencies, although they were being asked to perform their traditional roles better and faster. In other jurisdictions, private agencies assumed roles that were distinctly different from their roles in their past, and new, effective management structures were critical. YMCA of Sarasota County, Florida, which has successfully implemented Community-Based Care, strengthened its privatization-focused management capacity as a result of its experience as a pilot county. In many counties in Florida, however, newly created agencies, as opposed to long-standing entities such as YMCA, are assuming lead agency status. For these organizations, a strong management infrastructure must be built. Florida has attempted to address this issue through its Community-Based Care Readiness Assessment process, which guides agencies in developing their management infrastructures, and its use of transitional contracts that provide new lead agencies with time to establish all infrastructure elements.

In other initiatives, private agencies have experienced significant internal management challenges. Leadership issues surfaced early in Missouri as the Missouri Alliance attempted to implement the Interdepartmental Initiative. The arrival of a new executive director with strong management and child welfare skills in 2000 made an important difference in the ability of the alliance to function effectively as lead agency. Similarly, Creative Connections, in Hamilton County, Ohio, faced significant internal leadership challenges. It experienced five changes in the leadership of the program over a 3.5-year period. On the positive side, however, Creative Connections was based in a child welfare agency with a long history of service provision and a highly stable overall leadership structure. In Maine, CIP agencies, which principally were mental health services providers, had established management structures but limited experience in the area of child protective services. To address the need for child protection management experience, one of the agencies hired a former state public child welfare staff member to direct the new program.

Finally, adequate numbers of trained and skilled staff are essential elements in the infrastructure of any privatization initiative. The experiences of Maine; Hamilton County, Ohio; and Missouri illustrate the challenges that private agencies encounter in recruiting, training, and retaining staff with appropriate credentials, especially when new service delivery approaches are being implemented. Particularly when initiatives are designed to serve children with severe and complex needs, staffing may pose significant challenges. As an example, Beech Acres struggled to find the right staffing pattern for Creative Connections. In the contract renegotiation process, it proposed a staffing redesign that involved staff with increasing levels of skill and proficiency and that integrated more extensive staff development. Similarly, the contracting agencies in Maine struggled to recruit experienced staff and train them to conduct safety assessments and provide the range of needed services.

A transitional approach, as discussed in the next section, appears associated with strong management and staffing infrastructures. In Florida, for example, the transition for lead agencies over a six- to nine-month period permitted public staff to move into private agency positions in a coordinated manner. Private agencies' managers had the opportunity to integrate and fully train new staff, and public agencies were able to support staff in assuming new roles, such as quality assurance.

Adequate Financial Support for Start Up

In most jurisdictions, except Maine and Wayne County, Michigan, start-up funding was a concern for the private agencies as they designed new program approaches. In some programs, the lead agency received no start-up funding, such as in Hamilton County, Ohio; Kansas; and Missouri, where TSO received start-up funds but the lead agency did not. The private agencies often found that simultaneous efforts to develop an appropriate infrastructure and implement new programs created a serious financial drain on resources.

Initially, the Florida Community-Based Care initiative did not provide start-up funds for lead agencies. Recognizing the lead agencies' need for adequate capitalization, however, it began to provide such funding after the initial implementation phase of Community-Based Care. The Florida DCF supported legislative efforts that resulted in a budget increase to support provider capacity building, and it developed partnerships with local agencies and child advocacy groups to access funds through TANF. Nonetheless, the initiative continues to expect lead agency applicants to describe how they will create and fund the infrastructure for their Community-Based Care programs.

Strong Connections with the Community

The final infrastructure component, strong connections with the community, is more likely to be present when the community has been involved in planning the privatization initiative. Several jurisdictions found that efforts to change child welfare service philosophy and design have greater success when key community representatives are actively engaged with, understand, and support the initiative. Limited connections with key community stakeholders in Kansas—particularly the court system, service providers, and foster parents—worked against smooth implementation. Similarly, some of the challenges encountered by the Interdepartmental Initiative in Missouri may have been intensified by perceptions that the Missouri Alliance, not the community as a whole, was responsible for the effort.

Some jurisdictions successfully involved the community, with positive benefits for the program. In Florida, for example, community involvement has been a key element of Community-Based Care. Community involvement was a focus in the overall planning of the effort, and lead agency applicants must demonstrate strong community connections in their system of care designs. In particular, community alliances, modeled on Sarasota County's community involvement model, provide strong community linkages in all aspects of Community-Based Care initiatives. The functions of the community alliance include community-based needs assessments, joint planning, development of community-specific outcomes, and community education and advocacy. YMCA of Sarasota County identified community support for its service delivery model as one of the key factors in its success.

Similarly, in Hamilton County, Ohio, Creative Connections developed strong links with the community. It developed relationships with existing community-based service providers and worked to develop new services with current providers. In its efforts to improve the design of Creative Connections at the time of contract renegotiations, Beech Acres placed even greater emphasis on community connections to strengthen the implementation of its wraparound approach. Likewise, the Foster Care Permanency Initiative in Wayne County, Michigan, currently is emphasizing the involvement of key community stakeholders as it plans to move the initiative from pilot project to permanent status. Among the planned community outreach activities are training for the courts and for county caseworkers who process the incentive payments. Finally, the private agencies implementing CIP in Maine have emphasized community connections. The high rates of family acceptance of their services have been attributed, at least in part, to the private agencies' active involvement with their communities.

7. A "Go Slow" Approach Is More Realistic Than an "Overnight" Redesign

Privatization Initiatives That Have Comprehensive, Community-Based Planning Report Positive Results

Comprehensive planning processes and pilot testing were not used in every jurisdiction, but to the extent that such efforts were made, they appeared to be associated with positive results. Interestingly, the Reason Public Policy Institute (RPPI, 2000a), a leading think tank on privatization, urged that privatization initiatives be comprehensive in scope rather than incremental in the form of pilot programs. It warned that with incremental approaches, "The opponents of privatization will all gang up on the one unlucky manager who happens to have the only privatization in town" (RPPI, 2000a, p. 2). RPPI (2000a) concluded that "privatization is simply done, not studied"; governments should not "consider" privatization, but should develop requests for proposals with specific outcomes and "then see what you get back from the market" (p. 3). The experiences of these jurisdictions do not support this approach.

Kansas did not use a pilot project in preparation for statewide privatization. It did use a planning process, but that process was far more limited than the process used by Florida. The absence of a pilot project consistently has been criticized. The major complaint has been that because it failed to pilot test the service and cost assumptions, Kansas was not able to assess the potential negative effect of privatization on children, families, the courts, other service systems, and the child welfare system itself (Petr & Johnson, 1999). The rapid transition to privatization—with cases shifted from public agency to private agency in extremely short order—also undermined the predictability and quality of service and created significant problems in the early implementation stages (Kansas Action for Children, 1998).

Like the process used in Kansas, although confined geographically and limited to a smaller population, it was high-level administrative leadership, not community-based planners, who developed the Missouri approach. The Missouri RFP process closely tracks the advice of RPPI: The state simply issued an RFP and waited to see what it "got from the market." The market, however, produced one bidder, the Missouri Alliance, which then found itself attempting to implement the initiative on its own.

The five agencies in Hamilton County, Ohio, also moved quickly to establish the program that preceded Creative Connections. When the original lead agency, FCF Management, encountered significant financial problems, the county approached Beech Acres to assume responsibility programmatically and, to a significant degree, financially. The county agencies did not focus at that point on what could be learned from the FCF Management experience, which they could have treated as a pilot, other than to conclude that a significant sum of private money would be needed to make the effort possible.

Some jurisdictions, however, fully integrated community-based planning or pilot projects into their privatization efforts—apparently with positive results. Recognizing that time was needed to build consensus among the public agency, the private agencies, and the community, Wayne County, Michigan, devoted considerable time to planning and consensus building. It developed a pilot project that has been tested and gradually expanded over a period of five years with plans to move the initiative into permanent program status only after a full and thoughtful development of the effort.

Florida used both pilot projects and a comprehensive, community-based planning process. The state undertook a legislatively mandated privatization pilot project in 1996. The pilot played a significant role in demonstrating the importance of community involvement in the privatization effort and helped Florida identify some of the complexities it would need to address during statewide implementation. When the legislature mandated statewide privatization in 1998, it required DCF to implement a comprehensive planning process. That process involved focus groups and community forums across the state in which foster parents, children and youth in foster care, community-based representatives, and others participated. The state considers the planning process to be one of the hallmarks of its initiative.

Phasing-In Is Preferable to Immediate Full-Service Implementation

Participants in programs that were gradually ramped up gave more positive assessments of privatization than those in jurisdictions where implementation was rapid. These sentiments reflect the importance of time in implementing new initiatives that carry with them fairly radical changes in service philosophy, financing, and service delivery.

The respective experiences of Kansas and Florida illustrate the benefits of phasing in statewide initiatives. Petr and Johnson (1999) studied Kansas' early privatization efforts, which involved an almost overnight implementation process that was particularly problematic in the area of foster care. They found a number of negative effects as a result of attempting to implement radical system change over a very short period of time. Based on their findings, Petr and Johnson urged that privatization be phased in to provide private agencies with opportunities to recruit and train staff, develop necessary agreements with foster families and facilities, solidify relationships with the courts and other systems, and develop the information management systems necessary to track needed data. Kansas Action for Children (1998), after carefully assessing the effect of Kansas' rapid privatization approach, urged that the planning process for statewide privatization efforts take place over, at minimum, 18 months to two years.

In contrast to Kansas, Florida developed a phased-in approach to its Community-Based Care program. Florida worked with its 67 counties for several years to move them to Community-Based Care. The phasing in made it possible for counties believed to be unready for privatization to move in that direction. Florida also uses a Community-Based Care readiness assessment. It focuses on the lead agency's organizational stability, financial management, quality assurance and improvement capacity, data management systems, and model for service delivery; a transition contract with the lead agency; and, after a transitional period of six to nine months, a full service contract. Florida also was successful in educating the state legislature about the benefits of a go slow approach, resulting in legislative agreement to move the time frame for completion of privatization from January 1, 2002, to December 31, 2004. Florida also recently began experimenting with limited service contracts to allow lead agencies to test their systems and strategies with a small number of cases before assuming full responsibility for all child welfare services with a large population, an approach that might be considered a mini-pilot.

Similarly, Michigan adopted a phased-in approach to the privatization of foster care services in Wayne County. Because the payment structure was radically redesigned, FIA decided to do a dry run, beginning with a small project in Phase I (a 2-year period involving 4 agencies), expanding the effort conservatively in

Phase II (a 3.5-year period involving 6 agencies), and then planning county-wide implementation in Phase III (with 17 agencies). The state's approach to implementing the initiative statewide was similarly methodical, with careful assessments of the implementation of the program model for other urban areas and rural communities.

In the smaller initiatives by virtue of geography and population served, phasing in also appears to have benefits, although less dramatic ones than may be seen in the statewide initiatives. In Missouri, the contract for the Interdepartmental Initiative included a four-month start-up period for the Missouri Alliance to provide the alliance with an opportunity to build its infrastructure and capacity to comply with contractual obligations. In addition, through negotiations, the state and the alliance agreed to build the initiative's caseload over time. The phase in provided important benefits, but the adequacy of the four-month start-up period is questionable, particularly given the fact that the alliance was newly created and numerous issues remained to be resolved even after the partners finalized the contract.

Similarly, in Maine, preliminary steps were associated with CIP implementation. The state had implemented a pilot project in which private agencies provided case management services. That effort, however, was more limited than the initiative, as it did not include safety assessments of families. Maine implemented CIP itself statewide in less than one year, with child protective services responsibilities assumed by agencies with mental health backgrounds.

8. Information Systems that Produce a Range of Key Data Are Critical to Effective Privatization, but Typically, They Are Inadequate

Adequate Data Are Often Not Available for Determining Costs of Achieving Outcomes

The experiences of the privatization initiatives make clear that data are critical to determine the cost of services, calculate the cost benefits of new approaches to service delivery, establish outcomes and performance standards, and assess the extent to which agencies have achieved outcomes. With regard to cost data, USGAO (1998a) concluded that without complete and accurate data, it is not possible to determine payment rates that reflect the actual costs of providing services. Similarly, McCullough (2001) emphasized the importance of tracking the budgetary effect of privatization and managed care reforms at the systems level. She observed that without utilization and real-time cost information, it is difficult to anticipate the fiscal consequences of privatization, particularly if expectations are that money will be saved.

In Kansas, adequate cost data were lacking when the privatization initiative was begun, and, as a result, contractors could not make appropriate bids regarding the nature and scope of the work. Contractors needed, but could not obtain from the state agency, detailed information about such factors as costs and utilization rates, potential demand for services for very high-risk families, and the number of out-of-state educational and treatment placements that might be necessary. As subsequent events demonstrated, contractors seriously underestimated the financial resources needed to serve children and families. In a somewhat similar vein, the case rate in Hamilton County, Ohio, was not based on actual costs, but on available resources. The county agencies were well aware that the cost of care was considerably greater than the established case rate but expected Beech Acres to make up the difference.

More so than other jurisdictions that used a case rate approach, Missouri used historical cost data to calculate the case rate for the children to be served through the Interdepartmental Initiative. Unfortunately, the rate did not include certain real costs, such as case management services for children referred by the Division of Family Services, and Missouri calculated the case rate after allocations had been made to TSO and the risk pool. Missouri set the rate despite the use of data that proved it unacceptable to all potential bidders other than the Missouri Alliance.

Michigan also took a more methodical data-based approach to establishing a payment structure—one that proved more acceptable to contractors than the Missouri payment rate. Michigan began with the existing per diem rate for all children in foster care in Wayne County and increased that figure by 12%, largely to allay private agencies' fears that the new fiscal methodology would provide them with inadequate resources to meet their obligations under their new contracts. It then designed a payment structure that has proved particularly effective in promoting the achievement of positive outcomes.

Data also are essential for the development of performance-based standards. USGAO's (1998a) review of child welfare managed care initiatives highlighted the critical role of data in developing and revising performance-based standards, and RPPI (2000b) emphasized the role of data in the development of "rigorous performance standards for contracts." Nonetheless, only a few of the jurisdictions—notably Kansas and Michigan—used historical data to develop appropriate outcomes and performance measures.

Most Privatization Efforts Struggle to Develop Adequate Data Systems

USGAO (1998a) found that the development of management information systems was "the most difficult task" (p. 14) program officials faced as they implemented privatized managed care initiatives. McCullough and Schmitt (2002) similarly concluded that "current automated systems may not yet be up to the task" (p. 44) of meeting the necessary data collection and management demands of such initiatives.

Specifically, USGAO (1998a) expressed concern that many jurisdictions were using multiple, incompatible information systems. At the time of the USGAO study in Sarasota County, Florida, YMCA was directly connected to the state's two child welfare client and services information systems for its own management reports, and its own internal system was networked with the subcontractors to both enter and track client data. The three systems, however, were not integrated. As a result, the system required staff to enter the same information into each of the three systems and physically locate the three computer terminals side by side to ensure consistent data entry (USGAO, 1998a). Five years later, the data management situation in Sarasota County has improved, but a host of problems persist in linking Community-Based Care lead agencies to the state's troubled Home Safenet system.

In contrast to Florida, where there may have been too many incompatible data systems, Kansas had no management information system whatsoever at the time of the privatization of the state's foster care program. The system required staff to rely on handwritten reports from lead agencies to generate the automated reports needed to manage the effort (USGAO, 1998a). Interestingly, public agency representatives found that the system of using handwritten reports to generate data provided them with far more information than had previously been available about program performance (USGAO, 1998a).

As in Florida and Kansas, the agencies implementing privatized programs in other jurisdictions—Michigan, Maine, Missouri, and Hamilton County, Ohio—experienced numerous challenges in developing viable information management systems. These challenges vary but have common problems in generating and communicating complete, accurate data on individual children and families. In Michigan, for example, smaller agencies had difficulties tracking data on individual children, although over the five-year pilot project, their capabilities have improved. In Maine, CIP faced many information challenges because the private agencies did not have compatible information systems with one another or with the state.

Most Initiatives Have Only Limited Capacity to Aggregate Data to Assess the Program or Outcomes

One of the difficulties that many privatization efforts have encountered, in addition to developing the capacity to track data on individual children and families, is the aggregation of data to inform program development (McCullough & Schmitt, 2002). Aggregated data are essential to determining whether a program has achieved the relevant performance-based standards. The privatization initiatives studied here appeared to experience similar difficulties in building the capacity to aggregate data to allow an assessment of services and outcome achievement. The Missouri Alliance, for example, was able to produce aggregate data over time only on two outcome measures: placements at time of enrollment and at later points in time, and the extent to which children were maintained in community-based settings. It was not able to aggregate data from required instruments, such as the Childhood Severity of Psychiatric Illness tool that the state used for determining whether a child had serious behavioral health needs, or on any of the other indicators listed in its contract.

Some programs, however, demonstrated a strong data aggregation capacity. The Michigan Foster Care Permanency Initiative was able to aggregate data on a limited number of clearly defined outcomes standards and to use those data to refine the time frames within which the specified outcomes are to be achieved. YMCA in Sarasota County, Florida, and the Creative Connections program in Hamilton County, Ohio, were also able to develop data analysis systems that allowed data to be aggregated on program outcomes, although in both instances, this capacity took considerable time to develop.

Despite Problems with Data Analysis, Privatization Is Likely to Improve the Quality and Comprehensiveness of Data

Although data may largely be absent at the outset of privatization, indications exist that privatization improves the scope and quality of data available over time. In CWLA's (1999) survey of privatized child welfare initiatives, nearly half of the 47 identified programs had evaluation components. CWLA noted that:

> Perhaps one of the greatest benefits of current efforts will be the ability to generate more accurate data about service need characteristics of the populations, utilization patterns and trends over time, and costs that are linked to the attainment of certain outcomes. This alone may improve a system with historically inadequate and inaccurate data on which to base critical decisions. (pp. 6–7)

Despite the limitations discussed earlier, it appears that the privatization initiatives improved their abilities to collect and analyze data over time and demonstrated a stronger data collection and analysis capacity than the public agencies possessed prior to privatization.

Data relevant to program evaluation are now available in Kansas, and, in fact, these data have provided the foundation for further refinement of the family preservation, foster care, and adoption program outcomes and performance targets. Similarly, foster care outcome data are available in Wayne County, Michigan. In Florida, the lead agencies collect and analyze data on a range of community-specific indicators for program assessment purposes. In Hamilton County, Ohio, Creative Connections developed the capacity to report individual and aggregate data on children's overall role performance, community functioning, school functioning, and interaction with others, and to report aggregate data on children's placements at each level of care.

Of the jurisdictions studied, the Maine program appeared to have the least well-developed data analysis capacity. Although individual private agencies have developed data collection and analysis capabilities, no information system aggregates program data from the seven participating agencies and, as a result, a comprehensive picture of CIP is not possible.

9. The Extent to Which Privatization Is Viable Depends on Service Capacity

McCullough (2001) noted that privatization is based on an assumption that the existing service structure is adequate and that once funding is restructured and responsibilities reallocated, resources will be maximized to the benefit of those served. She also observed, however, that service capacity is underdeveloped in many communities and that financing reconfigurations, in and of themselves, do not address this issue. In many initiatives, it appears that designers made assumptions about the power of new fiscal methodologies to change systems without taking into account the critical role that service capacity plays in the change process. The experiences of these jurisdictions indicate that although adjusting fiscal incentives and penalties may improve certain aspects of service delivery systems, the system changes envisioned by privatization efforts cannot be made in the absence of strong service capacity.

Most of the jurisdictions that were studied here grappled with ensuring that needed services were available to clients. In some jurisdictions, the required array of services to be provided through the initiatives simply was not available. In some communities, the spectrum of services was heavily weighted at the more intensive end (residential and group care) with a far less-developed capacity for family support and family preservation services. In Missouri, for example, family foster care and in-home services were underdeveloped, which ultimately led the Missouri Alliance to provide those service directly, but the residential care capacity was more than adequate. In Hamilton County, Ohio, the reverse was true. Creative Connections succeeded in developing a range of community-based services, but it struggled to develop local residential care capacity that would make it possible to return children placed in other counties to Hamilton County.

In some communities, privatization enhanced service capacity. In Kansas, for example, rural and urban areas achieved greater service equity, particularly with regard to family preservation services. In Michigan, the Foster Care Permanency Initiative began with the provision of more traditional child welfare services, although with the expectation of heightened quality and timeliness, but then incorporated such services as supported visitation and foster parent mentoring—services not typically supported with child welfare funding. Similarly, the flexible funding approach of the Maine CIP supported an expansion of community-based services. YMCA, as lead agency for Sarasota County, Florida, developed strong local service capacity through partnerships with a range of service providers in the county. That said, YMCA has stressed that it is critical that any program's current service capacity be subject to a continuous quality improvement process that rigorously assesses the nature and scope of current services in light of clients' current and evolving needs.

As YMCA's focus on refining service capacity suggests, programs that use a lead agency approach must ensure the development of a provider network that responds to the needs of the children, youth, and families that the initiative serves. When service capacity at the outset is inadequate, the state expects lead agencies to develop new service options. As the experiences of Missouri and Hamilton County indicate, however, lead agencies may face serious barriers in attempting to develop a full array of services, because their contracts typically do not include provisions for the resources that lead agencies need to expand the service array (see McCullough, 2001).

At the same time, lead agencies may have limited choices in building service capacity. The Missouri Alliance found that community-based foster care resources were so extremely limited that the only viable option was to develop the service itself. This approach effectively met vital service needs, but it raised issues for the initiative regarding the extent to which it should become a "mega-agency" itself, rather than developing community-based collaborations. YMCA in Florida and Creative Connections in Ohio faced similar considerations. YMCA, for example, increased its direct service provision from 10% to approximately 20% of all

Community-Based Care services provided in Sarasota County. In Hamilton County, the Auditor for the State of Ohio criticized Creative Connections regarding its level of self-referrals.

Finally, service capacity issues arise in connection with the broader needs of children and families served through the child welfare system. McCullough (2001) wrote that privatization of child welfare services cannot resolve some of the underlying issues, such as parental mental illness, substance abuse, and incarceration, that have led to children's extended stays in foster care, lack of consistent success in reunification efforts, and difficulties achieving permanency for children through adoption. She also noted that from a service capacity standpoint, privatization cannot address these overarching concerns unless adequate access to other needed services exists, most notably mental health and substance abuse services for children in the child welfare system and their birthparents (McCullough, 2001). Although the initiatives acknowledged these realities to a greater or lesser degree, most struggled to develop strong connections with other service systems. Kansas and Florida, notably, have been successful in forging connections with the mental health systems in their communities.

10. Contracting Processes and Contracts Used in Privatization Initiatives Tend to Have Problems

Somewhat surprisingly, given the long history of contracting out in child welfare, many of the initiatives struggled to achieve meaningful competition through the bidding process, used contracting processes that proved less than effective, and developed contracts that were problematic in many ways.

Contracting for Privatization Initiatives Does Not Necessarily Result in Competitive Bidding

Many agree that contracting out as a privatization approach will be most effective when meaningful competition is secured in the bidding process (Pack, 1991). The Leadership 18 Group (2000) emphasized that a level playing field is necessary so that nonprofits may take full advantage of opportunities to bid on contracts in a competitive manner. Nonetheless, experience has shown that establishing a competitive process does not necessarily result in real competition. Studies have demonstrated that it is not uncommon that competitively bid contracts elicit responses from only one bidder (Schlesinger, 1986). The Missouri Interdepartmental Initiative, for example, anticipated contractual relationships with four agencies, but only one bidder responded to the RFP. Hamilton County made no effort create a competitive bidding environment. The five county agencies essentially recruited Beech Acres as lead agency because it brought not only programmatic expertise but independent financial resources to support the program. Lead agency status for Creative Connections has been the result of a sole source contractual arrangement—both when the Hamilton County agencies approached Beech Acres to assume responsibility for the program in 1998 and when they contacted the Indiana-based entity that assumed responsibility for the program in October 2002.

Compared with Missouri and Ohio, Kansas sought and achieved greater competition in its contracting process. In Kansas, meaningful competition existed (except for the adoption contract) for both the initial contract awards and the contract rebidding in 2000. Although the number of agencies that received family preservation contracts fell from five to two, suggesting a less competitive environment, the number of foster care contractors grew from three to five, suggesting livelier competition.

In Maine and Michigan, neither the actual level of competition nor the extent to which state's actually sought competition is clear. Initially, agencies submitted 32 proposals in response to the Maine RFP for CIP. Since the time of the initial award of contracts to seven agencies, however, Maine has not changed any contractors as the contracts have been renewed annually. Michigan initiated the pilot project through the efforts of one private agency that was subsequently joined by three other agencies in a noncompetitive process. In Phase II, five agencies submitted proposals to join the original contractors, and Michigan selected two. When the Foster Care Permanency Initiative becomes permanent in Phase III, the 17 foster care agencies currently providing services in Wayne County will participate.

Contracting Processes Vary in Effectiveness and Efficiency

A review of the processes used to contract out the privatization initiatives in this study suggests that the processes themselves were highly variable in terms of effectiveness and efficiency. Three of the initiatives used relatively effective processes. The Kansas process, particularly the 2000 rebidding of the contracts, was efficient, and the processes used in Maine and Michigan were straightforward contracting-out efforts. On the other hand, the remaining three programs used processes that proved less than effective, although at different points in the contracting process. In Missouri, the RFP involved repeated clarifications regarding information contained in the request, and as a result, the state changed the due date for proposals three times. In Florida, the request process was fairly clear and well developed, but inefficiencies plagued the contracting process. Although delineated in detail by the state, the contracting process was extremely variable from one county to another. In particular, variation existed in the final negotiation process, which, in some cases, involved the finalization of contracts by the state child welfare agency without the direct involvement of the lead agency. Finally, in Hamilton County, the contact renegotiation process became a protracted and futile effort for Beech Acres after it had invested substantially in Creative Connections over a four-year period. The programmatic details that Beech Acres developed over several months ultimately proved less important to the county than the risk-shifting provisions related to the case rate.

Privatization Contracts Are Fraught with Problems

Given the nature of contracting out, the contract is a critical feature. To serve as the effective basis for a privatization effort, contracts must include clearly defined expectations regarding the services to be provided, to whom they will be provided, and with what results, if monitoring is to play a meaningful role (Gormley, 1994–1995). The contracts of the jurisdictions largely failed to meet these standards, except for Michigan. In several cases, the contracts were extremely lengthy, unduly complicated, and overly focused on details that bore little relationship to critical issues. In some cases, contractual expectations were framed in ambiguous terms, making it impossible to determine what the private agencies were to do, what clients were to receive, and what results were to be produced (Sara Rosenbaum, personal communication, February 12, 2002). In one contract— Missouri's Interdepartmental Initiative—the problems posed by ambiguity were heightened by the use of highly technical language of questionable application to the initiative. The contract contained terms (subsequently integrated into the program itself) that were borrowed from the field of managed care. For example, *disenrollment,* generally understood in managed care parlance to be a negative outcome, was defined as a successful exit from the Interdepartmental Initiative. *Discharge,* typically understood in child welfare terminology to reflect a successful exit from services, was defined as a neutral outcome, reflecting neither success nor failure.

Many contracts had no clear articulation of how various requirements related to one another or how they ultimately supported the broad goals of the initiative. In some jurisdictions, the contracts focused on structural standards, such as staff credentials and competencies, which proved difficult to implement in light of the program design. In Hamilton County, Ohio, the program served children with such a broad range of severe needs, including autism, schizophrenia, and histories of sexual abuse, that it was not reasonable to expect that each staff member could demonstrate the many required professional competencies listed in the contract. Similar issues arose in Missouri where, because of difficulties in developing locally organized systems of care, the Missouri Alliance staff took on a variety of direct service functions that were distinctly different from the care management responsibilities stated in the contract.

Of particular note was the consistent failure of the privatization contracts to clearly articulate the interventions to be provided. The contracts typically failed to describe the required services, an oversight that intensified problems in appropriately pricing those services (Sara Rosenbaum, personal communication, February 12, 2002). The Missouri contract referred to the lead agency's responsibility to "recruit, develop and contract for a comprehensive array of community-based providers and resources"; the Hamilton County, Ohio, contract required that the lead agency "ensure provision of services at the appropriate Level of Care required by each enrolled child"; and the Maine contract required that "the provision of and/or arrangements for services outlined in the case plan" be "directly related to child abuse and its underlying causes."

In general, the contracts for the initiatives were problematic in a number of ways that made success elusive. Specifically, the contracts combined vague service obligations, poorly defined outcomes and performance measures, poorly specified roles and responsibilities (particularly for the public agency), and financial risk for the private agency. In sum, as noted by one contracting expert, the dynamic in many of the programs was one of inexperienced purchasing agents (public agencies) attempting to develop at-risk contracts with inexperienced sellers (private agencies) (Sara Rosenbaum, personal communication, September 30, 2002).

11. Monitoring Tends to Be Overdone or Underdone in Many Privatization Initiatives

The role of monitoring in privatization initiatives is a critical but complex one. Milward (1994) captured the complexities associated with monitoring—"Privatization occurs because severe capacity limitations force government to contract services it does not have the ability to provide" (p. 79), but the design of privatization policies, the implementation of privatization initiatives, and evaluation typically remain within government control. As Milward framed the question, "How can government be expected to effectively fulfill these functions when limited capacities led to privatization in the first place?" (p. 79). Similarly, Gormley (1994–1995) pointed out that although "vigilance and follow up" are essential in contracting out, "accountability continues to be the Achilles heel of many contracts" (p. 224). The problems in this area often arise in connection with staff shortages within government agencies and the lack of in-house expertise in managing contracts and conducting audits (Gurin, 1989; Kettl, 1993; Smith & Lipsky, 1992).

Nonetheless, particularly when privatization takes the form of contracting out, as is the case in child welfare privatization initiatives, the public agency is expected to retain a level of control and accountability for the services that private agencies provide. The responsibility for monitoring and oversight requires that the government retain the legal authority to effectively provide oversight; that it have the capacity in terms of expertise, staff, and funding to oversee private sector performance; and once evaluative criteria have been defined, that it determine private agency compliance with contractual requirements (USGAO, 1998b).

The privatization efforts that were studied for this book acknowledged the importance of monitoring. In fact, a wide variety of monitoring activities appeared in privatization contracts and in the operating procedures that were implemented in these initiatives. It was not unusual to find requirements for contract compliance, outcome monitoring, program monitoring, subcontractor monitoring, eligibility monitoring (particularly for Title IV-E and Medicaid), quality assurance activities, and independent evaluations. It also was not unusual to find that auditors' evaluations of states' monitoring of privatization initiatives fell short of expected standards (examples being the Auditor General's study in Florida and the auditor's report in Hamilton County, Ohio).

Considerable variation existed in the level of monitoring that actually took place in the initiatives. In Michigan, the public child welfare agency, working with the private agencies, developed a highly effective monitoring process focused on key outcomes. Kansas, Florida, and Michigan developed third-party evaluations to strengthen monitoring and evaluation.

In other cases, however, monitoring became so extensive that it presented serious programmatic issues. In the Missouri Interdepartmental Initiative, for example, Missouri placed great emphasis on monitoring the Missouri Alliance. TSO, rather than the public agencies that funded the effort, undertook that responsibility and apparently did so aggressively. The level of monitoring became so intensive that it undermined the Missouri Alliance's attempts to implement the new program. Eventually, the government reclaimed monitoring responsibilities, a step that stakeholders familiar with the program see as a highly positive development because the public agency's focus is much more on key programmatic and fiscal issues.

At the other end of the spectrum, monitoring appears to have been "underdone." Florida has had ongoing issues regarding the appropriate role of the state in monitoring and auditing, difficulties creating a monitoring system that addresses the unique features of community-based care, and problems building internal monitoring capacity within state systems that in the past, had not incorporated such functions. Although multiple monitoring requirements are in the Community-Based Care program, people have had concerns about the actual degree to which monitoring of program performance occurred. Similarly, some have had concerns in Maine that monitoring has not been adequate. To some degree, Maine's monitoring difficulties have been associated with an unclear articulation of program goals and shifting program emphases that largely have responded to public perceptions of the program. The recent focus on private agencies' face-to-face contacts with referred families, for example, was not the result of careful monitoring of program activity or outcomes but of negative media coverage.

12. Financial Problems Are Among the Thorniest Issues Privatization Efforts Confront

The fiscal arrangements in privatization initiatives frequently are highlighted as their most innovative features. Nonetheless, the financing structure—particularly in the context of risk-sharing arrangements—has been extremely challenging. Issues arise in relation to the underlying sources of funding for such efforts, the fiscal methodology, and the mechanisms to address the potential effect of risk sharing.

The Sources of Funding for Privatization Initiatives Varies

The core funding for privatization initiatives consistently has been from child welfare state and federal funds (McCullough, 2001). In various initiatives, however, other funding streams have been used: Medicaid (Title XIX of the Social Security Act), mental health and substance abuse block grant funds, funding under TANF, tobacco settlement funds, and, to a more limited extent, education and juvenile justice funds (McCullough, 2001). The jurisdictions studied reflected the same variability.

In Kansas, Michigan, and Maine, child welfare funding has supported the programs from their inception. Other initiatives have blended funds from multiple sources. Hamilton County, Ohio, for example, used funding from child welfare, mental health, alcohol and drug addiction, and mental retardation/developmental disability agencies, and from the juvenile court. Missouri used child welfare, juvenile justice, and mental health funding. In Missouri, however, funding will cease to be interdepartmental when the program is redesigned, and state and federal child welfare funding will provide the core funding in the future. In Florida, communities moving into Community-Based Care are expected to mobilize support from a range of funding sources (federal, state, and local) to meet the program's fiscal needs. Broward County, for example, plans to use tobacco settlement funds. Florida also has opted to use TANF funds to support the Community-Based Care program infrastructure in certain communities.

The relationship between the privatization initiatives and Medicaid was interesting. The role of Medicaid in financing services for poor children (the population of children largely served by child welfare systems in general) is well-recognized (McCarthy & Valentine, 2000). Other than in Maine, however, where the private agencies are providers of Medicaid-funded targeted case management services, the relationship between the studied initiatives and Medicaid, as a key funding source for many of the services to be provided through those initiatives, was not well developed. In Missouri, Medicaid contributed 18% of the case rate, but it was not clear whether that percentage appropriately reflected the actual level of Medicaid funding for the types of services provided by the initiative.

In some programs, such as Florida and Hamilton County, Ohio, the expectation was that the private agency serving as lead agency would maximize Medicaid funding for the services provided by the initiative. Such an approach is of concern, given the fact that private agencies do not control access to Medicaid-covered services, nor can they require Medicaid managed care organizations to serve children for whom the child welfare agency has primary service responsibility (Sara Rosenbaum, personal communication, September 30, 2002). Expectations that private agencies can finance privatization initiatives through Medicaid maximization, consequently, raise serious questions about the funding assumptions that have driven these programs (Sara Rosenbaum, personal communication, September 30, 2002).

Finding the Right Fiscal Methodology Is an Elusive Goal

Much remains to be understood about optimal approaches to the development and implementation of new payment methodologies in the context of privatization. USGAO (1998a), in its study of privatization efforts, noted that quality client and service-cost data were often absent and, as a result, public agencies had great difficulty establishing and implementing appropriate payment rates for providers, particularly prospective payment rates either in the form of capitated payments or case rates. Four years later, this study reached the same conclusion. Similarly, both USGAO and this study identified the need to continually revisit and adjust payment levels (and in some cases, risk-sharing provisions) as more current information is collected. This study, however, found that revisiting and adjusting payment levels based on data were not general practices. Typically, the pattern was, instead, that public and private agencies entered at-risk contracts without the data needed to price services. They then adjusted case rates based on no data or limited data, creating significant financial stresses for both the public and private sectors.

Consistent with the findings of McCullough and Schmitt (2002), the most common fiscal methodology found among the initiatives examined in this study was the case rate. The experiences of the studied jurisdictions in which case rates have been used suggest a lack of success in appropriately calculating an initial case rate level. In Kansas, for example, inadequate case rates had a dire financial effect, in the form of near or actual bankruptcy, on some private foster care agencies and on the agency that took lead agency responsibility for adoption services. After it became apparent that the case rate approach was not being successfully implemented, Kansas abandoned what was considered to be the most innovative feature of its effort and returned to a traditional payment methodology.

In Missouri, inadequate case rates similarly led to sizeable financial losses as the lead agency, a new business entity, struggled to implement a program within a very limited start-up period. Subsequent adjustments to the case rate failed to bring the rate into line with the actual cost of services. Missouri recently stated its intention to develop another fiscal methodology as an alternative to the case rate approach.

The problems in setting appropriate case rates were obvious in those jurisdictions where the population to be served was composed solely of a small number of children with severe needs. In Missouri and Hamilton County, Ohio, the fiscal effects of serving an extremely small number of children was heightened by the children's intense service needs; a no reject, no eject mandate; and poorly defined expectations regarding outcomes. This combination virtually guaranteed the failure of the financial risk approach (Sara Rosenbaum, personal communication, February 12, 2002). In neither of these programs was the case rate adequate (as initially established or subsequently revised), and in both cases, it is doubtful that the lead agencies could have continued to operate if other resources had not been available to them. In Missouri, the founding agency members of the Missouri Alliance invested their own funds to support the alliance's continuing operations. In Hamilton County, the effect of the inadequate case rate was softened only by Beech Acres' willingness to use its own endowment to subsidize Creative Connections. Its refusal to accept an inadequate case rate in the new contract ultimately led to termination of contract renegotiations and Beech Acres' decision to discontinue its involvement with the program.

It is important to note that Missouri calculated the case rate through a data-based process that was more rigorous than that used by most other jurisdictions (Michigan used a data-based approach in calculating the per diem rate and the incentive payments). Nonetheless, the case rate proved inadequate for a variety of reasons, including the exclusion of case management costs for children referred from the child welfare agency and the backing out of large sums of money to fund TSO and the proposed risk pool.

Florida adopted global budgeting, as opposed to a case rate, as the risk-based approach. This methodology requires lead agencies to assume full risk for the cost of all child welfare services and supports needed by children and families, regardless of how many clients in the area need services. Florida expected lead agencies to maximize the use of Medicaid-funded services and to mobilize a range of non-state revenues to cover the full cost of services.

Global budgeting has presented challenges that differ somewhat from the challenges posed by case rates. In Florida's global budgeting approach, clear budget data has been lacking, and, as a result, lead agencies have not been able to predict the actual funding levels for their programs. Delays in cost reimbursement have occurred as a result of problems with data management systems, further intensifying fiscal stresses for private agencies. Finally, as the overall costs of the program increased as more counties implemented Community-Based Care, many have had concerns about the adequacy of state funding for the program.

As an example of another approach, Maine developed a fixed sum contract, under which private agencies must provide services for a pre-established price. Maine calculated reimbursement rates on a geographical basis, but given the absence of data on anticipated referrals and the ambiguity regarding the services that must be provided, it is not possible to state definitively how Maine calculated the final fixed sums. At the same time, the contracts are silent as to the alternatives available to private agencies in the event of cost overruns, although it appears that the private agencies can approach the public agency for additional funds if needed (and they have done so successfully). Although the fixed sum contracts would suggest an at-risk approach, it appears that the public agency readily reallocates funding among contractors as financial issues arise.

Of all the jurisdictions, Michigan appeared to have the strongest fiscal methodology. Its combined use of reduced per diem payments and incentive payments to award performance has proven successful. The focus on incentive payments at key milestones in children's cases tied to successful achievement of permanency creates fiscal rewards for effective practice and successful outcomes. From a fiscal standpoint, the Foster Care Permanency Initiative agencies must qualify for the incentive payments to remain financially solvent because the per diem rate has been reduced to a level that both the public and private agencies know to be less than the cost of care. The fiscal incentives, consequently, play a powerful role in promoting desirable outcomes. They also create financial pressures that, it is important to note, have shaped practice but have not resulted in any participating agency experiencing serious threats to its fiscal viability.

As a final point, some have expressed concern that the adoption of new privatization financial methodologies may have an effect on the historical financial base of traditional nonprofit agencies that assume the role of lead agency or otherwise contract to provide services. Kansas Action for Children (1998), for example, noted that one of the flawed assumptions in the Kansas privatization initiative was that private agencies that contracted with the public agency would have the same level of community support that they enjoyed before privatization. Many of these private contractors found that with large public contracts in hand, they were perceived as needing less private support, and most of the private agencies experienced decreases in charitable giving. The contractors subsequently experienced a far more competitive environment among themselves for private dollars, volunteers, and other community support. By contrast, however, in Florida, an express expectation is that lead agencies for Community-Based Care will maximize financial support at the local level. In Sarasota and Broward Counties, the lead agencies appear to have been quite successful in mobilizing local support, a result that may be associated with the community-based focus of that privatization initiative.

Privatization Initiatives Rely on Fiscal Incentives and Penalties, but the Effects of Them Are Questionable

Several of the initiatives examined in this study incorporated financial incentives and bonuses tied to key outcomes or performance indicators. The initiatives took diverse approaches to these mechanisms. In some cases, as in Kansas, the state gave little attention to the use of financial penalties and incentives in relation to outcome achievement. In Missouri, by contrast, fiscal penalties and fiscal incentives were prominent contract features. Fiscal penalties ($6,600 per child replaced within 120 days of disenrollment), however, were approximately four times the rate of fiscal incentives ($1,600 per child who continued to satisfy disenrollment criteria for 120 days after disenrollment). In Hamilton County, Ohio, the contract set forth extensive penalties for the lead agency's failure to achieve specified indicators and benchmarks but placed no emphasis on fiscal incentives. Little evidence suggested that fiscal penalties affect outcome performance in any meaningful way.

Michigan's approach involved the use of fiscal incentives. Under the methodology for the Foster Care Permanency Initiative, agencies are paid a reduced per diem (substantially below the cost of care) and a lump sum payment at the time of referral, and they are eligible for significant incentive payments if they meet certain permanency milestones within specified periods of time. Although the contract has no express fiscal penalties, failure to qualify for an incentive payment has a direct negative financial effect on the private agency, because it will essentially be in a loss position in any case for which it does not collect incentive payments. The framing of the fiscal arrangements, however, in positive ways (incentive payments) as opposed to punitive ways (penalties), in addition to funding the incentive payments at fairly significantly levels, appear to have created a productive environment in which outcomes are being readily achieved.

Protecting Private Agencies Through Stop-Loss Provisions Tends to Be of Limited Practical Value

The jurisdictions used a number of approaches in an attempt to protect private agencies from extreme levels of financial loss, including risk pools and variations on stop-loss provisions in contracts. In many cases, the initiatives implemented provisions to attract private agencies to them. Nonetheless, in some cases, greater emphasis was placed on the design of these features than actual implementation. In other cases, the approaches either were not used, were not been fully tested, or were found to be useless.

In two jurisdictions, the contracts laboriously detailed protective mechanisms that were not implemented. In Missouri, for example, the contract described a risk pool in great specificity, but the state did not implement those contract provisions. When the Missouri Alliance faced financial problems in early implementation, it discovered that no mechanism existed to avail itself of needed resources, despite the fact that the risk pool funding had been subtracted from the pooled funds used to calculate the case rate. Similarly, in Hamilton County, Ohio, the contract described stop-loss provisions in extreme detail. The highly complex provisions appeared to play virtually no role in either the development or implementation of Creative Connections, nor the protection of Beech Acres from substantial losses. The proposed simplification of the stop-loss provisions in the negotiations for the new Creative Connections program seemed to indicate that both the public and private agencies recognized that protection from unreasonable risks of financial loss could be accomplished in a more straightforward, workable manner.

Instead of using contractual stop-loss provisions, Florida developed a risk pool and endorsed a shared earnings program. In 2000, the Florida legislature established a $4.5 million risk pool to protect lead agencies from extreme growth in caseloads beyond the lead agency's control. Views of this mechanism differ. The state points out that no provider has accessed the risk pool, as an indicator that lead agencies are experiencing fiscal stability. Others, however, note that it has not been made clear to lead agencies how they could use this assistance or what level of support they could receive. Florida recently added a statewide shared earnings program to address the potential financial risk that lead agencies could face if caseloads increased dramatically. Florida has not yet developed the approach or tested the level of protection that it may extend to private agencies.

As a final example of a protective approach, Kansas initially developed a shared risk corridor to allocate financial risk between the public agency and the lead agencies. It, however, provided inadequate protection for the foster care lead agencies. Only one of the initial three contractors remained within the corridor at the end of the first year of the contract. Kansas abandoned the approach in favor of increasing the case rate and creating an outside the case rate system, which itself was later abandoned in favor of a return to standard case rates.

13. Consumer Involvement Is Key in Privatization, But Is Often Not Explicitly Addressed

Organizations that have studied the essential features of initiatives that integrate privatization and managed care features consistently have highlighted the importance of consumer involvement. The Georgetown University Child Development Center (2001) identified consumer involvement as one of the essential elements of such efforts. The Leadership 18 Group (2000) similarly highlighted the need to ensure consumer involvement and protections in privatization efforts. Among the features that it outlined as critical in this regard were grievance and appeals mechanisms for consumers; requirements that clients be treated with respect and dignity; opportunities, whenever possible, for consumer choice of providers; evaluation of client satisfaction; and standards for management of private client information. McCullough and Schmitt (2002) noted that an increasing number of initiatives report goals related to child and family involvement in decisionmaking.

Consistent with the findings of McCullough and Schmitt (2002), most of the privatization efforts referred to "child and family involvement" as an initiative component. The extent to which clients were actually involved in the planning and implementation, however, appeared fairly limited. Some jurisdictions placed particular focus on consumer involvement. YMCA in Sarasota County, Florida, implemented a number of mechanisms to involve consumers in the evaluation of Community-Based Care, including annual parent and community surveys, interviews with children and youth when their foster care placements changed, and foster parent surveys. In Kansas, the third-party evaluation included a client satisfaction survey, although the low response rate made it difficult to draw definitive conclusions.

Other jurisdictions, however, struggled to implement consumer involvement mechanisms. In Missouri, consumer involvement has been limited to parents' participation in planning for their children. Parents become involved in the program only when their children are enrolled and the alliance forms a family support team. The Missouri Alliance has worked actively to ensure family involvement at that level. Only public agencies can refer children, however, leaving little room for families to advocate in behalf of their children for program services. Families are not involved in the referral process, nor are they permitted to attend meetings of the interdepartmental team. At the program design, implementation, and evaluation levels, families have not been significantly involved. The initiative never formed the proposed child and family advocacy committee, which might have given families a role in providing program input. The Missouri Alliance, however, recently focused on family involvement in an evaluation of the quality of its wraparound services.

In the case of Hamilton County, Ohio, consumer involvement was a central focus in the contract renegotiations regarding Creative Connections, reflecting a recognition that this program element needed greater focus. Beech Acres proposed to the county agencies a variety of consumer involvement activities, including parent support groups, parent advocacy training and coaching, and parent advocacy positions. Unfortunately, the county eliminated these proposed program changes when it approached an alternative contractor.

Recommendations

Based on the lessons learned from the six jurisdictions, communities considering privatized approaches to the delivery of child welfare services are advised to consider the following recommendations.

- When contemplating privatization, a community should take into account the goals of the privatization effort and, based on those goals, clearly specify:

  - the population to be served;

  - the model for privatization to be used, and if a lead agency model is selected, the types of agencies that will be eligible to serve in this role;

  - the roles and responsibilities of the public agency and the private agency; and

  - the fiscal methodology.

- Public agencies should not expect to save money through privatization. Cost savings are highly unlikely given the real costs of developing, implementing, and overseeing a privatization initiative and the costs associated with providing a full array of services to children and families under expectations of higher quality. Private agencies, however, should expect that public agencies will attempt to control costs through privatization and may design programs that shift the risk of financial loss to the private agency. In such cases, the private agency may be expected to finance the full cost of care with its own dollars or through other revenue sources.

■ Absent significant attention to the factors that undermine efficiency in the public sector, all parties should recognize that greater efficiency will not be achieved simply because a private agency has assumed primary responsibility for service provision.

■ At the outset, the initiative should use a few selected outcomes and associated performance targets. The outcomes should represent concepts to be measured in straightforward and simple terms. Outcomes and targets should be based on preprivatization program data or on baseline data developed during the initial implementation stage, as opposed to being arbitrarily defined with no demonstrable relationship to actual performance. Fiscal incentives should be tied to a limited number of key program outcomes.

■ Communities should recognize that privatization efforts require the commitment of high-level leadership over the long term and require concerted efforts to develop and sustain strong interpersonal relationships between public and private agencies. Without these factors, it is unlikely that a privatization initiative can be successfully implemented or sustained.

■ Attention should be given to carefully delineating the roles and responsibilities of the public and private agencies. It is not sufficient to detail the private agency's roles and responsibilities in relation to service delivery and accountability. The public agency's obligations—such as timely payment, responsiveness to providers' questions, and monitoring of outcomes—should be specified.

■ A strong infrastructure—characterized by a vision of the initiative shared by the public and private agency, an adequate management and staffing structure, financial support for start up, and strong connections with the community—should be the initial focus as communities move toward the implementation of any privatization initiative.

- A phased-in approach that gradually implements privatization through broad-based community planning, pilot projects, and/or transitional contracts should be used to ensure the successful implementation of the initiative.

- Service capacity should be a central focus in the planning and implementation of any privatization effort. The current service system should be realistically evaluated in light of clients' needs. Private agencies should receive needed support to develop an adequate service capacity, including linkages with other services systems such as the mental health and substance abuse treatment systems. Service capacity should be assessed on an ongoing basis by both the public and private agencies to ensure responsiveness to evolving client needs.

- Information management systems that produce cost, service, and outcomes data at the individual and aggregate levels should be developed and implemented as quickly as possible.

- In any privatization initiative involving contracting, the process of securing competitive bids should be carefully designed and consistently implemented. The process should clearly communicate the nature and scope of the program, the fiscal methodology, and the requirements of the private agency in terms of service provision and accountability. The process—from seeking bids to finalizing the contract—should be implemented in a consistent, predictable manner.

- Privatization contracts should be written in language that is understandable to the parties that will implement the requirements, particularly private agency administrators. Contracts should specifically state the services to be provided, to whom they are to be provided, and the results to be obtained. The obligations of both the private and public agency should be detailed.

- The public agency, which must remain accountable even as it privatizes services, should develop strong monitoring capabilities that ensure effective government oversight and assurance of contract compliance, compliance with standards of quality service provision (such as accreditation standards), and achievement of program outcomes.

- Any privatization initiative must have adequate funding. Privatization cannot be viewed as a way to provide services more cheaply or as a way to control costs. Reimbursement rates and schedules must be fair and equitable.

- At-risk contracting, which places private agencies at financial risk when the cost of services exceeds the predetermined rates or payment levels, should be viewed with considerable caution. Given the current state of knowledge regarding risk shifting in child welfare contracts, it is premature to use at-risk approaches whether in the form of case rates, capitated payments, or global budgeting. To the extent that such approaches are used, they should be subject to ongoing assessment based on the development of baseline cost and outcomes data and should be seen only as "working hypotheses."

- When at-risk contracting is used, private agencies should have viable protection against excessive levels of financial loss due to factors beyond the agency's control. Mechanisms such as stop-loss provisions should be carefully developed and fully implemented if they are to play a viable role in protecting private agencies against unacceptable levels of fiscal loss.

- Consumer involvement should be a key focus in program design, implementation, and evaluation. Specific mechanisms for involving consumers at all program levels should be developed and implemented.

Conclusion

Privatization is a tool that can be usefully employed in certain environments to enhance service provision. As Gormley (1994–1995) pointed out, however, governments should take care not "to select a hammer when they really need a wrench" (p. 231). Gormley also concluded that privatization efforts will be successful only if governments bring four key skills to the task:

1. matching good candidates for privatization with appropriate alternatives;

2. combining the public and private sectors in creative ways;

3. monitoring "to avoid unfettered discretion"; and

4. evaluating to "ensure that programs actually produce the desired results" (p. 231).

It appears that privatization in the arena of child welfare services—where contracting out has played a significant historical role—will continue to be pursued in a variety of ways. The case studies developed through this examination of privatization suggest that in some ways, these efforts have been successful, and in other ways, they have presented substantial challenges that have not been readily overcome. There has been some success in matching good candidates (private agencies) with the programs being designed by public agencies, and creative thinking has been clearly brought to many of the processes. On the other hand, many other aspects of these efforts proved inadequate. The financial methodologies frequently were unworkable, if not disastrous. Monitoring and evaluation posed significant difficulties, both for private agencies that were expected to comprehensively monitor and report on program achievement, and for public agen-

293

cies that were attempting to undertake new quality assurance roles. Finally, outcomes and performance measures proved to be a major hurdle for most of the programs. The desired results were often not clear, and the performance targets frequently were unspecified or were developed in the absence of validating data. These issues made it difficult to reach any viable conclusions about the success of the privatization efforts.

Although the positive aspects of privatization should not be underestimated, it is also important to place privatization in the broader context of service provision to low-income children and families—the clients generally served through child welfare programs. Starr (1988) wrote:

> [Privatization] reinforces the view that government cannot be expected to perform well....We commonly limit public services to a functional minimum and thereby guarantee that people will consider the private alternative a step up....The restricted quality of public provision is a self-reinforcing feature. Because the poor are the principal beneficiaries of many programs, the middle-class public opposes expenditures to produce as high a quality of service as they must pay for privately; and because the quality is held down, the poor as well as the middle class develop a contempt for the public sector and an eagerness to escape it. The movement toward privatization reflects and promotes this contempt, and therein lies part of its political danger. (p. 36)

Privatization cannot succeed by simply transferring to private agencies the constraints that have characterized public agencies' service provision to poor children and families. As this study has demonstrated, adequate support for services in the form of financial and human resources and a genuine commitment to quality are essential to any successful effort.

References

Allen, J. W., Chi, K. S., Devlin, K. A., Fall, M., Hatry, H. P. & Masterman, W. (1989). *The private sector in state service delivery: Examples of innovative practice.* Washington, DC: Urban Institute.

Alliance for Redesigning Government. (1996). *The Oregon option: Early lessons from a performance partnership on building results-driven accountability.* Washington, DC: National Academy of Public Administration.

American Federation of State, County, and Municipal Employees. (2000, August 28). Child welfare and privatization: Trends and considerations. Available from http://www.afscme.org/pol-leg/cwfs04.htm.

Ascher, K. (1987). *The politics of privatization: Contracting out public services.* New York: St. Martin's Press.

Atkan, C. C. (1995). An introduction to the theory of privatization. *Journal of Social, Political, and Economic Studies, 20*), 187–195.

Auditor General. (2001). Monitoring of community-based care providers of child welfare services by the Department of Children and Family Services, Operational audit (Report No. 02-033). Tallahassee, FL: State of Florida Auditor General.

Auditor of the State of Ohio. (2001). Hamilton County managed care performance audit. Columbus, OH: Author.

Bailey, R.W. (1987). Uses and, misuses of privitization. In S. H. Hanke (Ed.), *Prospects for privitization* (pp. 140–162). New York: Academy of Political Sciences.

Bardach, E., & Lesser, C. (1996). Accountability in human services collaboratives: For what? And to whom? *Journal of Public Administration Research and Theory, 6,* 197–224.

Barr, S., & McAllister, B. (1997, June 11). Downsizing cuts federal union representation: More postal employees covered. *Washington Post,* p. A21.

Barth, R. P. (1997). Effects of age and race on the odds of adoption versus remaining in long-term out-of-home care. *Child Welfare,* 74, 285–309.

Bates, E. (2000). *Private prisons.* Available from authors.

Beech Acres. (2001). Beech Acres—Creative Connections response to the State of Ohio performance audit of August 16, 2001. Available from authors.

Beecher, J. A. (1998). *Twenty myths about privatization.* Washington, DC: National Academy of Public Administration, Alliance for Redesigning Government.

Belsie, L. (2000, August 3). Kansas' bold experiment in child welfare. *Christian Science Monitor,* pp. 4–5.

Bendick, M. (1985). *Privatizing the delivery of social welfare services. Working paper #6: Project on the federal role.* Washington, DC: National Conference on Social Welfare.

Bendick, M. (1989). Privatizing the delivery of social welfare service. In S. B. Kamerman & A. J. Kahn (Eds.), *Privatization and the welfare state* (pp. 97–120). Princeton, NJ: Princeton University Press.

Bennett, R. (1990). *Decentralization, intergovernmental relations and markets: Towards a post-welfare agenda.* Oxford, UK: Clarendon Press.

Berger, V. (1999, March 22). Private prisons: Bad idea. *National Law Journal,* 21(30), p. A26.

Berger, P., & Neuhaus, R. (1977). *To empower people: The role of mediating structures in public policy.* Boston: University Press of America.

Bernstein, S. R. (1991). *Managing contracted services in the nonprofit economy.* Philadelphia: Temple University Press.

Blank, R. M. (2000, March). When can public policy makers rely on private markets? The effective provision of social services. *Economic Journal,* 110, 34–49.

Broskowski, A. (2001). *Report on cost indicators for child welfare services, Hamilton County, Department of Human Services.* Available from authors.

Bruns, E. J., Buchard, J. D., & Yor, J. T. (1995). Evaluating the Vermont system of care: Outcomes associated with community-based wraparound services. *Journal of Child and Family Services,* 4, 321–339.

Campbell, C. (2000, December 19). *Privatization, profits, and publicity—The new trinity.* Available from authors.

Casey Outcomes and Decision-Making Project. (1998). *Assessing outcomes in child welfare services: Principles, concepts, and a framework of core indicators.* Englewood, CO: American Humane Association.

Center for Assessment and Policy Development. (1999). *Some issues to consider in results-based contracting with service providers.* Bala Cynwyd, PA: Author.

Chi, K. S. (1994, July 17). Privatization in state government: Trends and options. Prepared for the 55th Training Conference of the American Society for Public Administration, Kansas City, MO.

Child Protection Report. (2002, February 28). Both public and private officials hope nice 'n' easy will get the job done, p. 33.

Child welfare database is long overdue. (2001, December 4). *Tallahassee Democrat,* p. A8.

Child Welfare League of America. (1999). *CWLA Managed Care and Privatization Child Welfare Tracking Project: 1998 state and county survey results.* Washington, DC: Author.

Child Welfare League of America. (1989). *Standards for services to strengthen and preserve families with children.* Washington, DC: CWLA Press.

Community-based care in Florida. (2001). *The Alliance,* 1(1).

Community Based Solutions Proposal. (2001). Available from authors.

Cooper, W. (2002, April 16). Alliance demands foster care answers. *Palm Beach Post,* p. 1B.

Cornell University Department of City & Regional Planning. (2000, December 19). The privatization debate: Proponents and opponents. Available from http://www.crp.cornell.edu/projects/restructuring/doc/privatization/.

Corrections Corp. pays $1.7 million settlement. (1999, March 1). *Atlanta Business Chronicle.,* p. 22.

Craig, C., Kulik, T., James, T., & Nielsen, S. (1998). Blueprint for the privatization of child welfare (Policy Study No. 248). Available from http://www.rppi.org/ps248.html.

Criswell, A. (2000, August 10). Foster care contracts: Testimony before the SRS Transition Oversight Committee, Kansas Legislature.

DeHoog, R. H. (1984). *Contracting out for human services—Economic, political and organizational perspectives.* Albany, NY: State University of Albany.

Donahue, J. (1989). *The privatization decision: Public ends, private means.* New York: Basic Books.

Feild, T. (1996). Managed care and child welfare: Will it work? *Public Welfare,* 54(3), 4–10.

Florida Department of Children and Families. (1999). *Community-Based Care implementation plan.* Tallahassee, FL: Author.

Florida Department of Children and Families. (2000a). *Community alliance resource book.* Tallahassee, FL: Author.

Florida Department of Children and Families. (2000b). *Florida Community Based Care evaluation 1999–2000.* Tallahassee, FL: Author.

Florida Department of Children and Families. (2001a). *CBC final report, quantitative research using program and department data sources, June 18, 2001.* Tallahassee, FL: Author.

Florida Department of Children and Families. (2001b). *Community-Based Care: Communities building better lives for families.* Tallahassee, FL: Author.

Florida Department of Children and Families. (2001c). Department of Children and Families quality improvement plan, Attachment L. Tallahassee, FL: Author.

Florida Department of Children and Families. (2002a). *A snapshot of Community-Based Care in Florida.* Tallahassee, FL: Author.

Florida Department of Children and Families. (2002b). *CBC readiness assessment.* Tallahassee, FL: Author.

Florida Department of Children and Families. (2002c). *Community alliance highlights, August 2002.* Tallahassee, FL: Author.

Florida Department of Children and Families. (2002d). *Community-Based Care highlights, 1998-2003.* Tallahassee, FL: Author.

Florida Department of Children and Families. (n.d.). *CBC readiness assessment.* Tallahassee, FL: Author.

Florida State University. (2001). *Evaluation of community-based care in foster care and related services in Florida.* Tallahassee, FL: Florida State University, School of Social Work.

For the kids sake. (2002, May 31). *St. Petersburg Times,* p. 12A.

Friedman, M. (1996). *A strategy map for results-based budgeting: Moving from theory to practice.* Washington, DC: Finance Project.

Georgetown University Child Development Center. (2001). *Meeting the health care needs of children in the foster care system: Framework of a comprehensive approach: Critical components.* Washington, DC: Author.

Gilbert, N. (1984). Welfare for profit: Moral, empirical and theoretical perspectives. *Journal of Social Policy,* 13, 338–346.

Gormley, W. T. (1994–1995). Privatization revisited. *Policy Studies Review,* 13, 215–234.

Governor's Blue Ribbon Panel on Child Protection. (2002). Tallahasee, FL: State of Florida. Available from http://www.cnn.com/2002/US/05/27/florida.child.report/index.html.

Greene, J. (2000, May 12). Prison privatization: Recent developments in the United States. Presented at the International Conference on Penal Abolition. Available from http://www.oregonafscme.com/corrections/private/prison_privatization.htm.

Grenz, C. (2001, August 30). Graves, contractors discuss concerns, issues facing foster care. *Capital-Journal,* p. 4.

Gummer, B. (1988). Managing in the public sector: Privatization, policy deadlock, and erosion of public authority. *Administration in Social Work,* 12(4), 103–118.

Gurin, A. (1989). Governmental responsibility and privatization: Examples from four social services. In S. Kamerman & A. Kahn (Eds.), *Privatization and the welfare state* (pp. 179–205). Princeton, NJ: Princeton University Press.

Hamilton County Creative Connections Contract. (2001). Available from authors.

Hanrahan, J. (1983). *Government by contract.* New York: Norton.

Hart, O., Shleifer, A., & Vishny, R. (1997). The proper scope of government: Theory and application to prisons. *Quarterly Journal of Economics,* 112(4), 1127–1161.

Hartley, K. (1986). Contracting out: A step toward competition. *Economic Affairs,* 6(5), 216–235.

Hatry, H. P. (1983). *A review of private approaches for delivery of public services.* Washington, DC: Urban Institute.

Hatry, H. P., & Durman, E. (1985). *Issues in competitive contracting for social services.* Falls Church, VA: National Institute of Governmental Purchasing.

Hoover, T. (2002, July 3). Governor signs bill requiring ministers to report child abuse. *Kansas City Star,* p. A3.

Jackson, V. H. (1995). *Managed care resource guide for social workers in agency settings.* Washington, DC: NASW Press.

James Bell Associates. (2000). *External evaluation of the Kansas child welfare system, year end report: January–December 1999.* Arlington, VA: Author.

James Bell Associates. (2001). *External evaluation of the Kansas child welfare system, July 2000–March 2001, FY 2001 third quarterly report.* Arlington, VA: Author.

Kamerman, S., & Kahn, A. (1989). *Privatization and the welfare state.* Princeton, NJ: Princeton University Press.

Kamerman, S., & Kahn, A. (1999). *Contracting for child and family services.* Baltimore: Annie E. Casey Foundation.

Kansas Action for Children. (1998). *Privatization of child welfare services in Kansas: A child advocacy perspective.* Topeka, KS: Author.

Kansas Action for Children. (2001). *The Kansas child welfare system: What are we? Where should we be going?* Topeka, KS: Author.

Kearny, K. (2000, October 3). Testimony before the Subcommittee on Human Resources of the House Committee on Ways and Means, Hearing on H.R. 5292, the "Flexible Funding for Child Protection Act of 2000." Retrieved on December 13, 2001 from http://waysandmeans.house.gov/humres/106cong/ 10-3-00/bb10-3kear.htm.

Kemp, R. L. (1991). *Privatization: The provision of public services by the private sector.* Jefferson, NC: McFarland.

Kestin, S. (2002a, January 7). Agency's system faces scrutiny: Computerized tracking project years behind and $198 million over budget. *Sun-Sentinel,* p. 1A.

Kestin, S. (2002b, September 24). Costly DCF files blasted. *Orlando Sentinel,* p. B1.

Kettl, D. (1993). *Sharing power: Public governance and private markets.* Washington, DC: Brookings Institute.

Kramer, R. M., & Grossman, B. (1987). Contracting for social services: Process management and resource dependence. *Social Service Review,* 61(1), 32–55.

Krueger, C. (2001, February 4). Social service overhaul may turn into a mess. *St. Petersburg Times,* p. 1D.

Krueger, C. (2002, May 4). Frustration extends to another family agency. *St. Petersburg Times,* p. 19.

Kuttner, R. (2000). Care, charity, and profit. *American Prospect,* May, 4.

LaFaive, M. (2000). *The tools of privatization: Benefits and pitfall to performance-based contracting.* Midland, MI: Mackinac Center for Public Policy.

Leadership 18 Group. (2000, March). *The profitization of social services policy statement.* Washington, DC: Catholic Charities.

Legislature of Kansas. (2001). *Performance audit report: The state's adoption and foster care contracts: Reviewing selected financial and services issues.* Topeka, KS: Legislature of Kansas, Legislative Division of Post Audit.

Linowes, D. F. (1988). *Privatization: Toward more effective government.* Chicago: University of Illinois Press.

Logan, C. H. (1991). *Well kept: comparing quality of confinement in a public and private prison.* Washington, DC: National Institute of Justice.

Lopez-de-Silanes, R., Shleifer, A., & Vishny, R. W. (1995). *Privatization in the United States* (Working Paper #5113). Cambridge, MA: National Bureau of Economic Research.

Lowery, D. (1982) The political incentives of government contracting. *Social Service Quarterly,* 63, 517–527.

Maine Department of Human Services. (1998). *Community Integration Program RFP.* Available from authors.

McCarthy, J., & Valentine, C. (2000). *Child welfare impact analysis: Health Care Reform Tracking Project: Tracking state managed care reforms as they affect children and adolescents with behavioral health disorders and their families.* Washington, DC: National Technical Assistance Center for Children's Mental Health, Center for Child Health and Mental Health Policy, Georgetown University Child Development Center.

McCullough, C. (1997). Child welfare: Defining the classical issues of managed Medicaid. *Behavioral Health Management, 17*(2), 14–21.

McCullough, C. (2001). *Testimony before the Florida Senate Committee on Children and Families, January 10, 2001.* Available from authors.

McCullough, C., & Schmitt, B. (2002). *2000-2001 Management, finance, and contracting survey final report.* Washington, DC: CWLA Press.

Mahlburg, B. (2002, May 11). Child tracking system is years late, over budget. *Sun Sentinel,* p. 98.

Markowitz, T. (2000). Florida: Community-based care evaluation, 1999-2000. Lawrence, KS: On the Mark.

McLean, J. (1999a, March 12). Foster care, adoption need funding infusion. *Capital-Journal,* p. 7.

McLean, J. (1999b, February 2). Jim McLean: Foster care crisis needs attention. *Capital-Journal,* p. 2.

Melia, R. (1997). *Private contracting in human services.* Boston, MA: Pioneer Institute.

Method, J. (2001, February 26). DYFS' Illinois counter part: Public mission, private solution. *Asbury Park Press,* p. A3.

Miles, D. (2000, September 27). Adoption funding woes discussed. *Topeka Capital Journal,* p. 3.

Milward, H. B. (1994). Nonprofit contracting and the hollow state. *Public Administration Review,* 54(1), 73–80.

Mission Interdepartmental Initiative contract. (1998). Available from authors

Moe, R. C. (1987, November/December). Exploring the limits of privatization. *Public Administration Review,* 47, 453–460.

Morgan, D. R., & England, R. E. (1988, November/December). The two faces of privatization. *Public Administration Review,* 979–987.

Moore, S. (1987). Contracting out: A painless alternative to the budget cutter's knife. In S. H. Hanke (Ed.), *Prospect for privatization* (pp. 116–139). New York: Academy of Political Science.

Moore, A. T. (1997). Privatization on a roll. *American Enterprise,* 8(6), 68–71.

More reforms in order for child protection system. (2002, June 2). *Tampa Tribune,* p. 2.

Motenko, A. K, Allen, E. A., Angelos, P., & Block, L. (1995). Privatization and cutbacks: Social work and client impressions of service delivery in Massachusetts. *Social Work,* 40, 456–462.

Mountjoy, J. J. (1999). The privatization of child welfare: Saving children, saving money. *Spectrum,* 72(2), 1–4.

Myers, R. (1997a, November 5). Judge questions program benefits: Privatization of child welfare programs center of controversy. *Topeka Capital Journal,* p. 8.

Myers, R. (1997b, November 25). SRS drafts plan to tackle child-welfare ills: Privatization has led to breakdowns, complaints allege. *Topeka Capital Journal,* p. 6.

National Association of Child Advocates. (2000). *Fact sheet: Privatization of human services—Is it the best choice for children?* Washington, DC: Author.

Neary, L. (2002, May 12). Florida officials plan to privatize child welfare services department by 2003. Washington, DC: National Public Radio. Transcript available from http://www.nexis.com/research/pnews/documentDisplay?_docnum=92&_ansset=A-WA-B...5/14/2002.

Nelson, J. I. (1992). Social welfare and the market economy. *Social Science Quarterly,* 73, 815–828.

Nightingale, D. S., & Pindus, N. (1997). *Privatization of public social services: A background paper.* Washington, DC: Urban Institute.

Office of Federal Procurement Policy. (1998). *A guide to best practices for performance-based service contracting.* Washington, DC: Office of Federal Procurement Policy, Office of Management and Budget, Executive Office of the President.

Office of Program Policy Analysis and Government Accountability (2001). *Justification review: Child protection programs, Florida Department of Children and Families* (Report No. 01-14). Tallahassee, FL: Florida State Legislature.

O'Looney, J. (1993, December). Beyond privatization and service integration: Organizational models for service delivery. *Social Service Review,* 501–534.

Pack, J. (1991). The opportunities and constraints of privatization. In W. T. Gormley, Jr. (Ed.), *Privatization and its alternatives* (pp. 281–396). Madison, WI: University of Wisconsin Press.

Perrin, E. B., & Koshel, J. J. (Eds.) (1997). *Assessment of performance measures for public health, substance abuse, and mental health.* Report of the Panel on Performance Measures and Data for Public Health Performance Partnership Grants, Committee on National Statistics, Commission on Behavioral and Social Sciences and Education, National Research Council. Washington, DC: National Academy Press.

Petr, C. G., & Johnson, I. C. (1999). Privatization of foster care in Kansas: A cautionary tale. *Social Work,* 44, 263–267.

Pierson, P. (1994). *Dismantling the welfare state? Reagan, Thatcher, and the politics of retrenchment.* Cambridge, UK: Cambridge University Press.

Pioneer Institute for Public Policy Research. (1997, May 1). Public versus private service delivery: A case study. *Center for Restructuring Government Newsletter.*

Poole, P. (2000, January 23). *Privatizing child welfare services: Models for Alabama.* Available from authors.

Port, B. (2001, February 25). City owes $16m for foster care. *New York Daily News,* p. 6.

Privatization's big test. (2002, January 14). *Sun Sentinel,* 16A.

Ranney, D. (2000a, September 27). Adoption agency, SRS admit to mistakes. *Lawrence Journal World,* p. 2.

Ranney, D. (2000b, November 13). Child welfare services in need. *Lawrence Journal World,* p. 6.

Ranney, D. (2001a, April 13). Foster care critics "go public." *Lawrence Journal World,* p. 1.

Ranney, D. (2001b, August 9). Graves weighs in on foster care crisis. *Lawrence Journal World,* p. 2.

Reason Public Policy Institute. (1999). *Privatization 1999: The Reason Public Policy Institute's 13th annual report on privatization.* Washington, DC: Author.

Reason Public Policy Institute. (2000a, December 19). *Political and organizational strategies for streamlining.* Available from http://www.privatization.org/Collection/PracticesAndStrategies/Political_and_Organizational_Strategies.html.

Reason Public Policy Institute. (2000b, December 19). *Privatization: Child welfare services*. Available from authors.

Reason Public Policy Institute. (2000c, December 19). *Types and techniques of privatization*. Available from http://www.privatization.org/Collection/WhatIsPrivatization/Privatization_techniques.html.

Reed, L. (1997, May 21). *The privatization revolution*. Presented at The Future of American Business, A Shavano Institute for National Leadership Seminar, Indianapolis, IN. Available from http://www.privatization.org/Collection/PrivatizationProsAndCons/privatization_revolution.html.

Reed, L. (2001, March 2). *Privatization works for social services too*. Midland, MI: Mackinac Center for Public Policy.

Rosenthal, M. G. (2000). Public or private children's services? *Social Service Review, 74,* 281–305.

Samson, C. (1994). The three faces of privatization. *Journal of the British Sociological Association,* 28(1), 79–90.

Savarese, R. (1999). *Speaking out: Don't privatize child welfare*. Available from http://www.ganinsvillesun.com/opinion/columns/03-02-99speaksavarese.html.

Savas, E. S. (1982). *Privatizing the public sector: How to shrink government*. Chatham, NJ: Chatham House.

Savas, E. S. (1987). *Privatization: The key to better government*. Chatham, NJ: Chatham House.

Savas, E. S. (1992). *Privatization for New York: Competing for a better future. The Lauder Report: A report of the New York State Senate Advisory Committee on Privatization*. Albany, NY: New York State Senate Advisory Committee on Privatization.

Scheslinger, M. (1986). Competitive bidding and states' purchase of services. *Journal of Policy Analysis and Public Management,* 5, 245–263.

Scheslinger, M. (1998). Mis-measuring the consequences of ownership: External influences and the comparative performance of public, for-profit, and private nonprofit organizations. In W. Powell & K. Clements (Eds.), *Private action and the public good* (pp. 85–113). New Haven, CT: Yale University Press.

Schuck, P. H. (1999). *Law and post-privatization regulatory reform: Perspectives from the US experience* (Working Paper #222). New Haven, CT: Yale Law School Program for Studies in Law, Economics, and Public Policy.

Sclar, E. D., Schaeffer, K. H., & Brandwein, R. (1989). *The emperor's new clothes: Transit privatization and public policy*. Washington, DC: Economic Policy Institute.

Seibel, B. (1998). Child welfare and managed care in Hamilton County, Ohio. In *Third national roundtable on managed care in child welfare services: Keeping the focus on kids: from ethics to implementation* (pp. 71–75). Englewood, CO: American Humane Association.

Smith, S. R., & Lipsky, M. (1992). Privatization in health and human services: A critique. *Journal of Health Politics, Policy and Law, 17*, 233–253.

Snell, L. (2000). *Child-welfare reform and the role of privatization* (Policy Study No. 271). Available from http://www.rppi.org/ps271.html

Starr, P. (1988). The meaning of privatization. *Yale Law and Policy Review, 6*, 6–41.

Stevens, B. J. (1984). *Relieving municipal services efficiently: A comparison of municipal and private service delivery.* Washington, DC: U.S. Department of Housing and Urban Development, Office of Policy Development and Research.

Stitt, C. B., Olsen, T. F., & Certo, D. (2001). *Submission to the Florida state legislature: Review of the Florida Department of Children and Families prototype "SunCoast" regionalization.* Indianapolis, IN: Competitive Government Strategies.

Sullivan, H. J. (1987, November/December). Privatization of public services: A growing threat to constitutional rights. *Public Administration Review, 47*, 461–467.

Testa, M. F., Shook, K. L., Cohen, L. S., & Woods, B. G. (1996). Permanency planning options for children in formal kinship care. *Child Welfare, 75*, 451–470.

Thayer, F. (1987). Privatization: Carnage, chaos, and corruption. In B. Carroll (Ed.), *Private means, public ends* (pp. 146–170). New York: Praeger.

Tobin, G. A. (1983, March). The public/private sector partnership in the redevelopment process. *Policy Studies Journal, 11*, 473–482.

Tuominen, M. (1991 September). Caring for profit: The social, economic, and political significance of for-profit child care. *Social Service Review, 450*–467.

University of Connecticut. (2000). *Arguments for and against private prison contracting.* Available from authors.

University of South Florida. (2002). *Evaluations of the Florida Department of Children and Families Community-Based Care initiative in Manatee, Sarasota, Pinellas, and Pasco Counties.* Tallahassee, FL: Florida Department of Children and Families, Office of Mission Support and Performance.

U.S. General Accounting Office. (1996a). *Child support enforcement: States' experience with private agencies' collection of support payments* (USGAO/HEHS-97-11). Washington, DC: Government Printing Office.

U.S. General Accounting Office. (1996b). *Studies comparing operational costs and/or quality of service* (USGAO/GGD-96-158). Washington, DC: Government Printing Office.

U.S. General Accounting Office. (1997). *Social service privatization: Expansion poses challenges in ensuring accountability for program results* (HEHS-98-6). Washington, DC: Government Printing Office.

U.S. General Accounting Office. (1998a). *Child welfare: Early experiences implementing a managed care approach* (HEHS-99-8). Washington, DC: Government Printing Office.

U.S. General Accounting Office. (1998b). *Privatization: Questions state and local decision-makers used when considering privatization options* (USGAO/GGD-98-97). Washington, DC: Government Printing Office.

U.S. General Accounting Office. (1999). *Agency performance plans: Examples of practices that can improve usefulness to decision makers.* Washington, DC: Government Printing Office.

U.S. Department of Health and Human Services. (1999). *Progress report to the Congress.* Available from http://www.acf.dhhs.gov/programs/cb/special/intro.htm

U.S. Department of Health and Human Services. (2000). *Title IV-E demonstration waivers.* Available from http://www.acf.dhhs.gov/programs/cb/waivers.htm.

U.S. Department of Health and Human Services. (2001). *National survey of child and adolescent well-being. Local child welfare agency survey: Report.* Washington, DC: U.S. Department of Health and Human Services, Commissioner's Office of Research and Evaluation and the Children's Bureau.

U.S. Department of Health and Human Services. (2002). *Child welfare outcomes 1999: Annual report.* Washington, DC: U.S. Department of Health and Human Services, Children's Bureau.

Usher, C. L., Gibbs, D., & Wildfire, J. (1999). *The rebound effect in child welfare reform: Secondary effects of success.* Englewood, CO: American Humane Association.

Whitt, J. A., & Yago, G. (1985, September). Corporate strategies and the decline of transit in US cities. *Urban Affairs Quarterly, 21,* 37-65.

Wulczyn, F., & Orlebeke, B. (1998). *Four case studies of fiscal reform and managed care in child welfare.* Chicago: University of Chicago Chapin Hall Center for Children.

Wulcyzn, F., & Sheu, E. (1998). *Setting capitated rates for child welfare programs.* Chicago: University of Chicago Chapin Hall Center for Children.

About the Authors

Madelyn Freundlich is Policy Director for Children's Rights, Inc., New York, NY. She formerly served as the Executive Director of the Evan B. Donaldson Adoption Institute and as General Counsel for the Child Welfare League of America. She is a social worker and lawyer whose work has focused on child welfare policy and practice for the past decade. She has coauthored a number of books on child welfare law and policy. She also has authored numerous articles on a range of topics, including the effects of welfare reform on foster care and special needs adoption, the role of race and culture in adoption, the use of Medicaid to finance services for children in foster care, interstate adoption law and practice, genetic testing in adoption evaluations, and confidentiality in child welfare practice. Ms. Freundlich holds master's degrees in social work and public health and a JD and LLM.

Sarah Gerstenzang is Policy Associate for Children's Rights, Inc., New York, NY. Ms. Gerstenzang holds a master's degree in social work from Columbia University. She is coauthor of an article entitled "Class Action Litigation: Judicial Reform of Child Welfare Systems in the United States," with Marcia Robinson Lowry and Madelyn Freundlich. Ms. Gerstenzang's professional interests include transracial foster care and adoptive placements, the foster parent–birth parent–agency relationship triad, the well-being of children in foster care, and foster care and class structure. She is also a foster/adoptive parent who is active in community-based foster care projects.